Study Guide

to accompany

Human Development

Updated Seventh Edition

James W. Vander Zanden
The Ohio State University

Revised by
Thomas L. Crandell
Broome Community College
and
Corinne Haines Crandell
Broome Community College

Prepared by
Craig Vivian
Monmouth College

Boston Burr Ridge, IL Dubuque, IA Madison, WI New York San Francisco St. Louis
Bangkok Bogotá Caracas Kuala Lumpur Lisbon London Madrid Mexico City
Milan Montreal New Delhi Santiago Seoul Singapore Sydney Taipei Toronto

McGraw-Hill Higher Education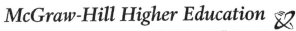

*A Division of The **McGraw-Hill** Companies*

Student Study Guide for use with
HUMAN DEVELOPMENT, UPDATED SEVENTH EDITION
JAMES W. VANDER ZANDEN, THOMAS L. CRANDELL, AND CORINNE HAINES CRANDELL

Published by McGraw-Hill Higher Education, an imprint of The McGraw-Hill Companies, Inc., 1221 Avenue of the Americas, New York, NY 10020. Copyright © The McGraw-Hill Companies, Inc., 2002, 2000, 1997, 1993, 1989, 1985, 1981, 1978. All rights reserved.

No part of this publication may be reproduced or distributed in any form or by any means, or stored in a database or retrieval system, without the prior written consent of The McGraw-Hill Companies, Inc., including, but not limited to, network or other electronic storage or transmission, or broadcast for distance learning.

This book is printed on acid-free paper.

1 2 3 4 5 6 7 8 9 0 VNH VNH 0 3 2 1

ISBN 0-07-282596-0

www.mhhe.com

TABLE OF CONTENTS

<u>STUDY GUIDE</u>

CHAPTER 1	Introduction	1
CHAPTER 2	Developmental Theories	21
CHAPTER 3	Reproduction, Hereditary and Genetics, and Prenatal Development	39
CHAPTER 4	Birth and Physical Development: The First Two Years	57
CHAPTER 5	Infancy: Cognitive and Language Development	75
CHAPTER 6	Infancy: The Development of Emotional and Social Bonds	91
CHAPTER 7	Early Childhood: Physical and Cognitive Development	107
CHAPTER 8	Early Childhood: Emotional and Social Development	125
CHAPTER 9	Middle Childhood: Physical and Cognitive Development	143
CHAPTER 10	Middle Childhood: Emotional and Social Development	163
CHAPTER 11	Adolescence: Physical and Cognitive Development	181
CHAPTER 12	Adolescence: Emotional and Social Development	199
CHAPTER 13	Early Adulthood: Physical and Cognitive Development	217
CHAPTER 14	Early Adulthood: Emotional and Social Development	233
CHAPTER 15	Middle Adulthood: Physical and Cognitive Development	251
CHAPTER 16	Middle Adulthood: Emotional and Social Development	267
CHAPTER 17	Late Adulthood: Physical and Cognitive Development	287
CHAPTER 18	Late Adulthood: Emotional and Social Development	305
CHAPTER 19	Dying and Death	323

Preface

TO THE STUDENT

Human Development is a course of study that will have practical and lasting effects on your own life. You will discover new and exciting insights into your own personal development as well as that of your family, friends, and acquaintances. The seventh edition of *Human Development* has been revised to incorporate the latest research findings and theories; and in the course of revision, the publisher has taken extra care to ensure that the book covers topics that are important to people of all ages and backgrounds.

Nevertheless, like any other course in college, the material in this textbook must be mastered in such a way that it can be recalled for classroom tests or in other situations where you may need to apply it (e.g., as a parent or professional). The purpose of this *Study Guide is* to help you accomplish this task and to achieve the best grades possible.

The *Study Guide is* intended to help you process the information presented in the textbook in a way that will make it more meaningful and memorable. This organization schema should be particularly beneficial to anyone who has been away from the formal classroom for any period of time.

Welcome to the field of human development! We believe you will enjoy all of the exciting topics and research-based information about human behavior in your textbook.

HOW TO USE THIS STUDY GUIDE

The student *Study Guide is* organized to coincide with the chapters of your textbook. Each chapter contains the following sections.

Introduction

The first section - the introduction - serves as a brief orientation to the material in the chapter. You can use the introduction in two ways: (1) to help you organize your thinking before reading the chapter or (2) to review what you have learned after having read the chapter.

Learning Objectives

The learning objectives provide you with a listing of the major topics for each chapter. Each objective corresponds to a major principle or concept discussed in the main text. The learning objectives often contain a key *term,* which will be *italicized.* (Key terms are also presented separately as matching questions in each chapter.) The highlighted key terms are considered to be significant concepts in developmental psychology. By carefully reading the learning objectives *before you* read the text chapter, you will know in advance what is expected of you.

Furthermore, the objectives can be particularly beneficial if your instructor gives essay-type questions or examinations, since essay questions may often resemble these objectives. Writing out answers to the objectives will give you practice in dealing with essay exams.

Self-Tests: Matching, Multiple Choice, Essay

One of the most effective ways to prepare for in-class examinations is to test yourself using questions similar to those you might find on an actual exam. Each self-test section of the Study Guide contains a set of sample questions - matching, multiple-choice, and essay items - that test your understanding of facts and concepts in the textbook chapter. You should test yourself on these questions; that is, try to answer them from memory *after you* have studied the material in the textbook chapter.

The multiple-choice conceptual questions are especially helpful as they force you to think about how to apply concepts in human development. Answering conceptual questions requires using your higher order thinking skills, as compared to answering simpler factual questions. However, you should expect to see both types of questions on examinations.

Answer Key

After you finish the self-test, use the answer key at the end of each chapter in the *Study Guide* to check your answers. The results of the self-test should then be used to determine whether you need to spend more time reading and reviewing the chapter. To help you restudy the questions you find troublesome, we have provided a text page reference for each answer.

Using this *Study Guide* Most Effectively

Step 1: **Preview.** Before reading each chapter in the textbook, read the introduction to the chapter in the *Study Guide*. Next, read and familiarize yourself with the chapter outline in the textbook and the learning objectives in the *Study Guide*. This will help you see the scope and direction of the material in the text. The *Study Guide* serves as an advance organizer (a bridge between old and new learning), enabling you to anticipate important issues, facts, and concepts in the textbook. This preview should take only a few minutes.

Step 2: **Read.** Break down the textbook into small study units, and read it one unit at a time. Preferably, each unit, and thus each learning session, should cover only about 7 to 9 pages of the text. As you read, use the blank space provided in the learning objectives to write out brief notes.

Merely reading a chapter passively does not mean that you have mastered it. Everything may seem to make sense as you read it; however, if you try to recall the material or summarize the main points, you will frequently find that terms, concepts, and names are not retrievable. On the other hand, by learning the key terms and by responding to the learning objectives, you will make the text more significant and hence easier to recall on a test (or, for that matter, in appropriate situations in real life).

Step 3: Review and Test Yourself After reviewing your notes in the learning objectives section, take the self-tests in the *Study Guide*. Check your answers against the answer key and correct your mistakes. Take the self-tests seriously. If you could not answer a question, do not merely look up the answer in the key. Find the textbook passage that answers the question, and reread that passage. Then re-answer the question. In this way, you will shore up any areas that need additional review and help store the information in long-term memory. This *Study Guide will* also be available in a computerized-disk version, if you prefer that method of review.

Step 4: Reread. Reread the textbook chapter, and then go through the self-test again. As you go through Step 4, you should find that the chapter material is more "connected" - and therefore much easier to remember.

Improving Your Memory

Try to *motivate* yourself before you begin to study. With your favorite subject, this is no problem. With a subject you don't like, try to set specific goals for your study period.

Select the material you think is most important to study. What has your professor stressed in class? Check your notes and handouts.

Organize the facts and concepts. You can't learn disorganized information. Organization is like a key that unlocks the information in your mind. Use categories or association. Are you learning the steps in a process? A list of causes?

Recite. Go over the material several times until you have mastered it. You have to do this to completely remember any material. Use your own words in studying: *paraphrasing* definitions and writing brief *summaries* of material are excellent study methods.

Review often. Several short periods with your study material are much more effective than one prolonged session.

Teach someone else. The best way to learn something is to teach it, so find a few people in the class and take turns teaching each other the material. You will learn it and, after having gone through the explanations with your friends, you will be able to answer questions in a more substantive manner.

Preface

LEARNING STYLES AND LEARNING DISABILITIES

Learning Styles

Keep in mind that not everyone learns in the same way. For example, some students understand information better when they see it in written form - they learn best from the textbook, the *Study Guide*, lecture notes, and handouts. Other students prefer to hear information - they learn best from listening to lectures, making and listening to tape recordings of lectures, making and listening to recordings of their own notes from the learning objectives and key terms sections of the *Study Guide*.

If you are using a study method that works for you and you are satisfied with the results you are getting (i.e., good grades), then stick with it. However, if you are struggling and seem to be spending too much time on your homework without satisfactory results, then you need to look at some alternative methods. For example, if you know information is easier for you to learn when you *hear* words rather than when *you see* them, you should be aware that most textbooks have been recorded on tape. Check with your college's library to see if *Human Development is* available in tape format.

You know yourself better than anyone else does; don't think that because one study technique works for another student it will necessarily work for you. By following the learning/study method that is most helpful to you, you will make the material more memorable and more retrievable at test time.

You may also be able to work directly with a tutor on your campus (this service is often provided free). Some colleges provide note takers for students who need this extra assistance. You may need to contact a counselor on your campus who assists students with learning disabilities.

Instructional Materials for Students with Visual or Learning Disabilities

If you know that you have a visual learning disability, you are eligible to get recorded books from a company called Recordings for the Blind. This library has a collection of textbooks on special tape available to *any* learner who is classified as legally blind, visually impaired, or learning disabled with visual perceptual difficulties.

Call (800) 221-4792 to get an application, which must be filled out by a school psychologist, private psychologist, physician, or local vocational testing agency. This is a short form in which the student's learning disability is identified by a professional. There is a fee for use of any materials.

Most college textbooks should be available. If a book is not yet on cassette, you *can make the request,* and they will hire a professional reader to prepare your text for you (expect a short wait).

Getting Recorded Textbooks for the Semester You Need Them

If you can find out at the end of each semester what textbooks you will need for the following semester, you should be able to get your books on 3/4-inch cassette on a timely basis. You can contact your college professors or college bookstore directly for the required reading list for the following semester. Textbook requests are usually turned in by November for the spring semester and by April for the summer sessions and fall semester.

The special cassette player that will play the 3/4-inch cassettes can be borrowed for free from your own state's Library for the Blind (usually located in your state's capitol). This recorder can be on loan as long as the student needs it.

Preface
TAKING AND PASSING CLASSROOM TESTS

Reducing Test Anxiety

Test anxiety can be defined as a feeling of helplessness before or during a test. It is important to realize that examinations cause many people to become anxious and that this is normal. Complete freedom from test anxiety is unattainable; and even if it were attainable, it would probably not be desirable. Low-to-moderate test anxiety before a test actually tends to have a positive effect on test performance.

However, if your test anxiety is so high that it prevents you from demonstrating what you have learned, then it becomes a problem and should be addressed. Unfortunately, such anxiety is usually a complex problem, which often cannot be traced to any single cause. Personality traits (e.g., a tendency to take risks), emotional states (e.g., a negative outlook and fear of failure), and personal needs and priorities (e.g., overemphasis on grades) can sabotage your performance on tests.

If you consistently experience test anxiety, we recommend that you make an appointment with someone in your college or university counseling center to discuss the problem and work out a procedure for dealing with it. College counselors are trained to help you assess the cause or causes of your test anxiety and to provide you with strategies for reducing it and for improving your performance on tests.

Learning to Be the Best Test Taker You Can Be

Students who are good test takers are able to prepare for tests efficiently and to take advantage of the characteristics of tests. For example, different tests (such as multiple-choice tests and essay tests) have different properties, which students can learn to recognize. In fact, your college library or bookstore should be able to provide materials dealing with the nature of tests and "test smarts"; one good such reference is *How to Take Tests* by Jason Millman and Walter Pauk (McGraw-Hill, Inc., New York). Some colleges also offer workshops or study sessions on how to take different kinds of tests.

Remember, instructors want your test scores to reflect what you have learned. If you do poorly because you do not understand the nature of the test, then the test becomes an obstacle rather than a tool for accurate assessment. Familiarizing yourself with various kinds of tests will help ensure that your grade will be determined by your learning.

Following are some strategies we suggest to help you prepare for and take tests, so that an examination will become a genuine opportunity for you to demonstrate what you have learned.

Intellectual Preparation

- Preparing for a test has intellectual, emotional, and physical aspects. Some strategies for *intellectual* preparation include:

- Attend classes.

- Follow the step-by-step procedure for using *Human Development* and the *Study Guide*. Remember that this procedure can be adapted for use with other textbooks and supplements.

- Schedule regular study sessions in a specific, quiet place; and set small, reachable goals for each study session.

- Study relevant quizzes and tests you have already taken.

Preface
- Become familiar, in advance, with the purpose and format of the test. Ask your instructor to give you information on what types of questions will appear.

- See yourself - realistically - as succeeding on the test.

Emotional and Physical Preparation

- Some strategies for preparing yourself emotionally and physically for a test include:

- Appreciate the usefulness of the test.

- Relax.

- Concentrate.

- Get a good night's sleep before the test.

- Eat a good meal before the test.

- Arrive early for the test, and come prepared with all necessary supplies (such as No. 2 pencils, pens, paper).

Taking the Test: General Strategies

- **Use time wisely.** Since the time allowable for taking the test is limited, it's important to use that time efficiently.

- Find out how long you have to complete the test.

- Look over the entire test briefly before you start to answer any questions. Find out which items yield the most points.

- Begin to work as rapidly as is possible with some reasonable assurance of accuracy.

- At the outset, complete items that you are confident answering. If you have enough time when you've completed the rest of the test, remember to return to these items.

- Work immediately, and quickly, on the items, which will yield the most points.

- If you become too nervous to work, stop briefly and use some relaxation techniques to calm yourself.

- If you have any time left when you've finished the test (after going back to any difficult items you skipped at the beginning), use it to reconsider and improve your answers. As a rule, however, don't change an answer unless you are absolutely certain that you misread the question initially or that you missed some important aspect of it. Your first answer is often the correct one.

Read all directions and questions carefully. Students often lose points simply because they haven't followed directions or because they have misinterpreted questions.

- Before you start writing, become familiar with the test directions.

- Pay particular attention to the directions that most influence how you will take the test.

Preface

- Ask the examiner for clarification when necessary.

- Keep the test directions in mind while you are answering the questions.

- Be careful to read each question "as is"--not as you might like it to be.

- Pay attention to any key terms that appear in the questions. If you are allowed to make your own notes on your exam paper, sometimes it helps to circle or highlight key terms in a question; this can help you pinpoint what the question is asking for.

- If you can write your own notes on the exam paper, it may be helpful in multiple-choice to cross out answers that you have eliminated as incorrect, and in matching sections to cross off items you've already paired up.

Taking the Test: Strategies for Specific Types of Questions

Multiple-choice items. The typical multiple-choice format consists of an incomplete sentence with several options for completing it or a question with several possible answers. (You may have to circle the correct choice, fill in a circle, or write its identifying letter or number in an answer space.)

- Read the fragment or question carefully, anticipate the answer, and then look for your anticipated answer among the choices.

- If the choices do not include the answer you anticipated, consider all the alternatives using a process of elimination. It can be helpful to treat the item as a "completion" question, covering all the choices and then uncovering one at a time.

- If, in a four-choice format, you have eliminated two of the choices but are undecided about the remaining two, treat each of the remaining two as a "true-false" question.

Matching items. The typical matching format consists of two sets of items to be paired off.

- As always, read the directions carefully.

- Count the number of items in each set.

- Determine the relationship between the two sets.
- Try the first item. If you can't find its "partner" in the second set, skip to the next item. Keep skipping until you find one matching pair, then go on until you find another pair, and so on.
- When you have matched all the items you know, use a process of elimination for the remaining items. If you are allowed to write your own notes on the exam paper, cross out the items you have already matched.

Completion items. The typical completion, or fill-in item, is a sentence with one or more blanks; you are to make the sentence read correctly by supplying whatever is needed in each blank. (You may be asked to write your answer in the blank itself or in a separate answer space.)

- Give a general answer if you don't know the specific answer.
- Examine the sentence for grammatical clues. (For example, *a* or *an* preceding a blank tells you that the answer is singular; *these* or *those* tells you that the answer is plural.)

Preface

True-false items. The typical true-false item is a statement which you are to identify as correct or incorrect. (You may have to write T or *true,* or *F* or false, in an answer space; or check off or circle T or *F.)*

- Remember the odds (50-50).
- As always, read each item carefully.
- Look for qualifiers *(not, new, recent,* etc.).

Essay items. An essay item may be phrased as a question ("Why did Freud believe that ... ?") or as an imperative ("Explain why Freud believed that. . ."). You are to write a full answer. Often, your answer will be graded not only for content but also for correct grammar and for the logic of your presentation. (Space may be provided for each answer; or all the essay items may be on a printed sheet, with answers to be written in an examination booklet or on your own paper.)

- When a test has more than one essay item, read each one carefully.

- If you are allowed to make notes on the exam paper, jot down beside each essay item the relevant points that occur to you. (Think back to your learning objectives.)

- If you can make notes on the exam paper, you may also want to highlight or circle parts of the question that indicate exactly what you are being asked to write about.

- Analyze the verbs in the item: *contrast, compare, describe, list, explain,* etc. Circle them for emphasis if that is permitted.

- Organize your answer before you start writing.

- If you are not sure of the best answer, quickly write down all your ideas.

- If you do not have enough time to write a full essay answer, give your answer in outline form.

- When you have finished an essay item, read it over. Check to be sure that you have followed each of the direction verbs you identified (you may have circled these, as noted above).

- Be sure that you write legibly.

A FINAL COMMENT

While this *Study Guide is* designed to help you learn the information in the main textbook, remember there are no shortcuts to effective learning and good grades - motivation, effort, practice, and endurance are the keys that will unlock your potential. Use this Study *Guide* as a learning tool to help you achieve your goal. Therefore, mark up the pages, make notes, jot down your thoughts about the learning objectives, and write in your answers to the self-tests.

As teachers of many college courses, we have found that the suggestions given above do help. We share them with you and welcome you to the Human Development course with our best wishes for your success.

Thomas L. Crandell, Ph.D. Craig T Vivian, Ph.D.

Chapter 1

Introduction

INTRODUCTION

Chapter 1 offers an overview of the developmental perspective, outlines basic concepts, and identifies various research methods. Several important topics are presented:

- The four goals of developmental psychologists. We will look at how psychologists try to describe, explain, predict, and control the developmental process.

- Frameworks for organizing information about human development. We will examine human development from the standpoints of major domains, processes, context, and timing.

- Urie Bronfenbrenner's ecological approach to development. This approach links the individual to social and cultural forces and shows connections between these forces and the individual.

- Cultural influences on human development. This section looks at the impact that culture has in shaping our conception of the life cycle.

- Historical "areas of concern" among developmentalists. This section highlights the critical questions of the past as well as their continuing influence on contemporary research.

- The scientific method. This section describes the scientific method and its importance for the field of development.

- Research methodology. This section presents detailed descriptions of the various research designs and methods used by scientists to study human nature.

- Ethical considerations. A framework is presented which highlights critical aspects of conducting research on human subjects.

Chapter 1   Introduction

LEARNING OBJECTIVES

After completing Chapter 1, you should be able to:

1. Explain what is meant by the study of *human development*.

2. Describe the four major issues focused on by scientists who study developmental psychology.

   -

   -

   -

   -

3. Name the three major domains within which development takes place, and give an example of each.

   -

   -

   -

4. Define the processes of *growth, maturation,* and *learning*. How is maturation different from growth, and how is learning different from maturation?

Chapter 1   Introduction

5. Explain what is meant by the *nature-nurture controversy* in terms of growth, maturation and learning.

6. Describe Bronfenbrenner's *ecological approach* toward understanding human development. Name the four levels of environmental influence on human development as presented in this model and give an example of each.

ecological approach

-

-

-

-

7. Describe why and how major events have affected different cohorts.

8. Name and describe the five steps employed in the scientific method.

Chapter 1   Introduction

-

-

-

-

-

9. Describe the following research designs, and identify the advantages and disadvantages of each.

longitudinal

cross sectional

sequential

10. Summarize the following terms as they relate to the *experimental design,* and provide an example of each:

independent variable

dependent variable

control group

experimental group

11. Define the main tasks of the *case study* and *social survey* methods of research design, and critically examine the advantages and disadvantages of each.

Chapter 1   Introduction

12. Explain the *naturalistic observation method* and define *time sampling* and *event sampling*.

13. Describe *cross-cultural studies,* and give an example of this type of research. List its advantages and limitations.

14. Understand and explain the significance of a correlational coefficient when r =

    - -1.00
    - .00
    - 1.00

15. Discuss what two guidelines must be followed when doing research on human subjects, and why.

Chapter 1   Introduction

WEB SITES

The following web sites deal with some of the major concepts and issues presented in Chapter 1. Additional resources can be found at the text's web site, at http://www.mhhe.com/crandell7.

Society for Personality and Social Psychology
http://www.spsp.org/

APA Division 9: The Society for the Psychological Study of Social Issues
http://www.spssi.org/

Experimental Psychology Lab on the Web
http://www.uni-tuebingen.de/uni/sii/Ulf/Lab/WebExpPsyLab.html

Journal of Cross Cultural Psychology
http://www.fit.edu/CampusLife/clubs-org/iaccp/JCCP/jccp.html

Society for Cross Cultural Research
http://www.fit.edu/CampusLife/clubs-org/sccr/

APA Ethical Principles and Codes of Conduct
http://www.apa.org/ethics/homepage.html

PsychWeb
http://www.psychweb.com/

The Inter-University Consortium for Political and Social Research (ICPSR)
http://www.icpsr.umich.edu/index.html

Historical Data Census 1790-1970
http://fisher.lib.Virginia.EDU/census/

Galaxy: Social Sciences
http://galaxy.einet.net/galaxy/Social-Sciences.html

Chapter 1 Introduction

SELF-TESTS

Matching

Match the key terms with their definitions:

a. age cohort
b. age strata
c. case-study method
d. cognitive development
e. control group
f. correlation coefficient
g. cross-cultural method
h. cross-sectional study
i. culture
j. dependent variable
k. development
l. developmental psychology
m. ecological approach
n. emotional-social development
o. event sampling
p. exosystem
q. experiment
r. experimental group
s. experimental method
t. extraneous variables
u. growth
v. hypothesis
w. independent variable
x. informed consent
y. learning
z. longitudinal method
aa. macrosystem
bb. master status
cc. maturation
dd. mesosystem
ee. naturalistic observation
ff. normative age-graded influences
gg. normative history-graded influences
hh. physical development
ii. random sampling
jj. right to privacy
kk. scientific method
ll. sequential methods
mm. selective attrition
nn. social norms
oo. social survey method
pp. time sampling

1. ____ a group of persons born in the same time interval

2. ____ a method used in studying the incidence of specific behaviors or attitudes in a large population of people

3. ____ a neutral standard against which the changes in the experimental groups can be measured

4. ____ a research approach in which scientists study the same individuals at different points in their lives

5. ____ a sampling technique in which each member of the population sampled has an equal probability of being chosen

6. ____ a series of steps we follow that allow us and others to be clear about what we studied, how we studied it and what were our conclusions

7. ____ a special type of longitudinal study focusing on a single individual rather than a group of subjects

8. ____ a study in which the investigator manipulates one or more variables and measures the resulting changes in the other variables to attempt to determine the cause of a specific behavior

9. ____ a technique of recording actions observed at particular time intervals

10. ____ a tentative proposition that can be tested

11. ____ an approach which proposes that the study of developmental influences must include the person's interaction with the environment, the person's changing physical and social settings, the relationship among those settings, and how the entire process is affected by the society in which the settings are embedded

12. ____ an environment that is "external" to the developing person

13. ____ assures participants that the information they share or behaviors that are recorded will be kept confidential

14. ____ expectations that specify what constitutes appropriate and inappropriate behavior for individuals at various periods in the life span

Chapter 1   Introduction

a. age cohort
b. age strata
c. case-study method
d. cognitive development
e. control group
f. correlation coefficient
g. cross-cultural method
h. cross-sectional study
i. culture
j. dependent variable
k. development
l. developmental psychology
m. ecological approach
n. emotional-social development
o. event sampling
p. exosystem
q. experiment
r. experimental group
s. experimental method
t. extraneous variables
u. growth
v. hypothesis
w. independent variable
x. informed consent
y. learning
z. longitudinal method
aa. macrosystem
bb. master status
cc. maturation
dd. mesosystem
ee. naturalistic observation
ff. normative age-graded influences
gg. normative history-graded influences
hh. physical development
ii. random sampling
jj. right to privacy
kk. scientific method
ll. sequential methods
mm. selective attrition
nn. social norms
oo. social survey method
pp. time sampling

15. ____ governs entry to many other statuses and makes its own distinct imprint on them

16. ____ investigates development by simultaneously comparing different age groups

17. ____ involves counting the occurrence of some specific behavior over a systematically spaced interval of time

18. ____ means that those subjects who drop out tend to be different from the subjects who remain in a study

19. ____ one of the most rigorously objective techniques available to science

20. ____ requires the researcher to obtain written consent to participate from each subject; this consent must be voluntary

21. ____ social layers within societies that are based on time periods in life

22. ____ some measure of the subject's behavior

23. ____ takes place through metabolic processes from within, and consequently, one of the most noticeable features of early development is the increase in size that occurs with changing age

24. ____ that branch of psychology that deals with how individuals change with time while remaining in some respects the same

25. ____ the factor that is manipulated in an experiment

26. ____ the group in which a researcher manipulates the independent variable or administers a treatment

27. ____ the interrelationships among the various settings in which the developing person is immersed

28. ____ the more or less automatic unfolding of biological potential in a set, irreversible sequence

29. ____ the more or less permanent modification in behavior that results from the individual's experience in the environment across the entire life span

30. ____ the numerical expression of the degree or extent of relationship between two variables or conditions

31. ____ the orderly and sequential changes that occur with the passage of time as an organism moves from conception to death

32. ____ the overarching cultural patterns of a society find expression in family, educational, economic, political, and religious institutions

Chapter 1   Introduction

33. ____ the social heritage of a people – those learned patterns for thinking, feeling, and acting that are transmitted from one generation to the next

34. ____ those changes that concern an individual's personality, emotions, and relationships with others

35. ____ those changes that occur in a person's body, including changes in weight and height; in the brain, heart and other organ structures and processes; and in skeletal, muscular, and neurological features that affect motor skills

36. ____ those changes that occur in mental activity, including sensation, perception, memory, thought, reasoning, and language

37. ____ those factors which may confound the outcome of the study, such as the age and gender of the subjects, the time of day the study is conducted, the educational attainment of the subjects, and so on

38. ____ when researchers compare data from two or more societies and cultures

39. ____ when researchers intensively watch and record behavior as it occurs but are careful not to disturb or affect the events under investigation

40. ____ research methods that involve measuring more than one cohort over time

41. ____ changes in an individual's social environment that are associated with his or her change in age

42. ____ historical events and trends that impact an age cohort's developmental experience

Multiple Choice

Circle the letter of the response that <u>best</u> completes or answers each of the following statements and questions.

Factual Questions

1. Psychologists who study orderly and sequential changes that occur in behavior with the passage of time are studying
   a. growth
   b. maturation
   c. development
   d. learning

Chapter 1   Introduction

2. The four major issues of developmental psychology are describing, explaining, predicting, and _____ developmental changes.
    a. modifying
    b. redirecting
    c. changing
    d. controlling

3. Which of the following domains of development entails changes in weight, height, organ structures and processes and skeletal, muscular, and neurological features?
    a. cognitive development
    b. physical development
    c. psychosocial development
    d. neurological development

4. Those changes that occur in mental activity, including sensation, perception, memory, thought, reasoning, and language, are studied in the field of _____ development.
    a. cognitive
    b. physical
    c. psychosocial
    d. evolutionary

5. Those changes that concern a person's personality, emotions, and relationships with others are known as _____ development.
    a. cognitive
    b. physical
    c. psychosocial
    d. evolutionary

6. Developmental psychologists studying psychosocial development are interested in
    a. perception
    b. mental activity
    c. personality formation
    d. motor skills

7. When an organism takes in a variety of substances, breaks them down into their chemical components, and then reassembles them into new materials, resulting in a change of size, this is called
    a. metabolic change
    b. mental change
    c. growth
    d. biochemical change

8. When a particular biological potential, such as the ability to walk, automatically unfolds in a set, irreversible sequence, we refer to this process as
    a. growth
    b. maturation
    c. learning
    d. development

9. The more or less permanent modification in behavior that results from the individual's experience in the environment is called
    a. cognitive overload
    b. maturation
    c. growth
    d. learning

10. An advocate of the ecological approach believes that the study of developmental influences must include
    a. a person's interaction with current technology
    b. the individual's changing physical and social settings
    c. how the process is analyzed by scientists
    d. all of the above

11. Which of the following consists of the interrelationships among the various settings in which the developing person is immersed?
    a. microsystem
    b. mesosystem
    c. exosystem
    d. macrosystem

12. Which ecological system includes the social structures that directly or indirectly affect a person's life, such as school, work, the media, government agencies, and various social networks?
    a. microsystem
    b. mesosystem
    c. exosystem
    d. macrosystem

13. An example of a normative age-graded influence on development would be an adolescent's
    a. experiencing a sudden religious conversion
    b. dropping out of school in 1930
    c. developing a severe case of acne
    d. finishing junior high school

14. Each generation's members experience certain decisive economic, social, political, and military events at similar junctures in life; these are referred to as
    a. normative age-graded influences
    b. normative history-graded influences
    c. nonnormative life events
    d. normative life events

15. Unique turning points at which people change some direction in their lives (such as divorce, winning the lottery, or being severely injured in an accident) are called
    a. normative age-graded influences
    b. normative history-graded influences
    c. nonnormative life events
    d. normative life events

Chapter 1 Introduction

16. When a developmental psychologist says that age is a master status, she means that
    a. roles are assigned independently of the person's age
    b. age governs entry to many other statuses over the life span
    c. as a person ages, he or she is afforded a higher status
    d. young men are assigned to the military in some cultures

17. A person's _____ functions as a reference point that allows people to orient themselves in terms of what or where they are within various social networks.
    a. educational status
    b. social status
    c. age
    d. financial status

18. The social heritage of a people (those learned patterns for thinking, feeling, and acting that are transmitted from one generation to the next) is called
    a. the life cycle
    b. culture
    c. social lifestyle
    d. social consequence

19. All societies are divided into social layers that are based on time periods in life, which psychologists call
    a. hierarchies
    b. layers
    c. age strata
    d. strata organization

20. In studying the historical changes in children's' lives, which of the following statements is true?
    a. School enrollments have declined overall in the U.S over the last 200 years.
    b. School enrollments have remained constant overall in the U.S. over the last 200 years.
    c. School enrolments have risen overall in the U.S. over the last 200 years.
    d. There has been no data collected.

21. Which of the following was not an area of concern of early developmentalists?
    a. cognitive development
    b. emotional development
    c. pathological development
    d. role of the self

22. Which of the following is not considered a step in the scientific method?
    a. formulating a hypothesis
    b. testing the hypothesis
    c. conducting a literature review
    d. disseminating the findings of the study to the scientific community

23. A hypothesis refers to a(n)
    a. prediction that can be tested by gathering appropriate information
    b. controlled lab experiment
    c. explanation of experimental data
    d. test to determine whether a prediction is correct

24. A benefit of the longitudinal method is that:
    a. the researcher studies all the same sample over the same period of time
    b. the researcher gains insight into the routes by which people turn out similarly or differently in adulthood
    c. a variety of social or economic events enters the picture, which makes this more interesting for the researchers
    d. some people drop out of the study, so the researcher has fewer subjects to work with

25. In the cross-sectional method
    a. the same group of subjects is repeatedly given the same test over a twenty year period
    b. surveys are administered to samples of people from around the country
    c. different groups and ages of subjects are observed at the same time
    d. the behavior of subjects in a laboratory environment is compared with their behavior in their natural setting

26. One of the major criticisms of cross-sectional studies is that
    a. they are costly and time-consuming to conduct
    b. it is difficult to keep in contact with all the subjects
    c. it is difficult to control the environment of the subjects between testing periods
    d. differences in social environment, intelligence, or diet make it difficult to compare groups

27. The sequential method approach
    a. relies mainly on the use of surveys
    b. always measures cohorts in ten year intervals
    c. involves measuring more than one cohort over time
    d. is used to compare different individuals sequentially

28. In the experimental method, the independent variable is
    a. a measure of extraneous behavior
    b. the variable being manipulated and is considered the causal factor
    c. administered only to the control group
    d. usually administered in the form of a paper-and-pencil test or a performance test

29. The case-study approach
    a. relies mainly on the use of surveys
    b. is exemplified by studies on maladjusted or emotionally disturbed individuals
    c. focuses on getting a representative sample of children
    d. is used to compare different individuals rather than groups

30. A developmental psychologist tries to determine whether a variable (e.g., instructional method) that he systematically manipulates affects another variable (e.g., IQ scores). This psychologist is using the _____ method.
    a. case-study
    b. cross-sectional
    c. experimental
    d. longitudinal

Chapter 1   Introduction

31. Researchers interested in studying the incidence of behavior in a large population might use a quantitative method known as
    a. the case study
    b. the cross-sectional study
    c. the Prodigy Polls
    d. the social survey method

32. Though naturalistic observation can provide a source of ideas for study, it is not a particularly strong technique for studying behavior because
    a. the researcher lacks control over the behavior being studied
    b. the subjects enjoy being observed
    c. the researcher usually interacts with the subjects
    d. the subjects usually want to be paid for their performance

33. In the cross-cultural method, researchers focus on
    a. comparison of data from at least five countries
    b. several neighboring families in a similar geographical area
    c. complex behaviors and customs
    d. culture rather than individuals

34. A positive correlation is defined as
    a. the positive identification of related data
    b. when two conditions occur and rise together
    c. a numerical relationship between two variables
    d. a change from -1.00 to +1.00

35. An important ethical guideline for human research emphasized by the authors of your text was that
    a. subjects should be required to continue in a study once they commit themselves
    b. subjects must sometimes be coerced to participate in an experiment
    c. the experimenter is responsible for conducting research with regard for the dignity and welfare of the participants
    d. deception should be used when full disclosure to subjects would be harmful to their egos

Conceptual Questions

1. A multidisciplinary approach to research in life-span development
    a. encourages a freshness of approach
    b. functions as a stimulus in advancing the frontiers of knowledge
    c. can encourage collaboration
    d. all of the above

2. Dr. Jones, a researcher, wishes to *explain* the specific determinants of a child's change in language. Which statement best represents the type of question she might ask when trying to *explain* this change?
    a. What is the role of learning in language acquisition?
    b. What is the nature of the speech?
    c. What are the language capabilities of a 6-month-old infant likely to be at 14 months of age?
    d. Can we control this change in language?

Chapter 1   Introduction

3. On the basis of previous research, a pediatrician decides to place children diagnosed with attention deficit hyperactivity disorder (ADHD) on a medication regimen including the drug Ritalin. This action is an example of
   a. control over behavioral development
   b. prediction of developmental change
   c. explanation of developmental change
   d. an unethical practice

4. A study is being conducted with preteen subjects examining their muscular development as puberty approaches. What domain is this study examining?
   a. physical development
   b. cognitive development
   c. psychosocial development
   d. evolutionary development

5. A psychologist's research on the memory strategies used by 7-year-old children is focusing on
   a. maturational development
   b. affective development
   c. psychosocial development
   d. cognitive development

6. The fact that in our society more adolescent females are giving birth to babies and becoming single parents before graduating from high school is being studied by psychologists specializing in
   a. physical development
   b. cognitive development
   c. psychosocial development
   d. evolutionary development

7. Which scenario illustrates an individual who is experiencing a developmental change in *growth*?
   a. A 7-month-old infant sits upright without support.
   b. An adolescent grows 6 inches taller over the course of a year.
   c. A young child decides not to touch the hot stove because he was burned when he did this before.
   d. A 12-year-old girl begins to ovulate.

8. A developmental psychologist discovers that girls begin menstruating only after they have reached a certain weight, body fat proportion, and height, and after other sexual changes have occurred. This psychologist might reasonably conclude that menstruation is controlled by
   a. learned readiness
   b. growth gradients
   c. maturational factors
   d. ecological factors

9. Of the following, which is the more or less permanent modification in behavior that results from the individual's experience in the environment?
   a. developing facial hair
   b. ovulating at age 13
   c. being able to sit up around 4 months of age
   d. becoming a concert pianist

Chapter 1   Introduction

10. Unlike American families one hundred years ago, in many families today the mother works outside the home, and close family relatives may be separated by substantial geographical distances. Developmental psychologists who view development from an ecological approach would explain these changes by referring to the _____ within which today's families exist.
    a. mesosystem
    b. exosystem
    c. macrosystem
    d. microsystem

11. An influence/event that impacts only one generation is of what type?
    a. normative age-graded influence
    b. normative history-graded influence
    c. nonnormative life event
    d. cross-generational life event

12. What type of conclusion is accurate concerning the impact of the parental generation on each new generation?
    a. Each new generation gathers more of its parents' cultural history.
    b. New generations typically replicate the views and perspectives of their elders.
    c. New generations are not necessarily bound to replicate their elder's views and perspectives.
    d. Cultural factors are paramount.

13. Which of the following best exemplifies age stratification?
    a. A lawyer is granted a personal parking space after being promoted to district attorney.
    b. Adolescents in all cultures reach puberty at relatively the same age.
    c. A 70-year-old woman is respected in her village because of her age.
    d. At 14 a young woman passes her driving test.

14. Age operates indirectly as a function of master status in which of the following cases
    a. being eligible to get a driver's license at age 16
    b. being able to vote
    c. going to college
    d. receiving social security benefits

15. Which of the following is acceptable according to social norms?
    a. a 2 year old having a temper tantrum
    b. an adolescent talking "baby talk" to his parents
    c. a 6 year old babysitting her younger siblings
    d. all of the above

16. Louis Terman conducted a study in which the intelligence test performance of the same group of children was assessed at different points in their lifetimes. This was a _____ study.
    a. sequential
    b. longitudinal
    c. cross-sectional
    d. time-sampling

17. The concept of adolescence as we know it today
    a. is a reflection of children's rights advocacy
    b. is the same all over the world
    c. emerged from changing social, political, and legal forces
    d. is evolving as a longer stage in life

18. A psychologist does a study in which she compares the IQ test performance of groups of 30-, 40-, and 50-year-old people. Each group's average score is lower than the preceding group's scores. The psychologist concludes that as people age, their test scores decline. This conclusion may be in error because
    a. this is a longitudinal study
    b. IQ tests are not valid measures of intelligence
    c. you cannot give the same IQ tests to people who vary in age
    d. the different age groups differed not only in age but also in cohort

19. A psychologist studies the emotional development of his son Raphael by recording the different ages at which different emotions appear. This research is an example of a(n)
    a. case study
    b. experiment
    c. naturalistic observation
    d. cross-sectional method

20. A group of students in a psychology class conduct an experiment in which the influence of an observer's presence on the subject's willingness to help is measured. The observer's presence is the
    a. dependent variable
    b. independent variable
    c. controlled variable
    d. varied variable

21. An experimenter is testing the effects of observed violence on children's behavior. One group of children views a violent cartoon. A second group views a humorous nonviolent cartoon. The third group is not exposed to any cartoon. The first group is a(n)
    a. experimental group
    b. control group
    c. comparison group
    d. observational group

22. A social psychologist is interested in measuring the attitudes of a group of high school teachers toward including intellectually and emotionally challenged learners in their classrooms. Which type of study would she be most likely to conduct?
    a. an experiment
    b. a naturalistic observation
    c. a survey
    d. a time-series study

23. A researcher did a study of children's prosocial behavior. He recorded the incidents in which children responded positively to another child in a preschool setting. The researcher was performing a(n)
    a. experiment
    b. longitudinal study
    c. case study
    d. naturalistic observation

24. A researcher wants to use the scientific method to determine the connection between shoe size and IQ. Which of the following steps will give him the most trouble?
    a. drawing conclusions
    b. making the findings available
    c. selecting a researchable problem
    d. formulating a hypothesis

25. A developmental psychologist is interested in comparing the attachment level to the parents of children raised on a collective Israel kibbutz with that of children reared in American farm families. This psychologist is using the
    a. cross-sectional method
    b. cross-cultural method
    c. naturalistic observation method
    d. cultural correlation method

Essay Questions

1. A set of identical twins has been discovered, and remarkably, they were separated at birth with one growing up in the United States while the other grew up in Nigeria. They are now in their mid-forties and lead very different lives. How would you use the ecological approach to examine the forces that have been at work in their lives, and how this might have affected their development?

2. Do you believe that there must be one "correct" method for doing developmental research. Why don't we find it and let it be the standard for future research?

3. Why do we divide development into different stages and "areas of concern," and what do we lose or gain by doing this?

Chapter 1   Introduction

ANSWERS FOR SELF-TESTS

Matching

1.	a	16.	h	30.	f
2.	oo	17.	pp	31.	k
3.	e	18.	mm	32.	aa
4.	z	19.	s	33.	i
5.	ii	20.	x	34.	n
6.	kk	21.	b	35.	hh
7.	c	22.	j	36.	d
8.	q	23.	u	37.	t
9.	o	24.	l	38.	g
10.	v	25.	w	39.	ee
11.	m	26.	r	40.	ll
12.	p	27.	dd	41.	ff
13.	jj	28.	cc	42.	gg
14.	nn	29.	y		
15.	bb				

Multiple-Choice

Factual

1.	c	13.	d	25.	c
2.	d	14.	b	26.	d
3.	b	15.	c	27.	c
4.	a	16.	b	28.	b
5.	c	17.	c	29.	d
6.	c	18.	b	30.	c
7.	c	19.	c	31.	d
8.	b	20.	c	32.	a
9.	d	21.	c	33.	d
10.	b	22.	c	34.	b
11.	b	23.	a	35.	c
12.	c	24.	a		

Conceptual

1.	d	10.	c	18.	d
2.	a	11.	b	19.	a
3.	a	12.	c	20.	b
4.	a	13.	c	21.	a
5.	d	14.	c	22.	c
6.	c	15.	a	23.	d
7.	b	16.	b	24.	d
8.	c	17.	c	25.	b
9.	d				

Chapter 2

Developmental Theories

INTRODUCTION

Chapter 1 explored the subject of human development and critiqued several research methods used in the study of various aspects of human development. Chapter 2 provides an in-depth analysis of major theoretical perspectives in regard to human development. The chapter presents a detailed discussion of the following:

- Psychoanalytic Theories. These illustrate the importance of early experience in personality development and the role of unconscious motivation. Freud's psychosexual stages, as well as Erikson's psychosocial stages of development, are examined within this context.

- Behavioral Theory. This stresses the part that learning plays in inducing individuals to act in the ways that they do. Skinner's basic tenets in regard to this perspective are highlighted.

- Cognitive Theory. This draws our attention to the importance of various mental capabilities and problem-solving skills that equip people with potent adaptive skills. Piaget's cognitive stages are examined within this context.

- Cognitive Learning. This emphasizes the information processing which allows individuals to perform discrete mental operations on incoming information and then store it for later processing.

- Ecological Theory. This looks at the interaction between the individual and the environment. Bronfenbrenner adds that development must be understood as the person immersed in a web of social, physical, and cultural spheres.

- Socio-Cultural Theory. The view that individual development must be aided by social interactions.

- Controversies. Several important controversies are presented, which increase one's understanding of the distinctions among the major theories of human development.

Chapter 2   Developmental Theories

LEARNING OBJECTIVES

After completing Chapter 2, you should be able to:

1. Define *theory*, and describe the functions that a theory serves.

2. Explain the central view of *psychoanalytic theory* and state Freud's view of the role of the unconscious.

3. Briefly describe Freud's five psychosexual stages.

    •

    •

    •

    •

    •

1. Distinguish between Erikson's psychosocial and Freud's psychosexual development theories.

Chapter 2 Developmental Theories

2. Name Erikson's nine stages of development, and describe the approximate time period during which each psychosocial stage occurs and the type of life crisis experienced.

   1.
   2.
   3.
   4.
   5.
   6.
   7.
   8.
   9.

1. Discuss the focus of *behavioral theory*, name its major proponents, and explain the significance of the following terms:

focus and proponents of behavioral theory

stimulus

response

classical conditioning

operant conditioning

reinforcement

behavior modification

Chapter 2 Developmental Theories

2. Summarize what is meant by *cognitive theory*.

3. Define the roles of the following as they relate to the process of cognitive development:

   schema

   assimilation

   accommodation

   equilibrium

4. Explain *cognitive learning*.

5. Explain Bronfenbrenner's $D=f(PE)$.

6. Explain the Chronosystem in Bronfenbrenner's model.

7. Explain Vygotsky's Sociocultural theory by describing the importance of

   Language

   Culture

   Social activities

Chapter 2   Developmental Theories

8. Explain how proponents of the *continuity* and *discontinuity* models view human development. Compare and contrast the *heredity* (nature) vs. *environment* (nurture) views of development.

9. Explain the complex interaction of hereditary (maturation) and environmental factors as proposed by Scarr and McCartney.

passive

evocative

active

10. Describe the importance of the findings from the Kagan Timidity Studies.

WEB SITES

The following web sites deal with some of the major concepts and issues presented in Chapter 2. Additional resources can be found at the text's web sit, at http://www.mhhe.com/crandell7.

American Psychoanalytic Association
http://apsa.org/

Freud Net
http://plaza.interport.net/nypsan/

Social Science Sites Useful in History
http://www.tntech.edu/www/acad/hist/socsci.html

The Social Psychology Network
http://www.wesleyan.edu/spn/

Cognitive Psychology
http://www.wesleyan.edu/spn/cognitiv.htm

The Jean Piaget Society
http://www.piaget.org/index.html

Celebrities in Cognitive Science
http://www.cudenver.edu/~mryder/itc_data/cogsci.html

Ethology and Evolutionary Psychology
http://evolution.humb.univie.ac.at/jump.html

Vygotsky
http://www.cudenver.edu/~mryder/itc_data/soc_cult.html#vygotsky

Twin Studies
http://www.twinspace.com/outlinestudy.html

Institute for Behavioral Genetics & Behavioral Genetics Association
http://ibgwww.colorado.edu/

SELF-TESTS

Matching

Match the key terms with their definitions:

a. accommodation
b. assimilation
c. behavior modification
d. behavioral theory
e. classical conditioning
f. cognition
g. cognitive learning
h. cognitive stages in development
i. cognitive theory
j. eclectic approach
k. ecological theory
l. environment
m. epigenetic principle
n. equilibrium
o. fixation
p. fraternal (dizygotic) twins
q. heredity
r. identical (monozygotic) twins
s. mechanistic model
t. operant conditioning
u. organismic model
v. psychoanalytic theory
w. psychosexual stages
x. psychosocial stages
y. reinforcement
z. response
aa. schema
bb. sociocultural theory
cc. stimulus/stimuli
dd. theory

1. ____ a model that focuses not on elementary particles but on the whole

2. ____ a model that represents the universe as a machine composed of elementary particles in motion

3. ____ a perspective which allows psychologists to select and choose from the various theories and models those aspects that provide the best fit for the descriptive and analytical task at hand

4. ____ a principle which states that each part of the personality has a particular time in the life span when it must develop if it is going to develop at all

5. ____ a process of stimulus substitution in which a new, previously neutral stimulus is substituted for the stimulus that naturally elicits a response

6. ____ a series of stages that all human beings pass through: oral, anal, phallic, latency, and genital

7. ____ a set of interrelated statements that provides an explanation for a class of events

8. ____ a technique that applies the result of learning theory and experimental psychology to the problem of altering maladaptive behavior

9. ____ a theory concerned with explaining the observable behavior of people – what they actually do and say

Chapter 2 Developmental Theories

a. accommodation
b. assimilation
c. behavior modification
d. behavioral theory
e. classical conditioning
f. cognition
g. cognitive learning
h. cognitive stages in development
i. cognitive theory
j. eclectic approach
k. ecological theory
l. environment
m. epigenetic principle
n. equilibrium
o. fixation
p. fraternal (dizygotic) twins
q. heredity
r. identical (monozygotic) twins
s. mechanistic model
t. operant conditioning
u. organismic model
v. psychoanalytic theory
w. psychosexual stages
x. psychosocial stages
y. reinforcement
z. response
aa. schema
bb. sociocultural theory
cc. stimulus/stimuli
dd. theory

10. ____ theory which looks at how we represent, organize, and transform information

11. ____ phenomena that elicit responses

12. ____ involves the inherited traits from our biological parents – physical, intellectual, social, and emotional development

13. ____ nine "crises" throughout the life span in which individuals resolve fundamental personal and social issues such as trust, identity, and autonomy

14. ____ sequential periods in the growth or maturing of an individual's ability to think – to gain knowledge and awareness of one's self and the environment

15. ____ theory which emphasizes the interaction between individuals and groups and/or cultures they are involved with

16. ____ the act or process of knowing

17. ____ the process of changing a schema to make it a better match to the world of reality

18. ____ the process of taking in new information and interpreting it in such a manner that the information conforms to a currently held model of the world

19. ____ the process of watching other people and learning new responses without first having had the opportunity to make the responses ourselves

Chapter 2 Developmental Theories

20. ____ the process whereby one event strengthens the probability of another event's occurring

21. ____ the result of balance between the processes of assimilation and accommodation

22. ____ the result when a fertilized egg, by some accident, gets split into two parts and each is essentially a carbon copy of the other

23. ____ the result when two eggs are fertilized by two different spermatozoa, and develop separately in the womb at the same time, and are born at the same time

24. ____ the tendency to stay at a particular stage

25. ____ the term Piaget used for cognitive structures that people evolve for dealing with specific kinds of situations in their environment

26. ____ the view that personality is fashioned progressively as the individual passes through various psychosexual stages

27. ____ what theorists have traditionally used for dividing behavior into units

28. ____ what theorists have traditionally used for dividing the environment into units

29. ____ a type of learning in which the consequences of a behavior alter the strength of that behavior

30. ____ a theory that looks at the relationship between the developing individual and the changing environment

Chapter 2   Developmental Theories

Multiple Choice

Circle the letter of the response that <u>best</u> completes or answers each of the following statements and questions.

Factual Questions

1. Which of the following is <u>not</u> characteristic of a theory?
    a. It is a set of interrelated statements.
    b. It suggests that development is directed from within.
    c. It serves as a stimulus to action.
    d. It is an attempt to make sense of our experiences.

2. The major function of a theory is to
    a. organize factual observations in a coherent way
    b. describe and catalog our behavior observations
    c. prove the correctness of our hypothetical formulations
    d. determine whether a behavior is innate or learned

3. Sigmund Freud's theory suggests that individuals pass through various _____ stages.
    a. ego
    b. oral
    c. psychosexual
    d. unconscious

4. According to Freud's view, the unconscious is important because
    a. many instinctual impulses are eliminated early in life
    b. we become aware of our instinctual but forbidden history through slips of the tongue, dreams, mental disorder, religion, art, literature, myths, etc.
    c. critical impulses occur during the child's first six years, which are an instinctual period in personality formation
    d. much of our behavior is motivated by unconscious drives

5. A major premise of Freudian theory is that fixation occurs when
    a. sex-role socialization takes place
    b. a person experiences a psychosocial crisis
    c. a person is frustrated or overindulged at a particular stage of development
    d. a biochemical imbalance exists at a stage of development

6. According to Freud, the latency period corresponds to which period of life?
    a. infancy
    b. adolescence
    c. middle childhood
    d. young adulthood

7. What is a criticism of psychoanalytic theory?
    a. It is too easy to evaluate by accepted scientific standards.
    b. The theory was based on inferences from Freud's adult patients.
    c. Freud worked with patients having healthy personalities rather than those with emotional difficulties.
    d. Freud's inability to define key concepts such as ego, id, and superego.

8. In contrast to Freud's concern with psychosexual development, Erik Erikson emphasized
    a. psychosocial development
    b. cognitive development
    c. sexual fixations
    d. critical periods

9. Erikson concluded that the personality continues to develop over the life span
    a. in five distinct epigenetic stages
    b. in nine stages while accomplishing meeting developmental tasks and resolving crises
    c. as a consequence of learning continually in one's environment
    d. by actively controlling one's destiny and using free will

10. Erikson indicates that _____ typically confront a crisis associated with identity vs. identity confusion.
    a. infants
    b. children
    c. adolescents
    d. adults

11. In Erikson's theory, a developing person is likely to have feelings of shame and doubt rather than autonomy when he or she
    a. develops an ego identity
    b. feels hopeless about impending death
    c. fails to receive recognition for school achievements
    d. has parents who are overprotective when learning to crawl, climb, walk, and explore

12. Behavioral theorists look at the interaction between
    a. classical and operant conditioning
    b. stimulus and response
    c. John Watson and B. F. Skinner
    d. conflicts and resolutions

13. Operant conditioning
    a. derives from preexisting reflexes
    b. controls behavior by changing the effect that follows
    c. requires introspection
    d. eliminates reflexes

14. Reinforcement occurs when
    a. two stimuli are paired together
    b. a stimulus is followed by a response
    c. one event strengthens the probability that another event will occur
    d. a response is initiated by a releasing stimulus

15. Behavior modification uses _____ to change behaviors
    a. phobias
    b. motivation
    c. diminished reflexes
    d. rewards and punishment

16. Those internal factors that are part of the process of thinking and reasoning (such phenomena as sensation, perception, imagery, retention, recall, etc.) are central to which theory of development?
    a. humanistic
    b. behavioral
    c. cognitive
    d. psychoanalytic

17. According to Piagetian theory, when a child engages in the process of assimilation, she
    a. is rewarded for responding accurately in a learning task
    b. processes new situations as if they were similar to previously experienced ones
    c. changes her old behavior when it no longer allows her to solve problems
    d. performs a new behavior without having had a previous opportunity to make the response

18. According to Piagetian theory, when a child engages in the process of accommodation, she is
    a. rewarded for responding accurately in a learning task
    b. conceptualizing new situations as if they were similar to previously experienced ones
    c. changing her previous conceptions when they no longer allow her to solve problems
    d. fitting old experiences into new ones

19. The process of accommodation and assimilation is essential to
    a. fixation
    b. equilibrium
    c. object permanence
    d. egocentrism

20. Children who rely solely on reflexes to interact with their environment are in Piaget's _____ stage.
    a. sensorimotor
    b. preoperational
    c. concrete operations
    d. formal operations

21. Cognitive learning, also known as social learning, refers to
    a. passive learning
    b. learning solely by direct experience
    c. intentional learning
    d. learning by observation and modeling

22. The difference between Field Theory and Bronfrenbrenner's Ecological Theory is the concept of
    a. personal habits
    b. environment
    c. locus of control
    d. development over time

Chapter 2   Developmental Theories

23. The socio-cultural theory emphasizes the link between the individual's development and
    a. historical context
    b. social interaction
    c. cultural values
    d. all of the above

24. In contrast to mechanistic models, organismic models of human development portray human beings as
    a. intrinsically active
    b. intrinsically passive
    c. developing in a continuous process
    d. mostly influenced by environmental factors

25. Children's genetic predispositions are coupled with their environment in three ways. Which is not a relationship as put forth by Scarr and McCartney?
    a. evocative
    b. destructive
    c. passive
    d. active

26. Studies on shyness (timidity) and the Minnesota Twin Project suggest that
    a. psychoanalytic theory is supported
    b. behavioral traits can be traced to a single gene
    c. hereditary aspects of behavior are supported
    d. new discoveries in microbiology and genetics show that parenting has the greatest influence on a child's behavior

Conceptual Questions

1. An adult is compulsively neat, orderly, and stingy. Freudian psychologists would say that this individual may have
    a. been weaned too early in the oral stage
    b. experienced a conflict related to toilet training in the anal stage
    c. never resolved his Oedipus conflict in the phallic stage
    d. been fixated at the guilt stage

2. Using psychoanalytic theory, which argument would support more natural weaning on the baby's own timetable?
    a. The child will develop a dislike for its parents.
    b. The child will fail to identify with the parent of the same sex.
    c. The child will continue to suckle, preventing excessive oral behaviors.
    d. The child is likely to develop a conformist personality.

3. Alex was severely criticized by his teachers whenever he failed to complete difficult math problems correctly. Now he feels that he is "stupid" in math. According to Erikson's psychosocial theory, which crisis is this indicative of?
    a. identity vs. role confusion
    b. autonomy vs. shame and doubt
    c. industry vs. inferiority

d. initiative vs. guilt

4. A couple feels the desire to start a family. Erikson would say they are in which stage?
   a. identity vs. role confusion
   b. generativity vs. stagnation
   c. industry vs. inferiority
   d. satisfaction vs. complacency

5. Peter has learned to associate a grimace on his mother's face with a "time out." If he gets anxious when his mother grimaces, his anxiety is due to
   a. the conditioning of that response
   b. learned shame and doubt
   c. his mother's face being a releasing stimulus
   d. negative reinforcement

6. Dr. Brown is studying retention and recall of vocabulary with preschoolers. What theoretical basis underlies this study?
   a. psychoanalytic
   b. behavioral
   c. cognitive
   d. psychosocial

7. A child has been successful in getting her way by screaming. One day, the child screams and is punished. According to Piaget, this should lead to _____.
   a. spanking
   b. schemation
   c. behavior modification
   d. disequilibration

8. Nguyen realizes when water is poured from a tall thin glass into a short wide glass, the same amount of water exists. Piaget would argue that Nguyen
   a. achieved the ability to conserve
   b. is demonstrating abstract thought
   c. is demonstrating object permanence
   d. is exhibiting egocentrism

9. A child in the *pre-operational* stage responds to this hypothetical problem: "If ice heated things, we could boil water by putting it in the _____."
   a. rain
   b. freezer
   c. refrigerator
   d. fire

10. Bandura's theory of information processing applies to which of the following scenarios?
    a. Luke observes a teacher interacting positively with the children who sit closest to her desk. He asks to move his desk near the teacher.
    b. Sara requests hypnosis to "look" at her unconscious childhood.
    c. A dog learns to sniff out cocaine in airports and is fed treats.
    d. A person with a phobia for snakes refuses to go to the zoo.

11. If a child is born deaf, cognitive psychologists would say this child will have difficulty
    a. modeling his parents' behavior
    b. learning by language experience
    c. going through Erikson's stages
    d. adapting biologically

12. Research on identical twins can be most helpful when studying which type of debate?
    a. mechanistic vs. organismic
    b. nature vs. nurture
    c. continuity vs. discontinuity
    d. operant vs. classical conditioning

13. Which of the following theorists viewed social interactions as the crucial "engine" of development?
    a. Sigmund Freud
    b. Omar Bradley
    c. Lev Vygotsky
    d. Jerome Kagan

14. Most behavioralists recognize which approach in understanding human development?
    a. psychoanalytic model
    b. mechanistic model
    c. organismic model
    d. eclectic model

Chapter 2 Developmental Theories

Essay Questions

1. Some people argue that theories do more harm than good in trying to understand human development. Furthermore, they argue that every well known theory is really just an attempt by one individual to understand himself or herself. Do you agree?

2. Examine and explain the reasons why someone might abuse alcohol or drugs from the point of view of nature and nurture, using one theoretical model for analysis.

3. Write a series of 4 short essays entitled "How I Became Who I Am" with each essay focusing on the following people:
   1. teacher
   2. thief
   3. queen or king
   4. fortune teller

Compare and contrast different theorists such as Piaget, Vygotsky, Bandura, Skinner, Erikson and Freud in order to understand the role of the environment, society, and the individual.

ANSWERS FOR SELF-TESTS

Matching

1. u
2. s
3. j
4. m
5. e
6. w
7. dd
8. c
9. d
10. i
11. l
12. q
13. x
14. h
15. bb
16. f
17. a
18. b
19. g
20. y
21. n
22. r
23. p
24. o
25. aa
26. v
27. z
28. cc
29. t
30. k

Multiple Choice

Factual

1. b
2. a
3. c
4. d
5. c
6. c
7. b
8. a
9. b
10. c
11. d
12. b
13. a
14. c
15. d
16. c
17. b
18. c
19. b
20. a
21. d
22. d
23. d
24. a
25. b
26. c

Chapter 2 Developmental Theories

Conceptual

1. b
2. c
3. c
4. b
5. a
6. c
7. d
8. a
9. b
10. a
11. b
12. b
13. c
14. d

Chapter 3

Reproduction, Heredity and Genetics, and Prenatal Development

INTRODUCTION

Whereas Chapters 1 and 2 examined the major developmental perspectives and theories, Chapter 3 illuminates the biological foundations of development. The chapter presents current research findings about the beginning of human development. Chapter 3 examines such important topics as the reproductive systems of males and females; the remarkable process of fertilization, growth and health factors crucial to prenatal development; the birth process; and possible complications of pregnancy and birth for mother, father, and child. Within this context, the following topics are covered:

- Reproduction. This includes a detailed section on how human beings are able to reproduce. Also explained and critically evaluated are the genetic testing and counseling methods available to assess development before birth.

- Heredity. This involves looking at the cellular level in order to understand the role that chromosomes, genes, and DNA play in passing on inheritances.

- Genetics. This section covers the Human Genome Project, principles of genetics such as dominant and recessive characteristics and phenotypes and genotypes. Also covered is genetic counseling and testing, and the methods of fetoscopy, amniocentesis, and ultrasonography.

- Cell Division. Examine the differences between mitosis and meiosis as well as the difference between autosomes and sex chromosomes.

- Prenatal Development. The three stages of prenatal development--germinal, embryonic, and fetal--are highlighted.

- Other Factors in Development. Environmental and teratological influences that can affect the developing organism are examined. These include drugs, disease, stress, HIV/AIDS, maternal age and the Rh factor.

Chapter 3   Reproduction, Heredity and Genetics, and Prenatal Development

---
LEARNING OBJECTIVES

After completing Chapter 3, you should be able to:

1. Describe some facts about a typical:

male's sperm production (location, locomotion, amount, when produced).

female's ova production (location, locomotion, amount, when produced).

2. Name and identify the function of the two male androgens.

3. Name and identify the function of the two female sex hormones.

4. Explain the journey of a mature ovum from where it is produced and the role of each body part through menstruation or fertilization (if that occurs).

5. Describe the process of fertilization.

Where does it takes place? Natural vs. Assisted Reproductive Technologies (ART)

How does conception occur?

How does the uterus prepare for pregnancy?

Chapter 3   Reproduction, Heredity and Genetics, and Prenatal Development

6.   Discuss different methods for conception.

In vitro fertilization (IVF)

Gamete intra-fallopian transfer (GIFT)

Zygote intra fallopian transfer (ZIFT)

Intracytoplasmic sperm injection (ICSI)

cytoplasm transfer

7.   Discuss different forms of birth control.

8.   Describe the Human Genome Project

9.   Explain the difference between genotype and phenotype.

10.   Describe each of the following diagnostic tests:

amniocentesis

ultrasonography

fetoscopy

chorionic villus biopsy

Chapter 3 Reproduction, Heredity and Genetics, and Prenatal Development

blood tests

11. Name the three stages of the *prenatal period*, identify the time period within which each occurs, and describe the main characteristics that define each stage.

-

-

-

12. Describe the development of the zygote during the early *germinal period*, and define the following:

mitosis

cleavage

blastocyst

endometrium

13. Identify what the layers of the cell wall mass of the *blastocyst* will eventually become.

ectoderm

mesoderm

endoderm

14. Discuss the growth and development of the embryo from the end of the second week until the end of the eighth week during the *embryonic period*.

growth

placenta

umbilical cord

early structure for all organs

recognizable human body

Chapter 3 Reproduction, Heredity and Genetics, and Prenatal Development

15. Define cephalocaudal and proximodistal development

16. Cite the impact of infectious and noninfectious diseases that might harm a fetus:

    rubella

    syphilis

    genital herpes

    AIDS (HIV)

    diabetes

WEB SITES

The following web sites deal with some of the major concepts and issues presented in Chapter 3. Additional resources can be found at the text's web site, at http://www.mhhe.com/crandell7.

Understanding Gene Testing
http://www.gene.com

Human Reproduction: Utah Division of Reproductive Endocrinology & Infertility
http://www-medlib.med.utah.edu/kw/human_reprod/

Why Pregnancy and Alcohol Don't Mix
http://www.aafp.org/patientinfo/pre_alco.html

Nature Genetics
http://genetics.nature.com/

Interactive Pregnancy Calendar
http://www.pregnancycalendar.com

Reproductive Health Resources
http://www.childbirth.org/articles/reprolinks.html

Infertility Resources
http://www.ihr.com/infertility/index.html

In vitro Fertilization and Related Procedures
http://www.ihr.com/ucsfivf/ivfgift.html

Embryo and Semen Freezing
http://www.ihr.com/ucsfivf/embfreez.html

The Kinsey Institute on Sex, Gender, & Reproduction
http://www.indiana.edu/~kinsey/

Chapter 3   Reproduction, Heredity and Genetics, and Prenatal Development

SELF-TESTS

Matching

Match the key terms with their definitions:

a. Abortion
b. Allele
c. amniocentesis
d. ARTs
e. autosomes
f. blastocyst
g. cephalocaudal development
h. CVS
i. Chromosomes
j. clone
k. DNA
l. dominant character
m. embryonic period
n. fallopian tube
o. fertilization
p. fetal period
q. fetoscopy
r. gametes
s. genes
t. genetics
u. genotype
v. germinal period
w. heterozygous
x. homozygous
y. human genome
z. in vitro fertilization
aa. meiosis
bb. menstruation
cc. miscarriage
dd. mitosis
ee. multifactorial transmission
ff. ovulation
gg. phenotype
hh. placenta
ii. polygenic inheritance
jj. proximodistal development
kk. recessive character
ll. sex chromosomes
mm. sex-linked traits
nn. teratogen
oo. ultrasonography
pp. uterus
qq. zygote

1. ____ a characteristic formed by different alleles

2. ____ a characteristic made up of alleles that are the same from both parents

3. ____ a gene at a given location on a chromosome

4. ____ a hollow, thick-walled, muscular organ that will house and nourish the developing embryo

5. ____ a map of the genetic makeup of each chromosome

6. ____ a noninvasive scanning procedure that allows physicians to determine the size and shape of the fetus and placenta, the amount of amniotic fluid, and the appearance of fetal anatomy

7. ____ a process that takes place in a dividing cell by which each new cell has the same number of chromosomes as the parent cell

8. ____ a single fertilized egg

9. ____ a trait determined by a gene located on a sex chromosome

10. ____ an invasive procedure whereby the physician inserts a thin catheter through the vagina and cervix and into the uterus, removing a small plug of villous tissue

11. ____ any agent that contributes to birth defects or anomalies

12. ____ development that commences with the brain and head areas and then works its way down the body

13. ____ development that occurs when tissues grow in opposite directions away from the axis of the primitive streak

14. ____ fertilization outside the body in a medical lab environment in an attempt to accomplish pregnancy

15. ____ long threadlike structures made of protein and nucleic acid that contain the hereditary materials found in the nuclei of all cells

16. ____ one allele (gene) that completely masks or hides the other allele

Chapter 3 Reproduction, Heredity and Genetics, and Prenatal Development

a. abortion
b. allele
c. amniocentesis
d. assisted reproductive technology (ART)
e. autosomes
f. blastocyst
g. cephalocaudal development
h. chorionic villus biopsy (CVS)
i. chromosomes
j. clone
k. deoxyribonucleic acid (DNA)
l. dominant character
m. embryonic period
n. fallopian tube
o. fertilization
p. fetal period
q. fetoscopy
r. gametes
s. genes
t. genetics
u. genotype
v. germinal period
w. heterozygous
x. homozygous
y. human genome
z. in vitro fertilization
aa. meiosis
bb. menstruation
cc. miscarriage
dd. mitosis
ee. multifactorial transmission
ff. ovulation
gg. phenotype
hh. placenta
ii. polygenic inheritance
jj. proximodistal development
kk. recessive character
ll. sex chromosomes
mm. sex-linked traits
nn. teratogen
oo. ultrasonography
pp. uterus
qq. zygote

17. ____ one commonly used invasive procedure conducted normally between the fourteenth to twentieth week of gestation to determine if the fetus is normal

18. ____ scientific technological options used to increase a woman's chance of becoming pregnant when conception does not occur through normal sexual activity

19. ____ term used when the cell division converts the zygote into a hollow ball of cells

20. ____ the 22 pairs of chromosomes similar in size and shape that each human being normally possess

21. ____ the twenty-third pair of chromosomes – one from the mother and one from the father – that determine the baby's sex

22. ____ the active biochemical substance of genes that programs the cells to manufacture vital protein substances

23. ____ the actual genetic makeup of an organism

24. ____ the discharge of the ovum from the follicle in the ovary

25. ____ the first stage of prenatal development which extends from conception to the end of the second week

26. ____ the maturing of an ovum and ovulation, and eventual expulsion of an unfertilized ovum from the body through the vagina

27. ____ the observable (or expressed) characteristics of an organism

28. ____ the organ formed from uterine tissue and the trophoblast of the blastocyst; it functions as an exchange terminal that permits entry of food materials, oxygen, and hormones and the exit of carbon dioxide and metabolic wastes

29. ____ the process by which the number of chromosomes in gamete-producing cells are reduced by one-half

30. ____ the recognition that environmental factors interact with genetic factors to produce traits

31. ____ the scientific study of biological inheritance

32. ____ the second stage of prenatal development which covers the period from the end of the second week to the end of the eighth week

33. ____ the term used when the zygote, embryo, or fetus is expelled from the uterus before it can survive outside the mother's womb

Chapter 3 Reproduction, Heredity and Genetics, and Prenatal Development

34. ____ the transmission of characteristics or traits for which a single gene is not responsible, but rather are determined by a large number of genes in combination

35. ____ the two kinds of mature sex cells that are involved in human reproduction

36. ____ the union (fusion) of a sperm and an ovum; it occurs in the upper end of the fallopian tube

37. ____ tubes leading from each ovary to the uterus; the location that fertilization occurs if sperm are present

38. ____ units on the chromosome that transmit inherited characteristics passed from biological parents to children

39. ____ when one allele (gene) is completely masked or hidden by the other allele

40. ____ the third stage of prenatal development extending from the end of the eighth week until birth

41. ____ a procedure that allows a physician to examine the fetus directly through a lens after inserting a very narrow tube into the uterus

42. ____ spontaneous or induced expulsion of the fetus

43. ____ an organism grown from a single somatic cell

Multiple Choice

Circle the letter of the response that <u>best</u> completes or answers each of the following statements and questions.

Factual Questions

1. Sex cells (sperm and ova) are called
    a. alleles
    b. genes
    c. gametes
    d. zygotes

2. A normal adult male's sperm production can be affected by
    a. health
    b. work
    c. temperature
    d. all of the above

Chapter 3 Reproduction, Heredity and Genetics, and Prenatal Development

3. A female produces immature ova in her ovaries while developing in her mother's womb. Between puberty and menopause, usually one ovum per month matures and is released. How many ova ultimately reach maturity?
    a. 40-50
    b. 400-500
    c. 400,000
    d. 400 million

4. The principal male sex hormones are
    a. estrogen and progesterone
    b. estrogen and testosterone
    c. testosterone and androsterone
    d. testosterone and semen

5. Sperm are produced in the man's body in winding tubules within the
    a. epididymis
    b. urethra
    c. testes
    d. fallopian tubes

6. During ejaculation, as the sperm pass out of the man's body through the penis, secretions that fuel and protect the sperm are also released from the
    a. seminal vesicles and prostate gland
    b. androgens and prostate gland
    c. prostate gland and urethra
    d. seminal vesicles and urethra

7. The primary female reproductive organs, the ovaries, produce mature ova and the female sex hormones
    a. estrogen and testosterone
    b. estrogen and progesterone
    c. progesterone and testosterone
    d. androsterone and progesterone

8. The journey of a mature ovum, if not fertilized, is
    a. ovaries, oviduct, uterus, cervix, vagina, vulva
    b. ovaries, oviduct, cervix, vagina, uterus, vulva
    c. ovaries, uterus, vagina, vulva, oviduct, cervix
    d. uterus, ovaries, oviduct, cervix, vagina, vulva

9. The optimal time for fertilization (conception) to occur within the menstrual (ovarian) cycle is
    a. at the beginning of the cycle
    b. at the middle of the cycle
    c. at the end of the cycle
    d. any time during the cycle

10. If unfertilized, the ovum degenerates after about how much time?
    a. 24 hours
    b. 5 days
    c. 14 days
    d. 28 days

Chapter 3   Reproduction, Heredity and Genetics, and Prenatal Development

11. Fertilization actually takes place in what female reproductive structure?
    a. ovaries
    b. oviduct (Fallopian tube)
    c. uterus
    d. vagina

12. According to your text, the newly fertilized ovum is now called a(n)
    a. embryo
    b. fetus
    c. conceptus
    d. zygote

13. About what percent of zygotes die shortly after fertilization?
    a. 10 percent
    b. 23 percent
    c. 33 percent
    d. 43 percent

14. If pregnancy fails to take place, the decreasing level of hormones lead to menstruation, about ____ days after ovulation.
    a. 2
    b. 5
    c. 7
    d. 14

15. During menstrual flow, what body structure secretes hormones into the bloodstream to "direct" another ovarian follicle to begin rapid growth?
    a. ovary
    b. pituitary gland
    c. uterus
    d. thyroid gland

16. Which of these is not an Assisted Reproductive Technology (ART)?
    a. ZIFT
    b. GIFT
    c. PREVEN
    d. ICSI

17. Long, threadlike structures made of protein and nucleic acid containing hereditary materials are known as _____?
    a. genomes
    b. chromosomes
    c. DNA
    d. genes

Chapter 3   Reproduction, Heredity and Genetics, and Prenatal Development

18. A medical diagnostic procedure, used by physicians to identify hereditary defects before an infant's birth that draws fluid from the sac surrounding the fetus, is called
    a. amniocentesis
    b. ultrasonography
    c. chorionic villus biopsy
    d. fetoscopy

19. Gametes differ from other cells in the body because they
    a. contain no chromatids
    b. contain one half the number of chromosomes that other cells have
    c. contain twice the number of genes that other cells have
    d. all of the above

20. Your mother and father are both Bb (dominant brown, recessive blue) concerning eye color. What is the probability that you have brown eyes?
    a. 100 percent
    b. 75 percent
    c. 50 percent
    d. 25 percent

21. The growth of the zygote and the establishment of a linkage with the support system of the mother is identified as what period?
    a. germinal
    b. embryonic
    c. fetal
    d. uterine

22. An absolutely essential growth process that begins within a few hours of fertilization and is a division of cells into identical cells (1 to 2, 2 to 4, 4 to 8, 8 to 16, 16 to 32, etc.) is called
    a. embriosis
    b. mitosis
    c. endotosis
    d. reproduction

23. As a result of cleavage, the zygote becomes transformed into a hollow ball of cells called the
    a. mitosis
    b. blastocyst
    c. chorion
    d. ectoderm

24. Normally the blastocyst "digests" its way through the rich lining of the uterine cavity called the _____ and gradually burrows into the wall of the uterus.
    a. oviduct
    b. cervix
    c. endometrium
    d. vagina

Chapter 3 Reproduction, Heredity and Genetics, and Prenatal Development

25. The internal cluster of cells that compose the blastocyst, the inner cell mass, produces the
    a. trophoblast
    b. amnion
    c. chorion
    d. embryo

26. During prenatal growth and development, the end of the second week to the eighth week is what period?
    a. germinal
    b. embryonic
    c. fetal
    d. uterine

27. The placenta is the organ that
    a. transfers maternal nutrients to the fetus
    b. protects the fetus against infectious organisms
    c. directly connects the fetal and maternal blood supplies
    d. connects the embryo to the vaginal wall

28. The principle that describes development as starting with the head and brain areas and moving downward is called
    a. cephalocaudal development
    b. proximodistal development
    c. teratology development
    d. progressive development

29. In which stage during prenatal development do the organs of the fetus assume their specialized functions?
    a. germinal
    b. embryonic
    c. fetal
    d. critical

30. During the 5th prenatal month, the mother generally begins to feel the spontaneous movements of the fetus (a sensation like a fluttering butterfly in the abdominal region) known as
    a. neuromuscular movement
    b. quickening
    c. embryonic activity
    d. prenatal movement

31. What percent of cattle fetuses produced by cloning die or abort between 35 and 90 days?
    a. 10
    b. 90
    c. 50
    d. 100

32. Most pregnancies end with the birth of a normal, healthy baby. However, about what percent of all conceptions result in spontaneous abortion?
    a. 0.5 to 1 percent
    b. 14 to 18 percent
    c. 5 to 10 percent
    d. 22 to 28 percent

33. Rh-negative disorder is one in which the infant may be given intrauterine transfusion because
    a. the mother develops a fever and a slight rash
    b. the mother forms antibodies that destroy the baby's incompatible blood cells
    c. the baby is born with an abnormally low white blood cell count
    d. the baby is separated from the placenta

Conceptual Questions

1. Ovum is to _____ as sperm is to _____.
    a. gamete; zygote
    b. estrogen; androgen
    c. prostate gland; uterus
    d. fertilization; gamete

2. You see a photograph of the largest human cell. What are you looking at?
    a. epididymis
    b. sperm
    c. ovum
    d. urethra

3. A woman is experiencing a sharp, constant pain near her left ovary in her lower abdomen. She had sexual intercourse about two weeks ago, and she suspects a pregnancy. She should see her doctor immediately because the blastocyst might be developing in the thin tubular structure that leads away from the ovary and *not* in the uterus (called an ectopic pregnancy). If this is the case, where is the blastocyst found?
    a. vulva
    b. vagina
    c. cervix
    d. oviduct

4. One of Janet's ovum was discharged 14 days ago and she has not had sexual intercourse in the past month. What can she expect will happen in the next few days?
    a. fertilization
    b. menstruation
    c. conception
    d. ovulation

Chapter 3   Reproduction, Heredity and Genetics, and Prenatal Development

5. A woman's obstetrician suggests to her that he needs to get a sample of amniotic fluid from her fetus. The obstetrician
    a. is performing in vitro fertilization
    b. intends to inseminate a surrogate mother
    c. may suspect that the fetus is genetically defective
    d. is looking at the shape and size of the fetus

6. A friend of yours thinks that she is pregnant because her period is two weeks overdue. If she is pregnant, she is probably at the
    a. end of the germinal period
    b. beginning of the fetal period
    c. middle of the embryonic period
    d. beginning of the germinal period

7. Regina, a first-time mother, tells you she is expecting quintuplets. What does this suggest to you?
    a. she is very fertile
    b. she is not very fertile and probably used assisted reproductive technology
    c. she has misused the contraceptive Depo Provera
    d. she has more than two ovaries

8. You find yourself looking at two cells and count 69 total chromosomes. What are looking at?
    a. two gametes
    b. one gamete and one other cell
    c. two other cells
    d. process of meiosis

9. Evelyn is informed by her pediatrician that her son has congenital deafness. She feels this probably occured because she
    a. married a man who had served in the Vietnam war and who handled Agent Orange containers
    b. smoked heavily throughout her pregnancy even though her doctor advised her to quit smoking
    c. shared intravenous needles with a friend
    d. used quinine when serving as a missionary in equatorial Africa

10. A pregnant woman's body produces antibodies that attack the baby's blood cells. Which of the following conclusions is most likely?
    a. The mother is Rh positive.
    b. The mother is affected by toxemia.
    c. The mother is a diabetic.
    d. The mother is hypertensive.

11. Which of the following statements most accurately represents your text's discussion of toxins in the workplace?
    a. The female's ova are more susceptible to damage from environmental cause than the male's sperm.
    b. The male's sperm are more susceptible to damage from environmental toxins than the female's ova.
    c. It makes sense to clean up the workplace not only for mothers but for fathers as well.
    d. Hazards in the workplace rarely contribute to reproductive problems.

Chapter 3   Reproduction, Heredity and Genetics, and Prenatal Development

12. Most spontaneous abortions will take place before which period of development?
    a. prenatal
    b. germinal
    c. embryonic
    d. cephalocaudal

13. If you were having a sonogram and wanted to know the sex of your child, what is the earliest that you could know?
    a. sixth month
    b. fifth month
    c. fourth month
    d. seventh month

Chapter 3 Reproduction, Heredity and Genetics, and Prenatal Development

Essay Questions

1. Give arguments for why and how a couple would "plan" when they were going to have a baby. What lifestyle changes might they consider?

2. Your best friend has six children and tells you she doesn't really want any more but can't figure out how to stop them from happening. Write a letter explaining to her reproduction, fertilization, and conception.

3. Someone writes a letter to the editor saying, "We should start practicing eugenics in order to create a better race of humans. After all, look what it's done for tomatoes." Having read the section on heredity and genetics, write a response that synthesizes both positive and negative aspects of "playing God."

Chapter 3 Reproduction, Heredity and Genetics, and Prenatal Development

ANSWERS FOR SELF-TESTS

Matching

1. w
2. x
3. b
4. pp
5. y
6. oo
7. dd
8. qq
9. mm
10. h
11. nn
12. g
13. jj
14. z
15. i
16. l
17. c
18. d
19. f
20. e
21. ll
22. k
23. u
24. ff
25. v
26. bb
27. gg
28. hh
29. aa
30. ee
31. t
32. m
33. cc
34. ii
35. r
36. o
37. n
38. s
39. kk
40. p
41. a
42. j

Multiple Choice

Factual

1. c
2. d
3. b
4. c
5. a
6. a
7. b
8. a
9. b
10. a
11. b
12. d
13. c
14. d
15. b
16. c
17. b
18. a
19. b
20. b
21. a
22. b
23. b
24. c
25. d
26. b
27. a
28. a
29. c
30. b
31. b
32. b
33. b

Conceptual

1. b
2. c
3. d
4. b
5. c
6. d
7. b
8. b
9. b
10. a
11. b
12. b
13. d

Chapter 4

Birth and Physical Development: The First Two Years

INTRODUCTION

Chapter 4 explores the period of infancy – the first two years of life – during which children interact with their environment to develop basic competencies. As children age, they are continuously forced to adapt to the demands of the world around them. Chapter 4 begins with an analysis of the abilities and behavior of neonates as expressed during the first two weeks following birth. The chapter then focuses on the two areas of development which are most profound during the first two years of life: physical growth and motor development. The chapter concludes with an overview of the senses.

- Birth. This is an in-depth look at the changes that occur for mother, father, and child during the birth process. Natural childbirth options that may promote family-infant bonding are also explained.

- Complications of Pregnancy and Birth. The chapter covers some of the complications that may arise during pregnancy, which might result in a Cesarean delivery, as well as the medical intervention available to help the mother and child.

- Newborn Behaviors and Abilities. This section includes an in-depth discussion of newborn behaviors and abilities, including sleeping, crying, feeding, and reflexes.

- Physical Growth. This generally occurs in an orderly fashion. However, not all parts of a child's body develop at equal rates. The brain grows rapidly during the first two years of life. Development in all children is known to follow the cephalocaudal principle as well as the proximodistal principle.

- Motor Development. This is highly complex in infants and is dependent upon the child's overall physical growth. Rhythmical behaviors, such as kicking and rocking, provide the basis for more skilled motor developments, such as crawling and walking. Locomotion evolves between eleven and fifteen months and represents the climax of a series of physical developments. The infant's acquisition of manual skills proceeds through a series of orderly stages.

- Senses. An overview is presented of the infant's ability to see, hear, taste, smell, and feel heat, cold, pressure, and pain. Research related to the significance of these senses is cited.

Chapter 4   Birth and Physical Development: The First Two Years

LEARNING OBJECTIVES

After completing Chapter 4, you should be able to:

1. Describe different birthing methods

psychoprophylactic method

Lamaze method

natural childbirth

2. Cite the changes that occur in the mother and the baby a few weeks before birth and during the three stages of birth.

fetal changes

maternal changes

labor

delivery

afterbirth

3. List the five conditions of the *Apgar scoring system*, and explain its rating system.
   -
   -
   -
   -
   -

Chapter 4   Birth and Physical Development: The First Two Years

4. Define what is meant by *parent-infant bonding*.

5. Explain the following risks to infants:

prematurity

postmaturity

drug-addicted mother

exposure to HIV

exposure to alcohol

exposure to chemicals

6. Briefly explain postpartum depression (PPD).

7. Discuss what is known about Sudden Infant Death Syndrome (SIDS).

Chapter 4   Birth and Physical Development: The First Two Years

8. Identify and describe the six types of *infant alertness states* illustrated by Wolff.

-
-
-
-
-
-

9. Describe the different aspects of motor development

rhythmic behavior

locomotion

manual skills

10. Discuss different aspects of vision and its development throughout infancy.

Acuity

Contrast sensitivity

Eye coordination

Tracking

Color vision

Face recognition

Visual constancy

Depth perception

Binocular vision

Chapter 4   Birth and Physical Development: The First Two Years

11. Explain Gibson's *visual cliff experiment*, and state its significance with respect to depth perception in infants.

12. Describe what is known about the neonate's ability to:

hear

taste

smell

feel heat

feel cold

feel pressure

feel pain

Chapter 4   Birth and Physical Development: The First Two Years

WEB SITES

The following web sites deal with some of the major concepts and issues presented in Chapter 4. Additional resources can be found at the text's web site at http://www.mhhe.com/crandell7.

Neonatology on the Web
http://www.neonatology.org/neo.links.html

American College of Obstetricians and Gynecologists
http://www.acog.org

The National Pediatric & Family HIV Resource Center (NPHRC)
http://www.pedhivaids.org

Genetic Conditions/Rare Conditions
(Support Groups and Information Page)
http://www.kumc.edu/gec/support/groups.html

Birth Defects Atlas of Ontario
http://www.hwc.ca/datahpb/dataLcec/chronic/doc/onatl.htm

Premature Birth Resources
http://www.dailyparent.com/dailyp/source/article/2265.html

SIDS Network
http://www.sids-network.org

Chapter 4 Birth and Physical Development: The First Two Years

SELF-TESTS

Matching

Match the key terms with their definitions:

a. afterbirth
b. anoxia
c. Apgar scoring system
d. birth
e. birthing centers
f. birthing rooms
g. cephalocaudal principle
h. cesarean section
i. colic
j. crowning
k. delivery
l. entrainment
m. failure to thrive
n. infancy
o. infant mortality
p. labor
q. lightening
r. locomotion
s. midwifery
t. natural childbirth
u. neonate
v. norms
w. obstetrician
x. parent-infant bonding
y. postmature infant
z. postpartum depression
aa. premature infant
bb. proximodistal principle
cc. psychoprophylactic method
dd. reflex
ee. rooming in
ff. shaken baby syndrome
gg. small-for-term infant
hh. states
ii. stillbirth
jj. sudden infant death syndrome (SIDS)

1. ____ a baby delivered more than two weeks after the usual forty weeks of gestation in the womb

2. ____ a baby weighing less than 5 pounds 8 ounces at birth or having a gestational age of less than thirty-seven weeks

3. ____ a condition of unknown cause of discomfort that causes some babies to cry for at least an hour or more, typically every day about the same time

4. ____ a continuum of alertness ranging from regular sleep to vigorous activity

5. ____ a method developed by an anesthesiologist to appraise the normalcy of a baby's condition at birth

6. ____ a method of childbirth in which women are encouraged to relax and concentrate on the manner in which they breathe when a contraction occurs

7. ____ a pattern of development that proceeds outward from the central axis of the body toward the extremities

8. ____ a physician who specializes in conception, prenatal development, birth, and the woman's post-birth care

9. ____ a process of interaction and mutual attention between parent and infant which occurs over time that builds an emotional bond

10. ____ a relatively simple, involuntary, and unlearned response to a stimulus

11. ____ a surgical delivery technique by which the physician enters the uterus through an abdominal incision and removes the infant

12. ____ an arrangement in a hospital whereby the newborn infant stays in a bassinet beside the mother's bed

13. ____ an awake, aware, and unmedicated delivery by the mother-to-be

14. ____ begins once the infant's head passes through the cervix and ends when the baby has completed its passage through the birth canal

Chapter 4 Birth and Physical Development: The First Two Years

a. afterbirth
b. anoxia
c. Apgar scoring system
d. birth
e. birthing centers
f. birthing rooms
g. cephalocaudal principle
h. cesarean section
i. colic
j. crowning
k. delivery
l. entrainment
m. failure to thrive
n. infancy
o. infant mortality
p. labor
q. lightening
r. locomotion
s. midwifery
t. natural childbirth
u. neonate
v. norms
w. obstetrician
x. parent-infant bonding
y. postmature infant
z. post partum depression
aa. premature infant
bb. proximodistal principle
cc. psychoprophylactic method
dd. reflex
ee. rooming in
ff. shaken baby syndrome
gg. small-for-term infant
hh. states
ii. stillbirth
jj. sudden infant death syndrome (SIDS)

15. ____ crib death; one of the leading causes of infant death and remains one of medicine's unsolved mysteries

16. ____ fetal death in the womb or death that occurs during labor and delivery

17. ____ hospital rooms where delivery will occur with a homelike atmosphere complete with wallpapered walls, window drapes, potted plants, color television, queen-sized bed and other comforts

18. ____ inadequate weight gain in an infant

19. ____ low-birth weight babies who are not pre-term

20. ____ motor development that proceeds from the head to the feet

21. ____ occurs when a baby's head is violently shaken back and forth or strikes something, resulting in bruising or bleeding of the brain, spinal cord injury, and eye damage

22. ____ occurs when the widest diameter of the baby's head is at the mother's vulva

23. ____ oxygen deprivation, often caused by an umbilical cord that has become squeezed or wrapped around the baby's neck during delivery

24. ____ primary care facilities that are used for low-risk deliveries because they lack high-tech equipment

25. ____ standards used for evaluating a child's developmental progress relative to the average of the child's age group

26. ____ the infant's ability to move itself, which climaxes in the ability to walk, typically between 11 and 15 months of age

27. ____ the legalized provision of prenatal care and delivery by midwives

28. ____ the newborn during the first two weeks following birth

29. ____ the period of the first two years of life

30. ____ the process of expelling the placenta and the remaining umbilical cord from the uterus through the vagina

31. ____ the rate of deaths of infants within the first year of life

32. ____ the repositioning of the infant – shifting downward and forward – which occurs shortly before birth

33. ____ the rhythmical contractions of the strong muscle fibers of the uterus which push the infant downward toward the birth canal

34. ____ the symbiotic relationship between a baby and his or her caregivers

Chapter 4   Birth and Physical Development: The First Two Years

35. ____ the disturbing thoughts and behaviors experienced by some new mothers as crying spells, depression, not sleeping enough or wanting to sleep too much, changes in appetite, anxiety, feelings of not being able to cope, thoughts of not wanting to take care of the baby or thoughts of wanting to harm the baby

36. ____ the transition between dependent existence in the uterus and life as a separate organism

Multiple Choice

Circle the letter of the response that <u>best</u> completes or answers each of the following statements and questions.

Factual Questions

1. The psychoprophylactic method of birthing derives from what famous theorist's insights?
    a. Doula
    b. Pavlov
    c. Mendel
    d. Freud

2. Natural childbirth refers to _____
    a. birth in the home
    b. an awake, aware, and unmedicated mother to be
    c. delivery of the baby by the father
    d. the mother giving birth outdoors and alone

3. What term is used to describe the stage in the birth process in which the strong muscle fibers of the uterus contract rhythmically, pushing the infant downward toward the birth canal?
    a. delivery
    b. afterbirth
    c. labor
    d. natural childbirth

4. Crowning occurs when the
    a. widest diameter of the baby's head is at the mother's vulva
    b. Braxton-Hicks contractions begin
    c. afterbirth is expelled from uterus
    d. Apgar test is performed

5. Women who use the psychoprophylactic method of childbirth
    a. use pain medication or spinal block to tolerate the uterine contractions
    b. use breathing and relaxation exercises during their labor
    c. become more affectionate toward their infants

d. have their babies delivered within a surgical environment

6. Dissatisfaction with the maternity care options provided by physicians has contributed to the legal revival in the United States of
    a. birthing rooms
    b. the couvade syndrome
    c. natural childbirth
    d. midwifery

7. Which of the following statements best describes family-centered hospitals?
    a. They separate the infant from the mother for a prolonged period so she can recuperate.
    b. They discourage new mothers from breast feeding their babies so other family members can feed the child.
    c. They allow the father to be an active member of the delivery team.
    d. They require the mother to use psychoprophylactic methods of delivery.

8. When fathers experience the "couvade syndrome" they are
    a. refusing to participate in child's birth and delivery
    b. protecting their fetus against the trauma of conventional birthing procedures
    c. experiencing pregnancy symptoms similar to those of their wives
    d. feeling a sense of loss following a miscarriage

9. According to the French obstetrician Frederick Leboyer, conventional hospital birth procedures
    a. may permanently damage the infant's nervous system
    b. produce high levels of stress hormones in the fetus
    c. increase the likelihood of delivering babies by cesarean section
    d. ensure that the newborn infant will have an adequate Apgar rating

10. A surgical procedure by which the physician enters the uterus through an abdominal incision and removes the infant is called
    a. epidural block
    b. suturemia
    c. the Lamaze method
    d. Caesarean section

11. A common difficulty encountered by premature infants is
    a. a negative Rh factor
    b. respiratory distress
    c. intestinal complications
    d. intracranial bleeding

12. Premature infants are defined as
    a. weighing less than 6 pounds 4 ounces
    b. being born with respiratory distress
    c. having a gestational age of less than 37 weeks
    d. none of the above

Chapter 4 Birth and Physical Development: The First Two Years

13. Which of the following has not been suggested as a possible cause of Sudden Infant Death Syndrome (SIDS)?
    a. breast feeding
    b. smoking
    c. bacterial infection
    d. brain defects

14. During the state that Peter Wolff refers to as "drowsiness," the infant
    a. is at full rest
    b. has occasional and rapid eye movement
    c. is relatively inactive but opens and closes its eyes intermittently
    d. has irregular respiration and frequent, diffuse motor activity

15. Which of the following descriptions would best characterize an infant's crying at the age of 9 months?
    a. fussy and irregular
    b. persistent and frequent
    c. punctuated by pauses
    d. rhythmic

16. One of the major advantages of breast versus bottle feeding is that breast feeding
    a. gives mothers more physical freedom
    b. protects the infant against infections
    c. immunizes babies by medication the mother receives
    d. gives babies better startle reflexes

17. Reflex responses in infants
    a. are primitive mechanisms that serve no useful biological function
    b. are generally necessary for human survival
    c. provide the infant's limbs with needed exercise
    d. are good indicators of neurological development

18. The two structures known to play a critical role in the growth regulation of children are
    a. the pituitary gland and the hypothalamus
    b. the pituitary gland and the cerebral cortex
    c. the subcortical level and the hypothalamus
    d. the left hemisphere and the right hemisphere

19. The lymphoid tissue shows its greatest development _____, whereas growth of the reproductive system peaks _____.
    a. prior to adolescence; during adolescence
    b. during adulthood; during adolescence
    c. after adolescence; before early adulthood
    d. during adulthood; during early infancy

Chapter 4 Birth and Physical Development: The First Two Years

20. Neurological research on brain development indicates that
    a. the corpus callosum in the newborn prevents passage of information between the two cerebral hemispheres
    b. rapid cortical development in infancy allows infants to develop more flexible and less stereotyped behaviors
    c. the right hemisphere is typically specialized for reasoning operations and speech control
    d. most reflexes, such as sucking and grasping, are organized in the cerebral cortex of the newborn's brain

21. According to the cephalocaudal principle, development proceeds
    a. from right to left
    b. from mother to infant
    c. from head to feet
    d. from left to right

22. Recent research on motor development in infants indicates that
    a. behaviors such as crawling emerge from the dynamic interplay of several developing capabilities
    b. capacities such as locomotion typically emerge in a linear manner
    c. the capacity for locomotion is independent of the child's overall physical growth
    d. the capacity for locomotion is unaffected by the child's interaction with the world around him

23. In learning to walk, children progress through a long sequence of developments, which
    a. progress in a sequence which follows the cephalocaudal principle
    b. are initiated by the infant's command of the trunk region
    c. surface most noticeably during the fourth month of life
    d. progress in sequence from hitching, to creeping, to crawling during the seventh month

24. Which of the following terms refers to the reception of information by our sense organs
    a. perception
    b. sensation
    c. gustation
    d. olfaction

25. Which of the following stimuli is least likely to attract the visual attention of an infant?
    a. facelike pattern
    b. colorful stripes
    c. plain shape
    d. black-and-white bull's-eye pattern

26. Which of the following terms describes the tendency for objects to look the same to us despite fluctuations in sensory input?
    a. depth constancy
    b. visual overlapping
    c. perception of form
    d. visual constancy

Chapter 4 Birth and Physical Development: The First Two Years

27. Eleanor Gibson's visual cliff experiment was designed to test an infant's ability to perceive
    a. color
    b. shape
    c. depth
    d. pattern

28. Infants' ability to tell the distances of various objects and to experience the world three-dimensionally is termed
    a. visual scanning
    b. binocular vision
    c. visual constancy
    d. shape constancy

29. William Condor and Louis Sander have videotaped neonate-adult interaction. They find that neonates
    a. do not possess a genetic predisposition for the acquisition of language
    b. synchronize (coordinate) the movement of their bodies to adult speech patterns
    c. hold their breath and tense their bodies when adults start to yell
    d. have an incompletely developed hearing apparatus resulting from vernix in the ear

30. When sweet fluid is put into the mouth of newborns, they
    a. decrease sucking speed
    b. use the expression sucking method
    c. display an increased respiration rate
    d. engage in increased limb movement

31. The four major cutaneous sensations are heat, cold, pressure, and
    a. taste
    b. smell
    c. pain
    d. sound

Conceptual Questions

1. You have been hired by a research agency to explore potential causes of Sudden Death Infant Syndrome (SIDS). According to current theories, which of the following exemplifies an area of research you would most likely examine?
    a. prenatal care
    b. reflexes
    c. brain development
    d. parental smoking

2. New parents observe that their baby girl's face is contorted, and she is making strong and intense vocalizations while moving about vigorously. According to Wolff, the infant is in which state?
    a. irregular sleep
    b. alert inactivity
    c. waking activity
    d. crying

Chapter 4 Birth and Physical Development: The First Two Years

3. Your friend Nakia is concerned because her baby cries frequently and makes her edgy. Nakia is concerned that she has "taught" her baby to cry. According to research,
   a. crying is a learned response
   b. crying is an unlearned response
   c. crying is a temperament problem
   d. crying is a comfort mechanism

4. Of the following techniques, which most clearly distinguishes American and Dutch parents in regard to their philosophies about how to foster an infant's mental and social growth?
   a. continuous stimulation vs. establishing a soothing routine
   b. breast feeding vs. bottle feeding
   c. visual stimulation vs. auditory stimulation
   d. immediate gratification vs. delayed gratification

5. You see an infant in a hospital that is premature and cries shrilly each time a nurse handles him. You might suspect the child:
   a. is an HIV baby
   b. is a crack baby
   c. has fetal alcohol syndrome
   d. is a normal, healthy baby

6. Select the group of terms that can be most logically placed in the same category.
   a. self-demand feeding, longer feeding intervals, vitamin D
   b. breast feeding, emotional and psychological rewards, antibody production
   c. schedule feeding, bottle feeding, fluoride supplements
   d. breast feeding, malnutrition, intimate contact

7. Monique decides that her infant should be breast-fed rather than bottle-fed. She wants to know how common breast feeding is today. You can tell her
   a. more women breast feed now than in 1900
   b. more women breast feed now than in 1956
   c. fewer women breast feed now than in 1946
   d. fewer women breast feed now than in 1956

8. A nursing mother tries to get her child to suck on the breast by pushing the child's head toward the breast. The child attempts to suck the mother's hand, thus indicating
   a. the orienting reflex
   b. dishabituation
   c. the rooting reflex
   d. breast sensitization

9. A baby has just received APGAR scores of 7 and 9. You can tell the parents that they should be
   a. relieved as this is within the normal range
   b. worried as this is below a perfect score
   c. unconcerned since you don't think this is a valid test
   d. concerned as the score has increased two points between readings

Chapter 4 Birth and Physical Development: The First Two Years

10. Your child appears very healthy, but he is much smaller than most children his age. The best advice might be to have your child's
    a. target-seeking rate monitored
    b. pituitary gland and hypothalamus checked
    c. testosterone levels checked
    d. doctor prescribe large doses of growth hormone to stimulate growth

11. Jasmine reports to her pediatrician that her son, Jeremiah, has grown almost an inch in the last 48 hours. Which of the following would most likely characterize Jeremiah's behavior in the days just prior to the growth spurt?
    a. very passive and withdrawn
    b. calm and placid
    c. fussy and agitated
    d. alert and curious

12. Lauren was able to read a first grade book when she was 2 years old. According to what we know about the development of the brain, which area of Lauren's brain is responsible for producing such giftedness?
    a. the subcortical level
    b. the temporal lobe
    c. the cerebral cortex
    d. the corpus callosum

13. Your 2-year-old child has recently undergone PET (positron emission tomography) scanning, which maps the brain's metabolic activity. The results will probably indicate
    a. the metabolic rate of your 2-year-old's brain approximates that of an adult's because of rapid increase in cerebral cortex activity.
    b. the metabolic rate of your 2-year-old's brain is about two-thirds that of an adult's brain
    c. the metabolic rate of your child's brain will never exceed that of an adult's brain
    d. the metabolic rate of your 2-year-old's brain approximates that of an adult's because of gradual increases in activity of the subcortical level of the brain

14. Sarah's parents kept a log of the various milestones she achieved in her motor development. They noted that Sarah learned to hold her head up before she acquired the ability to sit, and she learned to sit prior to learning how to walk. Sarah has expressed the
    a. proximodistal principle
    b. cephalocaudal principle
    c. stepping reflex
    d. phenomenon of hitching

15. When watching your 3-year-old son draw, you notice that he can coordinate the movements of his forearms, but his wrist is less coordinated. Your son is demonstrating the
    a. cephalocaudal principle
    b. effects of handedness
    c. proximodistal principle
    d. rhythmical behavior principle

Chapter 4 Birth and Physical Development: The First Two Years

16. Rhythmic behavior is to _____ as palm grasp is to _____.
    a. uncoordinated activity; voluntary motor control
    b. locomotion; self-stimulation
    c. locomotion; manual dexterity
    d. crawling; forefinger grasp

17. You are designing a clown costume for Halloween. If you want to maximize an infant's visual attention, you should
    a. use very dim pastel colors in the clown's mask
    b. paint two dark blue spots on the cheeks of the clown mask
    c. paint two straight lines on each cheek of the clown mask
    d. paint one brightly colored bull's-eye in the middle of the clown's mask

18. The results of a scientist's experiment revealed that the subjects perceived the target as a door even though its shape became a trapezoid as the door opened. This scientist has just recorded data to support which phenomenon?
    a. size constancy
    b. object constancy
    c. shape constancy
    d. color constancy

19. An 8-month-old infant creeps over to the top of the staircase. If the infant avoids creeping over the edge of the top step,
    a. she demonstrates visual constancy
    b. binocular vision has not yet occurred
    c. tactile information has been relied on more than visual information
    d. this is the visual cliff effect

20. A researcher conducting a corneal photography experiment with a group of various-aged babies observed that one of the babies focused on a very small portion of a figure. The researcher was most likely studying the eye of an infant in which age group?
    a. newborn
    b. 2 to 4 months
    c. 4 to 5 months
    d. over 5 months

21. A 4-month-old baby is shown two photographs, one of his mother's face and one of a stranger's face. We can reasonably infer that
    a. the infant cannot yet discriminate between familiar and unfamiliar faces
    b. the infant can distinguish his mother from somebody else
    c. the baby will inspect only the external features of the faces, such as the chin and ears
    d. the baby will not concentrate on the pictures because of his lack of visual preference for the human face

Chapter 4   Birth and Physical Development: The First Two Years

Essay Questions

1. Prepare a presentation for expectant parents informing them of what physical developments they can expect in their infant within the first two years.

2. Write a paper discussing options for birthing, and how each method and environment might have positive or negative consequences for different infants. Discuss at-risk infants and infants who need intervention.

3. Discuss the different way that birth affects parents (men and women), and how parents' decisions affect the birth experience as well as the infant's development.

Chapter 4 Birth and Physical Development: The First Two Years

---

ANSWERS FOR SELF-TESTS

Matching

1. y
2. aa
3. i
4. hh
5. c
6. cc
7. bb
8. w
9. x
10. dd
11. h
12. ee
13. t
14. k
15. jj
16. ii
17. f
18. m
19. gg
20. g
21. ff
22. j
23. b
24. e
25. v
26. r
27. s
28. u
29. n
30. a
31. o
32. q
33. p
34. l
35. z
36. d

Multiple Choice

Factual

1. b
2. b
3. c
4. a
5. b
6. d
7. c
8. c
9. b
10. d
11. b
12. c
13. a
14. c
15. c
16. b
17. d
18. a
19. a
20. b
21. c
22. b
23. a
24. b
25. c
26. d
27. c
28. b
29. b
30. a
31. c

Conceptual

1. d
2. d
3. b
4. a
5. b
6. b
7. b
8. c
9. a
10. b
11. c
12. c
13. b
14. b
15. c
16. d
17. d
18. c
19. d
20. d
21. b

Chapter 5

Infancy:
Cognitive and Language Development

INTRODUCTION

Chapter 5 explores the processes by which cognition and language develop during early childhood. Cognitive and language abilities are the most distinctive features of human beings; without them, we would be without culture. The chapter concentrates on the following topics:

- Cognitive Development. Individual differences in mental representation throughout infancy are shown to be developmentally continuous across childhood and even into adulthood.

- Piaget's Sensorimotor Period. Piaget explains the child's primary task of integrating motor and perceptual systems in order to begin the process of objectifying the world

- Learning. Learning is defined and its importance for how we make sense of the world around us is discussed.

- The Function of Language and Thought. The functional importance of language is discussed, with the emphasis on the role of language in facilitating communication as well as thought.

- The Relation of Language to Thought. This is examined in accordance with two opposing viewpoints: language as the mere container of thought and language as the determinant of thought.

- Theories of Language Development. Learning and interactionist theories are examined. These theories state that language is acquired through learning processes, as well as the opposing innateness theory, which views human beings as biologically "prewired" for language usage. Chomsky's nativist theory, whereby the basic structure of language is biologically programmed, is presented in detail.

- Language Development. The importance of early nonverbal behaviors, prelanguage, language production, and language reception in the communication process is discussed. The sequence of language development in children is examined, beginning with such early vocalizations as cooing and babbling, progressing into holophrastic speech, two-word utterances, and telegraphic speech.

Chapter 5   Infancy: Cognitive and Language Development

LEARNING OBJECTIVES

After completing Chapter 5, you should be able to:

1. List the three main criteria used to define *learning*.

    -

    -

    -

2. Summarize the findings from Sameroff's study of neonates' sucking techniques and their capacity to learn.

3. List and describe the three main characteristics of Piaget's *sensorimotor* period as they relate to cognitive development during the first two years of life.

    -

    -

    -

Chapter 5 Infancy: Cognitive and Language Development

4. Identify and explain Bruner's three modes of cognitive representation.

    •

    •

    •

5. Explain how the following two components can be used to predict cognitive competence in childhood.

decrement of attention

recovery of attention

6. Summarize the research on employing early intervention strategies with infants who are developmentally delayed, and discuss the positive and negative impacts of these findings.

7. State the two vital contributions that *language* makes to the human condition, and explain the functional importance of each.

    •

    •

Chapter 5 Infancy: Cognitive and Language Development

8. Describe the concept of "language as the container of thought."

9. Explain the "language as a determinant of thought" position.

10. Define and explain the benefits of each of the following concepts related to speech development.

caretaker speech

motherese in language development

interactional nature of caretaker speech

11. Discuss Chomsky's theory of language development, specifically defining the following terms.

language acquisition device (LAD)

surface structure

deep structure

transformational grammar

12. Discuss why twin studies are important to research on dyslexia and autism.

Chapter 5   Infancy: Cognitive and Language Development

13. Discuss the following elements in the *communication* process, and at what age these occur.

body language

gazing

pointing

paralanguage

language production

language reception

14. Describe the following features of early language development.

　　crying

　　cooing and babbling

　　holophrastic speech

　　overextension

　　two-word utterances

　　telegraphic speech

Chapter 5 Infancy: Cognitive and Language Development

WEB SITES

The following web sites deal with some of the major concepts and issues presented in Chapter 5. Additional resources can be found at the text's web site, http://www.mhhe.com/crandell7.

Cognitive & Linguistic Sciences: Brown University
http://www.cog.brown.edu/netscape3.html

Center for the Study of Language and Information: Stanford University
http://www-csli.stanford.edu/csli/index.shtml

Pediatric Associations & Societies
http://user.iworld.net/medmark/ped/

The National Academy for Child Development
http://www.nacd.org/

Deafax: Working with Technology
http://www.webcom.com/deafax/welcome.html

SIU-C Infant Cry Archive & Research
http://www.siu.edu/departments/coe/comdis/cryhome.html

Child Development Abstracts & Bibliography
http://www.blackwellpublishers.co.uk/asp/journal.asp?ref=0009-3939

PsycSite: Comprehensive
http://stange.simplenet.com/psycsite/html/body_online_info.htm#category

Small Fry Productions
http://www.small-fry.com/

Chapter 5 Infancy: Cognitive and Language Development

SELF-TESTS

Matching

Match the key terms with their definitions:

a. autism
b. babbling
c. caretaker speech
d. communication
e. conceptualization
f. critical period
g. expressive vocabulary
h. holophrase
i. language
j. language acquisition device (LAD)
k. motherese
l. object permanence
m. overextension
n. paralanguage
o. receptive vocabulary
p. sensorimotor
q. telegraphic speech
r. thought

1. ____ a relatively short period of time in which imprinting can take place

2. ____ a simplified, redundant, and highly grammatical sort of language

3. ____ a structured system of sound patterns (words and sentences) that have socially standardized meanings

4. ____ an inborn mechanism that takes all of the sounds, words, and sentences that an infant hears and then produces a grammar that is consistent with this data

5. ____ grouping perceptions into classes or categories on the basis of certain similarities

6. ____ language that is systematically modified by mothers and fathers when they are addressing infants and young people

7. ____ sequences of alternating vowels and consonants that resemble one-syllable utterances

8. ____ short, precise words in two-word or three-word combinations

9. ____ single words that convey different meanings depending on the context in which they are used

10. ____ the container for language that takes place independently of language

11. ____ the coordination of motor activities with sensory inputs

12. ____ the overgeneralization of a word beyond its core sense

13. ____ the process by which people transmit information, ideas, attitudes, and emotions to one another

14. ____ the stress, pitch, and volume of vocalizations by which we communicate expressive meaning

15. ____ when infants come to view a thing as having a reality of its own that extends beyond their immediate perception of it

16. ____ words that can be used correctly in speech

17. ____ words that can be understood

18. ____ a neurological disorder characterized by deficits in communication and social interaction

Chapter 5 Infancy: Cognitive and Language Development

Multiple Choice

Circle the letter of the response that best completes or answers each of the following statements and questions.

Factual Questions

1. The study of cognition includes all of the following except
   a. perception
   b. problem solving
   c. recall
   d. reactive reasoning

2. Learning involves a relatively permanent change in a capability or behavior that results from
   a. observation
   b. modeling
   c. experience
   d. conditioning

3. Arnold Sameroff conducted a study in which he was able to teach neonates to use one method of sucking (either expressive or suction) in preference to another. The learning was achieved through
   a. imitation
   b. observation
   c. punishment
   d. reinforcement

4. The developmental psychologist who contributed a great deal to our understanding of how children think, reason, and problem solve in developmental cognitive stages is
   a. Sigmund Freud
   b. Jean Piaget
   c. Noam Chomsky
   d. B. F. Skinner

5. The realization that objects continue to exist even when they are out of sight constitutes
   a. symbolic representation
   b. cognition
   c. object permanence
   d. object identity

6. According to Piaget, the infant comes to integrate the motor and perceptual systems during which period?
   a. motoperceptive
   b. preoperational
   c. sensorimotor
   d. somatosensory

Chapter 5 Infancy: Cognitive and Language Development

7. Which of the following are characteristic of Piaget's description of the early sensorimotor period?
    a. infants cannot internally represent the world
    b. infants cannot see that objects exist independently
    c. infants cannot coordinate grasping with visual cues
    d. all of the above

8. According to Jerome Bruner, what type of cognitive representation appears first in young children?
    a. ikonic
    b. enactive
    c. symbolic
    d. perceptual

9. Jerome Bruner indicates that children use mental images or pictures for representing the world. He refers to these as
    a. symbols
    b. enactive images
    c. ikonic images
    d. sign images

10. Which of the following has not been shown to be a consequence of maternal depression?
    a. intense mood swings
    b. an inability to discipline effectively
    c. a reduced capacity for nurturing
    d. the tendency for the child to exhibit a negative self-concept

11. Which of the following statements regarding the prediction of intelligence from cognitive performance in infancy is the most accurate?
    a. Modern psychologists believe that there is no continuity between early and later capabilities.
    b. Decrement and recovery of attention seem most indicative of intelligence in youngsters.
    c. Youngsters who tire more easily when looking at one object are less efficient processors of information.
    d. Youngsters who prefer familiar stimuli over novel stimuli are more efficient processors of information.

12. In this chapter, language is defined as
    a. a structured system of sound patterns that have socially standardized meanings
    b. a set of rules for joining words to form phrases and sentences
    c. the process by which people transmit information
    d. a system of categories used to organize perceptual input

13. The process of transmitting information, ideas, attitudes, and emotions to one another is termed
    a. conceptualization
    b. language
    c. communication
    d. reception

Chapter 5 Infancy: Cognitive and Language Development

14. Proponents who view language as a container of thought claim that
    a. language precedes thought
    b. thought is not possible without language
    c. language shapes thought
    d. thought takes place independently of language

15. Proponents who view language as the determinant of thought claim that
    a. language impedes thought
    b. thought is not possible without language
    c. language shapes thought
    d. thought takes place independently of language

16. Children approach the task of "word learning" equipped with preexisting _____ that limit the number of possible meanings for a new noun.
    a. cognitive biases
    b. conceptualizations
    c. language biases
    d. symbols

17. A psychologist who accepted the view that language determined thought would tend to emphasize the importance of
    a. paralanguage
    b. ikonic representation
    c. caretaker speech
    d. conceptualization

18. Interactionist theory is to _____ as innateness theory is to _____.
    a. nurture; nature
    b. learning; environment
    c. nature; nurture
    d. biological endowment; environment

19. In _____, parents systematically modify the language that they employ with adults when addressing young children.
    a. motherese
    b. caretaker speech
    c. conceptualization
    d. phonology

20. When a caretaker uses words such as "choo-choo" to signify a train, she is using
    a. caretaker speech
    b. baby talk
    c. motherese
    d. interactional speech

21. Nativists, such as Noam Chomsky, contend that the primary factor influencing language acquisition is
    a. the child's environment
    b. the interaction between the child and his or her caretaker
    c. learning processes
    d. the child's biological endowment

Chapter 5   Infancy: Cognitive and Language Development

22. Which of the following is a nativist criticism of learning theory views of language acquisition?
    a. Children's speech is not a mechanical playback of adult speech.
    b. Caretakers spontaneously develop a unique language system for communicating with children.
    c. Children understand only about one-half of the words spoken to them in motherese.
    d. The specialized anatomy of the vocal tract makes language possible.

23. Noam Chomsky pointed out that the world's languages have basic similarities in their composition, and he termed these similarities
    a. transformational grammar
    b. deep structure
    c. surface structure
    d. caretaker speech

24. Most psychologists agree that there is a _____ for language acquisition, but they disagree over the importance of _____.
    a. biological basis; parental input
    b. cultural basis; genetic factors
    c. cultural basis; biological factors
    d. biological basis; cognitive factors

25. The stress, pitch, and volume of words by which we communicate expressive meaning are referred to as
    a. language production
    b. kinesics
    c. paralanguage
    d. telegraphic speech

26. The best time to learn a new language is
    a. early in life
    b. when one enters kindergarten
    c. during middle school
    d. in college

27. Which of the following is in the correct sequence for language development?
    a. crying, babbling, cooing, holophrases
    b. crying, cooing, babbling, holophrases
    c. gurgling, babbling, cooing, holophrases
    d. making bubbles with saliva, crying, cooing, babbling

28. When a child uses the same single word to convey different meaning, depending on the context she is in, the child is using
    a. holophrastic speech
    b. transformational grammar
    c. symbolic syntax
    d. deep structures

Chapter 5   Infancy: Cognitive and Language Development

Conceptual Questions

1. Claire, a 6-month-old child, smiles and grows excited when she gazes at the teddy bear in her crib. However, when her mother accidentally covers the bear with a blanket, the child seems to forget about it and begins to play with something else. According to Piaget, the child is demonstrating _____ concerning the teddy bear.
    a. thought without cognition
    b. a learning disability
    c. lack of object permanence
    d. mental representation

2. An infant sees a ball under a chair; but when he crawls over to the side of the chair, the ball is not there. The infant is soon distracted by another toy. Psychologists who have revised Piaget's insights would say that this infant
    a. knew the ball still existed
    b. did not attribute permanence to objects
    c. had difficulty coordinating searching capabilities
    d. did not possess cognitive representation

3. A little girl hears the word "dog" and pictures her own dog Spot. She is using
    a. object permanence
    b. ikonic representation
    c. enactive representation
    d. symbolic representation

4. Eighteen-month-old Joey is not talking, and most of the time is unresponsive. During a visit, the grandparents witness the lack of communication and see Joey's inability to socialize with them. They are concerned Joey might have
    a. agoraphobia
    b. drug addiction
    c. autism
    d. anxiety attacks

5. Bridget's baby quickly becomes drowsy and inattentive when she rocks her or lays her down on the floor to watch television. However, the baby quickly becomes reanimated when an interesting sight or sound occurs in the room. We might reasonably predict that Bridget's baby will
    a. become impulsive and hyperactive
    b. become cognitively competent
    c. not differ substantially from other children during preschool years
    d. not display categorical perception

6. Monique is very concerned about how her behavior as a parent will affect her baby's intellectual development. Research suggests that Monique can best influence her infant's competence by doing all of the following except
    a. provide the baby with immediate positive feedback
    b. provide a nonrestrictive environment
    c. teaching math to her baby during the first year of life
    d. develop a secure parent-infant attachment

Chapter 5 Infancy: Cognitive and Language Development

7. Nathan, a 4-year-old, has been raised by overly ambitious parents who have pushed their son to gain academically oriented skills. We reasonably infer that Nathan
    a. may grow to dislike learning as a result of the pressures to learn
    b. will be more apt to undertake highly skilled activities
    c. will develop a higher intellect
    d. may benefit more from a structured preschool program

8. Marta is 8 months old and can picture her bottle, even though she doesn't yet know the word for it. Which theorist would accept this view of language and thought?
    a. Freud
    b. Piaget
    c. Vygotsky
    d. Mead

9. Joel has brought home a new dog for his family and wants to teach his young son how to call the dog. According to research on children's ability to conceptualize new words, Joel's son would most quickly learn which term?
    a. canine
    b. collie
    c. animal
    d. dog

10. Roseanne said to her baby "Hey, Anna! Anna! Where's the doggie? Where's the doggie? See. On the steps. See, over there on the steps!" This kind of language, where the focus is on the location of an object, is representative of which form of parental speech?
    a. baby talk
    b. caretaker speech
    c. caregiver speech
    d. motherese

11. Nancy is a depressed mother and primary caretaker for her new baby. She speaks to her infant very little, and uses unexaggerated intonation.   She is slow to respond to her child's early attempts at vocalization. We can reasonably infer that Nancy's child
    a. will acquire language in much the same manner as the child of a healthy, happy mother
    b. will suffer a delay in language acquisition
    c. will have an overdeveloped language acquisition device
    d. will remain unaffected by her mother's depression

12. In speaking to her 8-month-old baby, a mother uses shorter words, more pointing, more repetition, more exclamations (e.g., "gee," "gosh"), and more diminutives (e.g., "bunny" vs. "rabbit") than when talking to her 5-year-old. This simplified speech
    a. is intended to develop the child's language acquisition capabilities
    b. improves the child's object permanence ability
    c. attributes conceptual ability to the baby and by doing so facilitates language acquisition
    d. is pleasing to the parent but has no effect on the child because children this age have only productive speech

Chapter 5 Infancy: Cognitive and Language Development

13. Which statement in regard to language acquisition is most consistent with the nativists' viewpoint?
    a. Language is acquired directly through learning processes.
    b. Experience dictates the development of language.
    c. Humans are biologically "preprogrammed" for language usage.
    d. Learning and biology interact to determine language.

14. Your child uses word constructions such as "all gone sticky" and "gooder." This type of language supports the
    a. learning theory position
    b. Piagetian position
    c. nativist position
    d. linguistic relativity position

15. Tony observed that his baby was able to alter the stress, pitch, and volume of his vocalizations when angry. Tony was witnessing his son's ability to use which form of communication?
    a. metalanguage
    b. paralanguage
    c. language reception
    d. telegraphic speech

16. Keiko, a 6-month-old, has just begun to make her first babbling sounds. According to what is known about the development of babbling sounds in babies, which sound is Keiko least likely to utter first?
    a. a nasal such as *n* or *m*
    b. a single-stop consonant *d, t,* or *b*
    c. vowel sounds such as "eh"
    d. a consonant such as *l, r, f,* or *v*

17. Tony, who has normal hearing, lives with deaf parents who communicate by sign language. Tony suffers severe asthma and is confined to his home where no English is spoken. By the time he is 4 years old, Tony will
    a. probably not speak English
    b. not understand English or sign language
    c. have learned English through daily television exposure
    d. be fluent in sign language and English

18. A child says the word "mama" when she wants to be fed. The child also uses the word "mama" to communicate that she wants to be let out of her crib. The child's use of the word "mama" could be described as a(n)
    a. overgeneralization
    b. body language
    c. transformational rule
    d. holophrase

19. Sara, a toddler, uses sentences such as "go store" and "more cookie." This child is probably using
    a. general syntax rules
    b. telegraphic speech
    c. compound speech
    d. functional speech

Chapter 5 Infancy: Cognitive and Language Development

Essay Questions

1. It has been said that "Language is what makes us human." What tasks does language permit us to do that other animals cannot do, and how do these tasks contribute to our development?

2. Compare and contrast the idea of language as container of thought with language as determinant of thought using the information you have on children's language acquisition.

3. Observe two children and an adult with child – each having a conversation. Discuss similarities and differences in these conversations, and the implications of these differences for children.

Chapter 5 Infancy: Cognitive and Language Development

ANSWERS FOR SELF-TESTS

Matching

1. f
2. k
3. i
4. j
5. e
6. c
7. b
8. q
9. h
10. r
11. p
12. m
13. d
14. n
15. l
16. g
17. o
18. a

Multiple Choice

Factual

1. d
2. c
3. d
4. b
5. c
6. c
7. d
8. b
9. c
10. b
11. b
12. a
13. c
14. d
15. c
16. a
17. d
18. a
19. b
20. b
21. d
22. a
23. b
24. a
25. c
26. a
27. b
28. a

Conceptual

1. c
2. c
3. b
4. c
5. b
6. c
7. a
8. b
9. d
10. d
11. b
12. c
13. c
14. c
15. b
16. d
17. a
18. d
19. b

Chapter 6

Infancy:
The Development of Emotional and Social Bonds

INTRODUCTION

Chapter 6 illustrates the importance of children's early years in shaping their psychological and social well-being. The chapter covers several domains, including:

- The Development of Emotion. The role of emotion is discussed, and research pertaining to the emotional life of children is presented.

- Theories of Personality Development. Five different theories are presented: psychoanalytic, psychosocial, behavioral, cognitive, and ecological.

- Social Bonds. The objects, functions, and formation of the attachment process are illustrated, as well as the effect of early attachment patterns on later relationships.

- Temperament. The interaction between a child's temperament and the parents' child-rearing practices is examined.

- Early Parenting. Different aspects of parenting are considered: the role of the mother and father, and multiple mothering are all discussed regarding the child's psychosocial development.

- Other Factors. The effects of day care, siblings, and grandparents on the child's emotional, social, and intellectual development are also covered.

- Negative Influences. The effects of poverty, abuse, and neglect are presented.

LEARNING OBJECTIVES

After completing Chapter 6, you should be able to:

1. Discuss the role of emotions in development and list three functions of emotions

    1.
    2.
    3.

2. Cite different views of personality development associated with:

Freud

Erikson

Skinner

Bronfenbrenner

Piaget

3. Define the term *attachment* and describe the three stages of attachment.

attachment

-

-

-

Chapter 6 Infancy: The Development of Emotional and Social Bonds

4. Describe the concept Emotional Intelligence

5. Describe the difference between intrapersonal and interpersonal intelligences

6. Summarize the findings from Ainsworth's research procedure called the *strange situation* and describe the following types:

securely attached infants

avoidant infants

resistant infants

disorganized/disoriented infants

7. Briefly summarize what is known about the development of *stranger anxiety* in children, and state when it seems to appear.

8. Briefly list children's developing *emotion*s as they appear in an orderly fashion in the course of maturation using Izard's differential emotions theory and Campos's theory about emotional development.

9. List and briefly describe the functions of attachment according to ethologists.

-

-

-

-

10. Define *temperament* and discuss Alexander Thomas' views on individual temperaments:

difficult

slow to warm up

easy

11. Explain Alexander Thomas' "goodness of fit" theory.

Chapter 6 Infancy: The Development of Emotional and Social Bonds

12. Explain the roles of father and mother in caregiving.

13. Discuss different perspectives on the importance of early childcare practices.

14. Describe *multiple mothering*, and examine its effects on young children.

15. Explain which children are more likely to become the victims of maltreatment and abuse.

16. List signs adults should look for when suspecting child abuse or neglect, or some symptoms displayed by children who are maltreated.

Chapter 6 Infancy: The Development of Emotional and Social Bonds

WEB SITES

The following web sites deal with some of the major concepts and issues presented in Chapter 6. Additional resources can be found at the text's web site at http://www.mhhe.com/crandell7.

Preschoolers
http://www.kidsource.com/kidsource/pages/Preschoolers.html

The Nature of Children's Play
http://www.kidsource.com/kidsource/content2/nature.of.childs.play.html

Inclusion in the Preschool Setting
http://www.earlychildhood.com/articles/inclpres.html

National Research Center on the Gifted and Talented
http://www.gifted.uconn.edu/nrcgt.html

Federal Interagency Forum on Child and Family Statistics
http://www.childstats.gov/

Head Start & Early Head Start Programs
http://www.acf.dhhs.gov/programs/hsb/goals.htm

Erik Erikson & Psychosocial Development
http://snycorva.cortland.edu/~ANDERSMD/ERIK/sum.html

National Fatherhood Initiative
http://www.fatherhood.org/

The Child Abuse Prevention Network
http://child.cornell.edu/capn.html

The ABCs of Safe and Healthy Child Care: An Online Handbook for Child Care Providers
http://www.cdc.gov/ncidod/hip/abc/abc.htm

Chapter 6   Infancy: The Development of Emotional and Social Bonds

SELF-TESTS

Matching

Match the key terms with their definitions:

a. attachment
b. child abuse
c. emotion
d. emotional intelligence
e. intrapersonal intelligence
f. interpersonal intelligence
g. multiple mothering
h. neglect
i. reactive attachment disorder
j. separation anxiety
k. social referencing
l. strange situation
m. stranger anxiety
n. temperament

1. ____ a technique consisting of a series of eight episodes in which researchers observe infants in an unfamiliar playroom

2. ____ a wariness of strangers

3. ____ an affectional bond that one individual forms for another and that endures across time and space

4. ____ an arrangement in which responsibility for a child's care is dispersed among several people

5. ____ distress shown when a familiar caregiver leaves

6. ____ feeling that motivates, organizes and guides perception, thought, and action

7. ____ non-accidental physical attack on or injury to children by individuals caring for them

8. ____ abilities such as being able to motive oneself, persisting in the face of frustrations, controlling impulses and delaying gratification, empathizing, hoping, deregulation one's moods to keep distress from overwhelming the ability to think

9. ____ the absence of adequate social, emotional, and physical care

10. ____ the practice whereby an inexperienced person relies on a more experienced person's interpretation of an event to regulate his or her subsequent behavior

11. ____ inappropriate social behaviors due to abandonment and deprivation

12. ____ the ability to understand and manage oneself

13. ____ the relatively consistent, basic dispositions inherent in people that underlie and modulate much of their behavior

14. ____ the ability to understand and manage other people

Chapter 6 Infancy: The Development of Emotional and Social Bonds

Multiple Choice

Circle the letter of the response that <u>best</u> completes or answers each of the following statements and questions.

Factual Questions

1. According to Erik Erikson, the development of which of the following is the essential task of infancy?
    a. independence
    b. a sense of self-worth
    c. a basic trust in others
    d. the feeling of belonging

2. The physiological changes, subjective experiences, and expressive behaviors that are involved in feelings is termed
    a. temperament
    b. emotion
    c. self-esteem
    d. social referencing

3. Child neglect is best defined as
    a. an intentional physical attack on a child by the parent
    b. an injury that is purposely inflicted on the child by the parent
    c. the absence of adequate social, emotional, and physical care
    d. severe injuries associated with physical abuse of children

4. Studies of parents who abuse their children reveal that the parents
    a. expect very little from their children
    b. are exclusively from lower socioeconomic levels
    c. were themselves abused as children
    d. usually suffer from severe psychotic tendencies, untreatable through counseling

5. The practice whereby an inexperienced person relies on a more experienced person's interpretation of an event to regulate his or her subsequent behavior is
    a. accommodation
    b. modeling
    c. imprinting
    d. social referencing

6. Which of the following statements is the most accurate according to Izard's differential emotions theory?
    a. All the basic emotions are in place at birth.
    b. At birth, the inner feelings of babies are limited to shyness, contempt, and guilt.
    c. Emotions are not preprogrammed on a biological clock.
    d. Each emotion has its own distinctive facial pattern.

Chapter 6 Infancy: The Development of Emotional and Social Bonds

7. Izard has found that infants normally express shyness as well as self-awareness
   a. shortly after birth
   b. around 4 to 6 weeks of age
   c. around 6 to 8 months of age
   d. by about their first birthday

8 What is the main disagreement Joseph Campos has with Carroll Izard regarding emotions?
   a. in fact they have no disagreement
   b. Campos believes that children actively construct emotions
   c. Campos believes that all the basic emotions are in place at birth
   d. Campos believes that all the basic emotions are preprogrammed to occur at specified times

9. The relatively consistent, basic dispositions inherent in people that underlie and modulate much of their behavior are referred to as
   a. temperament
   b. attachment
   c. person permanence
   d. emotion

10. The attachment behavioral system does the following
    a. encourages youngsters to avoid people
    b. leads to maintaining proximal contact with adults
    c. gives the child feelings of security to explore
    d. encourages interaction with others after initial wariness subsides

11. According to Thomas's categories of temperament, a baby that has a low activity level, adapts very slowly, and tends to be withdrawn would be classified as a(n) _____ baby.
    a. difficult
    b. easy
    c. slow-to-warm-up
    d. passive

12. Thomas refers to the match between the characteristics of infants and their families as
    a. temperament
    b. attachment
    c. social bonding
    d. goodness of fit

13. A major finding about temperament and child-rearing practices is
    a. children are active agents in their own socialization process
    b. parents are the product of the children they are trying to rear
    c. both a and b
    d. neither a nor b

14. The bond that one individual forms for another and that endures across time is referred to as
    a. attachment
    b. temperament
    c. person permanence
    d. social referencing

Chapter 6 Infancy: The Development of Emotional and Social Bonds

15. Which of the following is identified as an indicator of specific attachment in infants (the 3rd stage of attachment)?
    a. separation distress
    b. bonding
    c. maternal deprivation
    d. developmental psychopathology

16. A child who cries in the presence of unknown people is probably exhibiting
    a. neglect
    b. object relations anxiety
    c. attachment anxiety
    d. stranger anxiety

17. The ongoing relationships infants have with mothers, fathers, grandparents, and siblings is called their
    a. social framework
    b. social network
    c. social attachment
    d. social permanence

18. Which of the following is not a function of attachment?
    a. The child learns to cling to the primary caregiver.
    b. The child learns about the world.
    c. It provides the child with emotional security.
    d. It allows the child to enter into social relationships with other human beings.

19. The ethologist John Bowlby says that attachment behaviors are
    a. learned behaviors from one's environment
    b. formed from proximity and contact with adults
    c. innate biological tendencies ready to be activated
    d. reciprocal and derive from a reinforcing relationship with the mother

20. According to learning theories of attachment, the mother is initially a
    a. biologically preprogrammed magnet for the child
    b. punishing source for the child
    c. hindrance to the child's acquisition of gender identity
    d. neutral stimulus for the child

21. Research by Ainsworth indicates that
    a. there is no correlation between early maternal caregiving and patterns of attachment behavior
    b. the avoidant mothers of resistant infants are often inconsistent, insensitive, and rejecting
    c. attachment patterns do not vary from culture to culture
    d. early attachment behaviors are not indicative of later social and cognitive development

22. Which of the following statements is the least accurate regarding the research on stranger anxiety?
    a. It seems to be common among 8-month-old infants.
    b. Infants show significantly more "wary" behaviors than their mothers do.
    c. It is a developmental milestone that normally occurs in children.
    d. Children tend to react to strangers with acceptance.

23. Emotional intelligence includes such abilities as
    a. social gratification
    b. impulse control
    c. excessive stress promotion
    d. sensory deprivation

24. Absentee fathers seems to affect
    a. girls more than boys
    b. boys more than girls
    c. girls and boys equally
    d. neither boys or girls

25. Current research on the role of the father indicates that
    a. men lack the potential to be as good caretakers of children as women
    b. fathers are more likely than mothers to hold their babies and look at them
    c. fathers smile more at their babies than mothers
    d. babies drink less milk when fathers do the bottle feeding than when mothers do

26. Concerning parenting responsibility, which of the following is not a trend that has emerged in the United States over the past thirty years?
    a. More children reside in fatherless settings.
    b. Fathers are taking a more active role in childcare and household tasks since more women work outside the home.
    c. Mothers still provide most of the child care and perform most of the household tasks.
    d. Fathers are likely to be "weekend" parents.

27. One of the most consistent findings about a father's absence in the home is
    a. girls from fatherless homes exhibit poorer moral judgment
    b. deterioration of a boy's school performance
    c. deterioration of a daughter's school performance
    d. the older the child is when he or she loses the father, the greater the impairment

28. The arrangement in which responsibility for a child's care is dispersed among several people is termed
    a. extended caregiving
    b. communal parenting
    c. multiple parenting
    d. multiple mothering

29. Regarding the research on child day-care centers, which statement is most accurate?
    a. Day-care children are very different from their home-raised counterparts in regard to their intellectual, social, and emotional development.
    b. Day-care children appear to be less attached to their mothers than children raised at home.
    c. Most infants with working mothers spend the day in a day-care center.
    d. High-quality day care is an acceptable alternative childcare arrangement.

Chapter 6 Infancy: The Development of Emotional and Social Bonds

Conceptual Questions

1. An adoptive mother tells a therapist, "My 2-month-old doesn't show any special preference for me. I think she doesn't love me." Such a declaration indicates that the
    a. child has probably developed maternal deprivation syndrome
    b. mother may abuse the child when the child doesn't satisfy her needs
    c. mother has psychotic tendencies and should be institutionalized
    d. child is demonstrating the first stage of attachment behavior

2. You are a first grade teacher. A child in your class arrives at school early and wants to stay after school to help you clean up the room. This behavior may be
    a. the way the child deals with separation anxiety
    b. an indication of secure attachment to the mothering figure
    c. an indicator of recent maternal deprivation
    d. a potential warning sign of child abuse and neglect

3. Roxanne's 1-year-old son looks at her for guidance before he allows a photographer to take his picture. When his mother smiles at him, the child remains at ease until the camera flicks. Roxanne's son has demonstrated
    a. specific attachment
    b. person permanence
    c. social referencing
    d. stranger anxiety

4. Dionne's baby daughter, Celine, was scolded because she would not share any of her toys with her twin sister. After being reprimanded, her facial expression appeared to convey a look of guilt. According to Izard's differential emotions theory, Celine is likely to be
    a. 4 to 6 weeks
    b. 3 to 4 months
    c. 1 year old
    d. 2 years old

5. Your nephew is 8 months old. You are a psychology major interested in assessing his emotional development. You might expect that your nephew will
    a. lift his arms when his mother bends over to pick him up and gurgle when his mother says "Hi"
    b. primarily display either surprise or sadness, particularly if he has never seen you
    c. respond in a stereotypical way toward you even when you change your facial expressions
    d. approach you if you raise your eyebrows and wrinkle your nose

6. During the Foster's annual Easter egg hunt, Beth overhears her young son, Matthew, say that he no longer believes in the Easter bunny. According to the Greenspans' stage theory on children's emotional development, Matthew's ability to tell fantasy from reality represents which stage?
    a. stage three
    b. stage four
    c. stage five
    d. stage six

Chapter 6 Infancy: The Development of Emotional and Social Bonds

7. A 2-year-old will not let his mother out of his sight without expressing rage or anxiety. Erikson suggests that this child
    a. has had a deficient parenting style
    b. has a disposition he was born with
    c. has not resolved issues of trust satisfactorily
    d. has a chemical imbalance in his brain

8. Frank's infant son, Albert, usually has a cheerful disposition and is able to adapt quickly to novel situations and people. Alexander Thomas's research on temperament suggests that Albert would be classified as a(n) _____ baby.
    a. passive
    b. slow-to-warm-up
    c. easy
    d. low maintenance

9. An infant is more likely to approach, follow, and cling to her mother than to her father. These behaviors indicate
    a. unfocused expression and excitement
    b. a specific attachment
    c. an insecure attachment
    d. arousal by all parts of the environment

10. You are concerned because your 8-month-old does not seem to feel distressed when you leave the house. Your sister, who is a full-time homemaker, says that her children showed separation anxiety at 6 months of age. On the basis of research evidence, you might conclude that
    a. because you work, separation is a more common event for your infant, and thus he reacts less to it
    b. your child has probably developed person permanence, whereas your nephews have not
    c. your nephews are showing indiscriminate attachment, whereas your child is showing specific attachment
    d. your child has not been imprinted by a social network of other adults

11. Tanya is concerned because her infant son, Marlon, becomes visibly upset, cries loudly, and stops playing with his toys whenever she leaves his room. A developmental psychologist would respond to Tanya's concern by saying that Marlon is expressing a normal tendency for infants termed
    a. indiscriminate attachment
    b. person permanence
    c. stranger anxiety
    d. separation distress

12. David placed his infant daughter, Mariah, on the rug so she could crawl around. Mariah became visibly upset, and she started to cry. David picked Mariah up into his arms, she immediately began to smile, then David cuddled her. To suggest that David and Mariah were genetically predisposed for such behavior offers support for which developmental paradigm?
    a. learning perspective
    b. social perspective
    c. ethological perspective
    d. behavioral perspective

Chapter 6 Infancy: The Development of Emotional and Social Bonds

13. Which of the following statements is consistent with the learning theory view of attachment?
    a. Behaviors that promote proximity are important in the natural selection process.
    b. Attachment develops through the process of socialization, whereby children acquire a need for the presence of the parents.
    c. Parents are genetically predisposed to provide caretaking behavior.
    d. The human face is an innate releasing stimulus for smiling.

14. Stephanie and her mother are visiting a friend for the first time. Stephanie plays happily until her mother leaves to get some coffee. She starts to cry but quickly stops when her mother returns. What type of attachment does she have with her mother?
    a. secure
    b. avoidant
    c. resistant
    d. ambivalent

15. Pierre is a 1-year-old who is securely attached to his mother. Which of the following statements is the least accurate?
    a. He has received consistent, sensitive, responsive mothering.
    b. Pierre is likely to develop into an unselfish toddler and will acquire normal social skills.
    c. He is likely to develop good cognitive skills.
    d. As he ages, Pierre will lack the ability to care for his younger siblings because he demands too much attention from his mother.

16. Dana is out with her father when a woman she does not know approaches them rapidly. Dana starts to cry. Her crying probably signifies
    a. wariness of strangers
    b. attachment to her mother
    c. separation distress
    d. attachment to her father

17. Chelsea is 11 months old when her mother drops her off at the local day-care center for the first time. Based on what is known about wariness of strangers, predict how Chelsea would most likely respond upon meeting her new caretaker for the first time?
    a. She will cry because she has achieved the developmental milestone of a "fear of the stranger."
    b. She will become visibly upset because she believes that her mother is abandoning her.
    c. She will cling to her mother and withdraw from looking at the stranger.
    d. She will greet the stranger with acceptance and exhibit friendly responses.

18. Alex was raised in an institution until the Romanos adopted him at the age of 4. He will probably
    a. experience no mental deficiency whatsoever
    b. attain a higher IQ score after adoption
    c. attain a normal IQ score after he is reared in a normal family environment
    d. remain unaffected by the processes of institutionalization and adoption

Chapter 6 Infancy: The Development of Emotional and Social Bonds

19. Your 1-year-old son displays distress when you leave him at the day-care center. Developmental psychopathologists would probably say that
    a. your son will be more likely than other children to have psychiatric difficulties as an adult
    b. your son was displaying the early precursors of a bipolar mood disorder
    c. this behavior was an ethologically significant and normal part of your son's attachment behavioral system
    d. the duration, frequency, and intensity of his behavior would need to be assessed before its significance could be determined

20. On a typical day, Vanessa's mother shares mothering with several other individuals, including Vanessa's aunts, grandmothers, older cousins, and neighbors. This illustration of diffused nurturance is termed
    a. maternal deprivation
    b. motherese
    c. secondary mothering
    d. multiple mothering

Essay Questions

1. A friend tells you that attachment occurs between any two animals or people who are brought together. Explain why this is not true based on your understanding of the course, objects and functions of attachment.

2. You must settle an argument between two friends who disagree over whether it is emotion or intellect that ensures survival of our species. What are the arguments for emotion? For intellect?

3. A set of twins are forced to spend each day in separate care environments. One must stay in a day care facility at her mother's place of employment. The other stays with her father for half the day and with her grandmother at home for the other half. Discuss the advantages and disadvantages of these two arrangements.

Chapter 6 Infancy: The Development of Emotional and Social Bonds

ANSWERS FOR SELF-TESTS

Matching

1. l
2. m
3. a
4. g
5. j
6. c
7. b
8. d
9. h
10. k
11. i
12. e
13. n
14. f

Multiple Choice

Factual
1. c
2. b
3. c
4. c
5. d
6. d
7. c
8. c
9. a
10. b
11. c
12. d
13. c
14. a
15. a
16. d
17. b
18. a
19. c
20. d
21. b
22. b
23. b
24. b
25. b
26. d
27. b
28. d
29. d

Conceptual
1. d
2. d
3. c
4. d
5. d
6. d
7. c
8. c
9. b
10. a
11. d
12. c
13. b
14. a
15. d
16. a
17. c
18. b
19. c
20. d

Chapter 7

Early Childhood:
Physical and Cognitive Development

INTRODUCTION

Chapters 4, 5, and 6 dealt with the period of infancy. Chapter 7 is the first of two chapters focusing on early childhood – the time between ages 2 and 6. During this period, children acquire autonomy, evolve new ways of relating to other people, and gain a sense of themselves and their effectiveness in the world. Several vital topics are examined, including:

- Physical Growth and Health Concerns. Underpinning cognitive and social skills are continued physical growth and the perfection of gross and fine motor skills that promote coordination of movement. The expansion of their physical world allows children the opportunity for affecting their environment. Health issues such as asthma, Hiv, and diet are also examined.

- Cognitive Development. Various forms of intelligence are discussed, as is the nature-nurture controversy surrounding the level of an individual's intelligence. The early development of intelligence is traced in accordance with Piaget's observations. More recent research concerning children's conceptual foundations for learning is also presented.

- Information Processing and Memory. Early memory, information processing, metacognition, and metamemory are discussed in detail. The memory strategies of categorizing and rehearsing are illustrated in this section as well.

- Cognitive Foundations for Social Interaction. The ways in which children acquire conceptions of role and self are discussed. Roles provide social guidelines which define an individual's obligations as well as expectations. The self provides an individual with the capacity to observe, respond to, and direct his or her morals and behavior.

Chapter 7   Early Childhood: Physical and Cognitive Development

---

LEARNING OBJECTIVES

After completing Chapter 7, you should be able to:

1. Describe physical growth and motor skill development in early childhood regarding:

rate of growth

self-stabilizing quality

impact of coordination

2. Briefly explain aspects of sensory development of children from 2 to 7 years old.

3. Discuss the role of nutrition in developing children.

4. Describe the implications of changing demographics on children's health.

5. Briefly explain the developing cognitive abilities of children from 2 to 7 years old.

intelligence

intelligence as a general factor (Binet)

intelligence as a composite of abilities   (Spearman)

the two-factor theory of intelligence

Gardner's 9 intelligences (intellectual profile)

intelligence as a process

intelligence as information processing

6. Psychologists have conflicting views about the impact of heredity and environment on intelligence. Briefly describe the following positions:

heredity (nature) is significant

major findings from studies of identical and fraternal twins

nurture (environment) is significant

contemporary scientific consensus

Bouchard (1990)

Jencks' (1972) gene-environment covariance

7. Define what Piaget meant by the *preoperational period* and characterize the thinking of the preoperational child by describing:

use of symbols

conservation performance

centering

state vs. transformational reasoning

nonreversibility

egocentrism vs. sociocentrism

8. Describe critiques of Piaget's work based on the following examples:

talking and communication

altruistic (prosocial) behavior

9. Discuss recent research on children's theory of mind.

10. Discuss the conceptual foundations for learning in young children regarding:

causality

number concepts

11. List signs of atypical cognitive development.

Chapter 7 Early Childhood: Physical and Cognitive Development

12. Describe the components of language acquisition.

phonology

morphology

syntax

pragmatics

semantics

13. Define Vygotsky's Zone of Proximal Development (ZPD).

14. Explain the hypothesis of childhood amnesia.

15. Define each of the five major systems of memory.

procedural

working

perceptual representation

semantic

episodic

16. Describe the following information related concepts:

recall

recognition

facilitation of relearning

sensory information storage

short-term memory

long-term memory

17. Explain how *memory* occurs, and distinguish between:

metacognition

metamemory

18. Describe rehearsal and categorizing as memory strategies, and discuss the Rossi and Wittrock study.

Chapter 7 Early Childhood: Physical and Cognitive Development

WEB SITES

The following web sites deal with some of the major concepts and issues presented in Chapter 7. Additional resources can be found on the text's web site, at http://www.mhhe.com/crandell7.

Preschool Page
http://www.kidsource.com/kidsource/pages/preschoolers.html

Childhood Obesity
http://www.kidsource.com/kidsource/content2/obesity.html

Child Health Guide
http://www.kidsource.com/kidsource/content/hg/index.html

Helping Your Child be Healthy & Fit
http://www.kidsource.com/kidsource/content/healthy.html

Spoken Language Problems
http://www.kidsource.com/LDA/spoken_language.html

Brain Development Research for Young Children & Their Families
http://www.kidsource.com/kidsource/content4/brain.development.html

Language Development & Young Children
http://www.kidsource.com/kidsource/content4/growth.chart/page1.html

School Readiness & Children's Developmental Readiness
http://www.kidsource.com/kidsource/content3/School.Readiness.p.k12.2.html

Resources on Multiple Intelligences
http://real.org/know/interactive.htm

The Montessori Foundation
http://www.montessori.org/

Chapter 7 Early Childhood: Physical and Cognitive Development

SELF TESTS

Matching

Match the key terms with their definitions:

a. centration
b. conservation
c. egocentrism
d. expressive language
e. implicit understanding
f. intelligence
g. long-term memory
h. memory
i. metacognition
j. metamemory
k. morphology
l. phonology
m. pragmatics
n. preoperational period
o. receptive language
p. reversibility
q. semantics
r. sensory information storage
s. short-term memory
t. syntax
u. theory of mind
v. two-factor theory of intelligence
w. zone of proximal development

1. ____ helping children with tasks that are a little too hard for them to accomplish alone
2. ____ a stage of cognitive development typified by an egocentric view of the world
3. ____ refers to a child's failure to recognize that operations can be turned back to an earlier state
4. ____ the knowledge of certain principles
5. ____ the term used when a word changes form
6. ____ the type of language that can be used in different social contexts
7. ____ the ability to understand that others see the world differently from oneself
8. ____ a global capacity to understand the world, think rationally, and cope resourcefully with the challenges of life
9. ____ a lack of awareness that there are viewpoints other than one's own
10. ____ a theory which concludes that there is a general intellectual ability employed for abstract reasoning and problem solving
11. ____ deals with the meaning of words as well as the rules for combining words together meaningfully
12. ____ individuals' awareness and understanding of their memory processes
13. ____ individuals' awareness and understanding of their own mental processes
14. ____ language that can be produced
15. ____ language that can be understood
16. ____ refers to the way that words must be ordered in a sentence
17. ____ requires the recognition that the quantity or amount of something stays the same despite changes in appearance
18. ____ the process whereby preoperational children concentrate on one feature of a situation and neglect other aspects

114

Chapter 7 Early Childhood: Physical and Cognitive Development

19. ____ the retention of information for a very brief period, usually not more than 30 seconds

20. ____ the retention of information for an extended period of time

21. ____ the retention of what has been experienced

22. ____ the stage of language development where children move beyond two-word sentences and begin to display a real understanding of the rules that govern language as well as mastering the different sounds within the language

23. ____ when information from the senses is preserved in the sensory register just long enough to permit the stimuli to be scanned for processing, generally less than two seconds

Multiple Choice

Circle the letter of the response that best completes or answers each of the following statements and questions.

Factual Questions

1. The most accurate statement regarding physical growth is that
    a. children grow in an even, sequential pattern
    b. the only time of fast growth is in the teen years
    c. about twice as much growth occurs between the ages of 1 and 3 as between the ages of 3 and 5
    d. slender children tend to grow faster than the average, while broadly built children grow more slowly

2. Which of the following is not a correct statement concerning children's coordination?
    a. Some 5 percent of youngsters have noticeable difficulties with coordination.
    b. Clumsy boys have just as many friends as their coordinated peers.
    c. Children with coordination problems are at a greater risk for significant social problems.
    d. Motor skills form a large part of a youngster's self-concept.

3. In terms of activity performance, which of the following would be an example of a motor-skill developmental delay for a typical 3-year-old?
    a. cannot ride a tricycle
    b. cannot turn pages of a book
    c. cannot use a scissors to cut straight line
    d. cannot copy squares

4. At age 5, a child's brain will
    a. weigh 30 percent of an adult's
    b. weigh 60 percent of an adult's
    c. weigh 90 percent of an adult's
    d. weigh 99 percent of an adult's

115

5. In 1993 the majority of deaths (52 percent) for children ages 5-14 were due to
   a. malnutrition
   b. abuse
   c. injuries
   d. suicide

6. Wechsler's description of intelligence is
   a. the possession of a fund of knowledge
   b. a capacity for acquiring knowledge and functioning rationally and effectively
   c. a type of metamemory
   d. the retention of what has been experienced

7. Who is the psychologist who viewed intelligence as a general ability and devised the first widely used intelligence test?
   a. Charles Spearman
   b. David Wechsler
   c. J. P. Guilford
   d. Alfred Binet

8. Spearman advanced an opposing view of intelligence; that is, intelligence is
   a. a single, general intellectual capacity
   b. a general intellectual ability employed for reasoning and problem solving with special factors peculiar to given tasks
   c. identified as 120 distinct factors
   d. seven distinct intelligences: linguistic, logical-mathematical, spatial, musical, body-kinesthetic, and two forms of personal intelligence

9. Psychologists who view intelligence as a process, as compared to an ability, are not so much interested in _____ we know, but in _____ we know.
   a. what; how
   b. why; how
   c. how; what
   d. what; when

10. Research done by Sternberg, who has an information-processing view of intelligence (where people can solve problems in everyday life as well as on tests), holds that
    a. some skills are trainable
    b. gifted children can ignore irrelevant information
    c. gifted and nongifted children can improve their performance
    d. all of the above

11. Based on data on IQ performance from family resemblance studies, Bouchard and his colleagues found that which correlation was the highest?
    a. between parent and child, same sex
    b. between dizygotic, same sex twins
    c. between monozygotic twins, reared together
    d. between monozygotic twins, reared apart

12. A numerical expression of the degree of relationship between two variables (events, conditions) which tells the extent to which two measures tend to go together is called the _____ coefficient.
    a. standard deviation
    b. median deviation
    c. correlation
    d. mean covariance

13. Environmentalists, who believe intelligence is learned, contend that studies of adopted children are biased because adoptive agencies traditionally attempt to place these children in an environment that is
    a. economically superior to the one in which they were born
    b. geographically different from the one in which they were born
    c. religiously, ethnically, and racially similar to the one in which they were born
    d. linguistically similar to the one in which they were born

14. Sociologist C. Jencks has introduced the third element of gene-environment interaction to the nature-nurture controversy, which is
    a. associated primarily with genetic factors
    b. associated primarily with environmental factors
    c. a result of the combining of genes and environment
    d. a measure of family resemblance

15. Piaget said children first develop the capacity to represent the external world internally through symbols during which period?
    a. preoperational
    b. sensorimotor
    c. concrete operational
    d. formal operational

16. The concept that the quantity or amount of something stays the same regardless of changes in its shape or position is called
    a. conservation
    b. transformation
    c. roles
    d. centering

17. Recent critiques of Piaget's theory focus on a child's ability to
    a. talk to others
    b. decenter
    c. be sociocentric
    d. be preoperational

18. Wellman's research on the theory of mind reveals that 3-year-olds can
    a. predict people's future actions
    b. explain their past actions
    c. both a and b
    d. neither a nor b

Chapter 7 Early Childhood: Physical and Cognitive Development

19. Children around 7 and 8 years old are able distinguish between cause and effect, known as
    a. causality
    b. recall
    c. inherent knowledge
    d. recognition

20. Contemporary developmental psychologists (in contrast to Piaget) in measuring children's counting capabilities, would support that
    a. there is no connection between the acquired ability to count and operations the child is capable of
    b. preschoolers seem to have an implicit understanding for number concepts
    c. counting is not an "easy" cognitive task for young children
    d. young children seem to possess some basic knowledge of "quantity" after they acquire such knowledge from their experiences

21. When a child understands that words must go in a specific order, then they have grasped
    a. morphology
    b. phonology
    c. syntax
    d. pragmatics

22. Chomsky's LAD stands for
    a. language assimilation development
    b. linguistic appropriation device
    c. linguistic accelerated development
    d. language acquisition device

23. Vygotsky's concept, known as the zone of proximal development (ZPD) states that
    a. development takes place at the approximate zone of human interaction
    b. children's developmental zone is approximately between the ages of 2 and 7
    c. tasks that are learned alone are better understood than those learned with others
    d. tasks that are too difficult to master alone are mastered with the help of a skilled partner

24. Information from the senses is preserved just long enough to permit the stimuli to be scanned for processing. This provides a relatively complete, literal copy of the physical stimulus and best describes
    a. short-term memory
    b. sensory information storage
    c. long-term memory
    d. rehearsal

25. Individual awareness and understanding of one's mental process is _____; whereas understanding one's own memory processes is _____.
    a. short-term memory; long-term memory
    b. metacognition; short-term memory
    c. metamemory; metacognition
    d. metacognition; metamemory

Chapter 7 Early Childhood: Physical and Cognitive Development

26. A memory strategy that helps children organize information for recall and includes rhyming, clustering, and ordering is
   a. rehearsal
   b. categorizing
   c. meta-rehearsal
   d. syntax recall

27. Piaget asserts that _____ is the foundation for social interchange in children.
   a. egocentrism
   b. reciprocity
   c. autonomy
   d. morality

Conceptual Questions

1. Andy is a 6-year-old boy who has had coordination problems since he was a toddler. His parents and school officials are concerned about the impact of his clumsiness because studies seem to predict that Andy
   a. will not enjoy athletics as he ages
   b. will have fewer friends than his coordinated peers
   c. will not achieve as well academically
   d. will seriously injure himself eventually

2. You are a first grade teacher, and you give your students a battery of aptitude tests. Their performance on each test is highly correlated with their performance on all their other tests. Therefore you might conclude that your test battery
   a. successfully tapped into the *g* factor
   b. successfully tapped into the *s* factor
   c. was not valid because it measures only composite factors
   d. measured primarily mental abilities

3. According to the hereditarian position, we would expect the correlation between the IQ scores of two unrelated children living in the same home to be
   a. higher than the correlation of fraternal twins raised in separate homes
   b. about the same as that of unrelated children raised in separate homes
   c. very high, because the same environment causes people to be similar
   d. unpredictable because we know nothing of their biological backgrounds

4. There is a positive correlation between the number of bars in a city and the number of churches; that is, as the number of bars increases, so does the number of churches. One would be in error to suggest that an increase in bars causes more churches, or that the churches cause the bars to open. This is because
   a. the correlation coefficient isn't high enough
   b. churches are only associated with activities of high moral standards
   c. the positive correlation doesn't mean causation
   d. all of the above

5. Stephen claims that his mother gave his brother a bigger piece of cake than he got. However, Stephen is pacified when his mother cuts his piece in two. He defiantly says to his brother, "Now I've got more." Stephen's statement shows
   a. good perspective-taking ability
   b. sociocentric behavior
   c. associative learning but no conceptual learning
   d. lack of conservation

6. A young child sees two rows of pennies and says that each row contains five pennies. When the bottom row is spread out, she says that it has more pennies, which could be considered an example of
   a. centration
   b. encoding
   c. reversibility
   d. metamemory

7. When asked what to get Daddy for his birthday, a preoperational child might suggest something like candy or a toy. This is due to the fact that
   a. they are people-oriented
   b. they are egocentric
   c. they are deeply affected
   d. they are altruistic

8. Stephanie, 18 months, sees her mother looking out the window. Stephanie goes over and points to a bird outside. She might be demonstrating
   a. non-egocentric behavior
   b. egocentrism
   c. centering
   d. typical sharing

9. Christine has just told Michael, her 3-year-old, that they are going to give Daddy a surprise party. When Michael sees his Daddy the day before the party, he shouts, "Are you surprised?!" Michael is exhibiting
   a. altruistic behavior
   b. theory of mind
   c. lack of theory of mind
   d. environmental adaptiveness

10. Many current developmental psychologists disagree with Piaget's views that young children have limited understanding of cause and effect. According to these contemporary researchers, which of the following statements would a typical 4-year-old make?
    a. "The street makes the car go."
    b. "If I cry, Mommy will come."
    c. "The moon comes to look at me."
    d. "The river runs because it is happy."

Chapter 7   Early Childhood: Physical and Cognitive Development

11. If intelligence is primarily determined by environmental factors, Kamin would say
    a. fraternal twins will be more similar to one another than regular siblings
    b. fraternal twins raised in differing environments would be more similar to one another than regular siblings
    c. identical twins who were highly intelligent would also be highly creative
    d. more could be done to improve people's abilities through education and social arrangement

12. Julie, a 40-year-old woman, is concerned about memory loss because she can only recall bits and pieces of her life up until the 4th grade. After that, she remembers events very clearly. Her neighbor, a psychologist, has told her not to be concerned, as this phenomenon is called
    a. selective recall
    b. childhood amnesia
    c. normal aging forgetfulness
    d. sensory information overload

13. Serge is a college student "cramming" for a final exam in psychology (consisting mainly of recognition of terminology and definitions). Although he received an "A" on his exam in May, he is surprised to learn in June that he could not remember the definition of many terms. Serge's retention of information is described as
    a. long-term memory
    b. working memory
    c. focused memory
    d. semantic memory

14. A second-grade child realizes that she will have to spend more time studying words she has misspelled than words she can spell correctly. This child is using
    a. sensory information storage
    b. recognition memory
    c. metacognition
    d. metamemory

15. A child is trying to remember her new friend's name, and she repeats it over and over. The child is using
    a. rehearsing
    b. metamemory
    c. a clustering form of categorization
    d. a serial ordering form of categorization

16. Dee states that she is intrapersonally intelligent. This means she will display
    a. knowledge of how to deal with others
    b. knowledge of how to deal with herself
    c. knowledge of people's minds
    d. knowledge of herself

17. According to the theory of mind research, a 3-year-old would not be able to play a practical joke on someone because he or she would not understand
   a. what humor is
   b. that people's actions stem from representations of the world
   c. that the environment is objective reality
   d. cause and effect

18. When a child learns to read by engaging in that activity with an adult over time, Vygotsky would say that is an example of
   a. language acquisition device
   b. decentering
   c. zone of proximal development
   d. theory of mind

19. When a child says, "Let me see my phone number, so I'll remember it," she is using
   a. metanarrative
   b. metatheory
   c. metacognition
   d. metamemory

20. The reason that a young child cannot differentiate between something done accidentally or intentionally is due to
   a. morality based on deception
   b. morality based on perception
   c. morality based on reciprocity
   d. morality based on context

Chapter 7   Early Childhood: Physical and Cognitive Development

Essay Questions

1. You are going to play a game of 20 questions with some children aged 5 to 10 and adults. What would you expect to happen during the course of the game? Which group would become bored first?

2. A professor explains to the class that there is only one type of memory, anything that can be recalled is a memory. Explain why you think this is not an adequate view of memory.

3. You step on a 5 year-old's toy and break it. Will the child believe it was an accident or intentional? How can you convince the child she is right or wrong?

ANSWERS FOR SELF-TESTS

Matching

1. w	9. c	17. b
2. n	10. v	18. a
3. p	11. q	19. s
4. e	12. j	20. g
5. k	13. i	21. h
6. m	14. d	22. l
7. u	15. o	23. r
8. f	16. t	

Multiple Choice

Factual

1. c	10. d	19. a
2. b	11. c	20. b
3. b	12. c	21. c
4. c	13. c	22. d
5. c	14. c	23. d
6. b	15. a	24. b
7. d	16. a	25. d
8. b	17. c	26. b
9. a	18. d	27. b

Conceptual

1. b	8. a	15. a
2. a	9. c	16. d
3. d	10. b	17. b
4. c	11. d	18. c
5. d	12. b	19. d
6. a	13. b	20. b
7. b	14. c	

Chapter 8

Early Childhood: Emotional and Social Development

INTRODUCTION

Chapter 7 focused on the expanding physical and cognitive competencies of preschool children. In Chapter 8, the early childhood years are once again examined, with primary emphasis on the process of emotional development and socialization. The main topics in Chapter include:

- Emotional Development. The ability to express more subtle emotions occurs as well as the ability to engage in forms of symbolic emotional communication such as play.

- The Development of Self. The development of self includes forms of self-awareness and self-esteem.

- Gender Identification. It is at this time that gender roles and gender identity begin to form.

- Family Influences. Specific parenting determinants and various child-rearing practices are discussed. Baumrind's four parenting styles and their effects on children's behavior are examined. Research is cited on effective parenting as well as on the sexual abuse of children. The impact of single-parent families and divorce on parents, as well as on children, is illustrated in detail. The final issue focuses on sibling relationships and their role in the socialization process.

- Peer Relationships. This section discusses children's peer relationships and friendships. The role of children as reinforcing agents and behavioral models for one another is examined, as is the importance of play in the child's personal and social development. The subject of aggression is addressed, with an emphasis on the effects of media violence on the behavior of the nation's youth. Finally, the impact of preschools and Head Start programs on both parents and children is summarized, and a guideline for selecting a preschool is presented.

Chapter 8   Early Childhood: Emotional and Social Development

LEARNING OBJECTIVES

After completing Chapter 8, you should be able to:

1. Describe how *emotions* are displayed and regulated among children.

2. Describe how children link feelings with thoughts.

3. Discuss the child's growing sense of *self*, defining ecological and interpersonal self.

4. Discuss how psychologists assess *self esteem*.

5. Distinguish between *gender role, gender identity,* and *sexual orientation* as they relate to gender identification.

6. Briefly summarize the following theories regarding the acquisition of *gender identity*.

psychoanalytic theory (Freud)

Chapter 8 Early Childhood: Emotional and Social Development

cognitive-learning theory

selective reinforcement

Bandura's research

cognitive-developmental theory (Kohlberg)

self-socialization

gender schemes

7. Appraise the research on the effects of fathers and mothers on gender typing.

8. Define *socialization* and briefly discuss the role of the family in early human development.

9. Identify and briefly discuss Belsky's three major determinants of parental functioning.
   -
   -
   -

Chapter 8 Early Childhood: Emotional and Social Development

10. Outline the major dimensions underlying child-rearing and *socialization* practices, and discuss the effects of each of these practices and combination of practices on children's behavior.

warmth-hostility

control-autonomy

combinations

consistency in discipline

11. Analyze each of the following parenting styles. Explain how each contributes to the development of socially responsible and independent behavior from Baumrind's research.

authoritarian

authoritative

permissive

harmonious

12. On the basis of Baumrind's research, discuss the impact of spanking on children.

13. Describe the effects of sexual abuse on children

Chapter 8   Early Childhood: Emotional and Social Development

14. Identify some of the difficulties that each of the following people experience with parenting (e.g., parent-child contact and communication, changes in behavior of parents as well as in children at the time of divorce).

single parents

divorced parents

children of divorced parents

gay or lesbian parents

15. Summarize the research findings on sibling relationships with regard to:

birth order

pioneering function

firstborn

middle children

laterborn

family size

confluence theory

resource dilution hypothesis

sex of siblings

"dethroning'

16. Characterize the qualitative changes that occur in *peer* friendship patterns.

17. Describe research findings on aggressive behaviors in children.

18. Describe the purpose and effects of the Head Start program.

19. Discuss the research on children's antisocial behavior.

20. Discuss the media's influence on children's behavior.

Chapter 8   Early Childhood: Emotional and Social Development

WEB SITES

The following web sites deal with some of the major concepts and issues presented in Chapter 8. Additional resources can be found on the text's web site, at http://www.mhhe.com/crandell7.

Erik Erikson & Psychosocial Development
http://snycorva.cortland.edu/~ANDERSMD/ERIK/sum.HTML

Assessment of Temperament - ERIC Digest
http://ericae.net/edo/ED389963.HTM

Concepts about Child Development from the American Psychological Association
http://www.apa.org/concept/children.html

Early Childhood Development from Age 2 to 6
http://www.ecdgroup.com/archive/ecd06.html

Early Head Start National Resource Center
http://www.ehsnrc.org/

National Head Start Organization
http://www.ehsnrc.org/headstrt.htm

Early Childhood
http://www.earlychildhood.com/links.html

National Association for the Education of Young Children
http://www.naeyc.org/

American Library Association Links for Parents and Caregivers
http://www.ala.org/alsc/parents.links.html

SELF-TESTS

Matching

Match the key terms with their definitions:

a. aggression
b. authoritarian parenting
c. authoritative parenting
d. confluence theory
e. emotion
f. gender
g. gender identity
h. gender roles
i. gender stereotypes
j. harmonious parenting
k. initiative vs. guilt
l. joint custody
m. permissive parenting
n. peers
o. play
p. resource dilution hypothesis
q. scaffolding
r. self
s. self-concept
t. self-esteem
u. socialization

1. ____ being classed male or female

2. ____ a person's own sense of self-worth or self-image

3. ____ a set of cultural expectations that define the ways in which the members of each sex should behave

4. ____ an arrangement whereby both parents share equally in the making of significant child-rearing decisions and share in regular childcare responsibilities

5. ____ attempts to shape, control, and evaluate a child's behavior in accordance with traditional and absolute values and standards of conduct

6. ____ behavior that is socially defined as injurious or destructive

7. ____ distinguished by parents that seldom exercise direct control over their children in an attempt to cultivate an egalitarian relationship

8. ____ distinguished by providing a non-punitive, accepting, and affirmative environment in which the children regulate their own behavior as much as possible

9. ____ exaggerated generalizations about male or female behaviors

10. ____ firm direction for a child's overall activities but gives the child considerable freedom within reasonable limits

11. ____ individuals who are approximately the same age

12. ____ states that in large families resources get spread too thinly, to the detriment of all the offspring

13. ____ supports a child's learning through intervention and tutoring that provide helpful task information attuned to the child's current level of functioning

14. ____ the conception that people have of themselves as being male or female

15. ____ the image one has of oneself

Chapter 8   Early Childhood: Emotional and Social Development

16. ____ the process of transmitting culture, transforming children into functioning members of society

17. ____ the psychological changes, subjective experiences, and expressive behaviors that are involved in such feelings as love, joy, grief, and anger

18. ____ the stage when children strive exuberantly to do things and to test developing abilities, sometimes reaching beyond their competence

19. ____ the system of concepts we use in defining ourselves

20. ____ the view that the intellectual development of a family is like a river, with the input of each family member flowing into it

21. ____ voluntary activities that are not performed for any sake beyond themselves

Multiple Choice

Circle the letter of the response that <u>best</u> completes or answers each of the following statements and questions.

Factual Questions

1. The process of transmitting culture to one's children so they can become functioning members of society is called
   a. acculturation
   b. socialization
   c. tempering
   d. social transformation

2. The system of concepts we use in defining ourselves is best termed
   a. the self
   b. expectations
   c. social categories
   d. role

3. The self-conceptions that people have as being male or female are called
   a. gender roles
   b. genetic genders
   c. biological sexes
   d. gender identities

Chapter 8   Early Childhood: Emotional and Social Development

4. Which theory proposes that a child is bisexual at birth but heterosexual identity develops more firmly as the child resolves conflicting feelings of love and jealousy and begins to identify with the parent of the same sex?
   a. psychoanalytic
   b. cognitive learning
   c. cognitive-developmental
   d. behavioral

5. According to Albert Bandura, children determine which behaviors are appropriate for each sex by
   a. watching the dominant parent in their primary environment
   b. watching the behavior of many male and female models
   c. watching clearly defined sex roles in cartoons
   d. playing with certain toys and games

6. "I am a boy; therefore, I want to do boy things; therefore, the opportunity to do boy things is rewarded." This best describes the position of which of the following theories?
   a. psychoanalytic
   b. social modeling
   c. cognitive-developmental
   d. none of the above

7. According to the evidence, who plays the most critical role in encouraging "femininity" in females and "masculinity" in males in U.S. society?
   a. mothers
   b. grandparents
   c. fathers
   d. preschool teachers

8. According to Gilmore's study (1990), fathers' absence from many U.S. homes during the son's formative years may lead to which of the following
   a. less secure sense of masculinity
   b. exaggerating male behavior
   c. developing androgynous behavior
   d. negative attitudes toward women

9. Which of the following is not included in Jay Belsky's framework for family functioning
   a. mother-child
   b. parenting practices
   c. socioeconomic staus
   d. marital relations

10. Referring to Schaefer and Becker's four combinations of the warmth-hostility and control-autonomy dimensions of parenting, which style of parenting is associated with impulsive, disobedient, aggressive, delinquent behavior?
    a. warm-restrictive
    b. warm-permissive
    c. hostile-restrictive
    d. hostile-permissive

Chapter 8 Early Childhood: Emotional and Social Development

11. Which statement concerning parenting is least accurate according to the chapter?
    a. Unpredictable discipline is the most effective.
    b. Aggressive children usually have the most permissive parents regarding aggression.
    c. Boys are less inclined to obey mothers.
    d. The majority of parents agree that a spanking is sometimes necessary.

12. According to Diana Baumrind's analysis of parental authority, an authoritative parent is best described as one who
    a. stresses obedience and conformity to rules in a disciplined environment
    b. allows the child to regulate his or her own behavior
    c. prefers forced discipline but allows children to make the rules
    d. provides firm direction but allows the child freedom within limits

13. Baumrind found that the least self-reliant, explorative, and self-controlled children were those with parents who were
    a. permissive
    b. authoritative
    c. harmonious
    d. authoritarian

14. _____ supports a child's learning through intervention and tutoring that provide helpful task information attuned to the child's current level of functioning.
    a. Permissive parenting
    b. Scaffolding
    c. Socialization
    d. Harmonious parenting

15. Which statement is the most accurate regarding the sexual abuse of children?
    a. Sexually abused children are usually afraid to tell others about their experiences.
    b. Most research has dealt with the sexual abuse of males.
    c. Most victims of childhood sexual abuse recover from patterns of psychological shame within a few years.
    d. There is a decrease in the number of male victims of childhood sexual abuse.

16. Which of the following scenarios most closely illustrates an example of a child asserting his individuality when told to put his toys away?
    a. When told to put his toys away, the child does so.
    b. The child leaves the area without doing so.
    c. The child ignores the request completely.
    d. The child responds that he is "still playing" with the toys.

17. Studies by McClelland and colleagues have indicated that
    a. toilet training, spanking, and breast feeding influences what people think and do as adults
    b. how parents feel about their children has an important influence on what their children think and do as adults
    c. parents who employ good child-rearing techniques are more likely to raise children who have healthy personalities as adults
    d. parents whose child-rearing techniques are inconsistent are more likely to raise children who become aggressive adults

Chapter 8 Early Childhood: Emotional and Social Development

18. The most important message from the Harvard Child-Rearing Study is
    a. read to your children often
    b. enjoy your children and love them
    c. spank your oldest child once a week
    d. there are "set patterns" that work in nearly all parent-child relationships

19. Single-parent families tend not to be characterized by
    a. higher delinquency rates among the children
    b. poorer school adjustment of the children
    c. more serious economic problems
    d. male heads of households

20. Which statement is the least accurate about research on the effects of divorce?
    a. The first year after the divorce is equally stressful for both parents.
    b. Divorced parents communicate less well with their children than parents in intact families.
    c. Poor parenting seems most evident for divorced mothers one year after divorce.
    d. Single-parent families usually experience increased stress and difficulties during the second year of divorce compared with the first year of divorce.

21. Researchers find the quality of children's relationship with _____ is the best predictor of their post-divorce adjustment.
    a. their mother
    b. their siblings
    c. both parents
    d. their father

22. With respect to school achievement, social adjustment, and delinquent behavior, the differences between children from one-parent and two-parent homes of comparable social status are
    a. small
    b. moderate
    c. very large
    d. large

23. Studies of sibling relationships have demonstrated that
    a. a child's position within the family doesn't affect his or her development
    b. each child has a unique microenvironment
    c. siblings often have similar personality traits
    d. sibling interactions usually are less important after high school

24. Which of the following is not a finding from a cross-cultural study of firstborns conducted by Rosenblatt and colleagues?
    a. Firstborns receive more respect from siblings and society.
    b. Firstborns are more likely to be given control of property and power in society.
    c. Firstborns often have elaborate birth ceremonies.
    d. Firstborns often cannot act as caretakers for siblings because they are usually in positions of power and authority and don't have time.

Chapter 8   Early Childhood: Emotional and Social Development

25. Confluence theory (now under scrutiny by other researchers) as described by psychologist Zajonc says
    a. the conflicts siblings tend to have with each other influence the intellectual growth of siblings
    b. the more older siblings a child has, the lower his or her intellectual level
    c. each additional child improves the intellectual climate within a family
    d. the oldest sibling experiences the richest intellectual environment

26. The theory that in large families the resources get spread thin to the detriment of the offspring is called
    a. confluence theory
    b. crucial resource theory
    c. resource dilution theory
    d. developmental delay theory

27. Studies of peer relationships of children indicate that
    a. 4-year-olds spend about one-third of their time playing with peers
    b. by 18 months of age, social play predominates
    c. spontaneous peer reinforcement decreases with age
    d. more social interaction takes place among acquainted toddlers

28. As children grow older, their aggressiveness becomes
    a. more diffused and less directed
    b. less oriented toward temper tantrums
    c. less retaliatory in response to others' aggression
    d. less verbal

29. Which of the following is not an accurate finding from studies of children's aggressive behavior?
    a. When an aggressive response is followed by passive behavior by the victim, the aggressor is reinforced to victimize again.
    b. When aggressive behavior is followed by punishment, aggressors move to other victims.
    c. Children's aggressive behavior comes from home influences.
    d. More aggressive children, particularly boys, report that aggression brings rewards.

30. Media violence fosters aggressive behavior in all of the following ways except
    a. Media violence provides opportunities for children to learn new aggressive skills
    b. Television violence affords occasions for vicarious conditioning.
    c. Watching television violence weakens children's inhibitions against violence.
    d. Television violence links aggression to success in life.

Conceptual Questions

1. Your child is playing with an imaginary friend. This usually indicates
    a. psychosis
    b. underlying cognitive changes
    c. dissatisfaction with real friends
    d. all of the above

2. Your child shows evidence of emotional self-regulation, can express feelings in complex ways, plays cooperatively, but hasn't started constructing a gender identity. Her most probable age is
   a. 4 ½
   b. 3
   c. 6
   d. 2

3. Sam wears clothes that are not traditionally masculine or feminine. Sam's hair is not done in a way that is indicative of a man's style or a woman's style. Sam likes to fish, play baseball, knit, and take ballet lessons. Sam is not conforming to
   a. gender identity
   b. gender roles
   c. gender
   d. gender bias

4. A girl grows up never once seeing the genitals of another person, so she is unaware of the physical differences between boys and girls, but she still has a strong sense of gender identification. Which theory of gender identity development will this case undermine?
   a. cognitive learning
   b. psychoanalytic
   c. cognitive development
   d. ecological

5. Theresa is a 5-year-old whose mother rarely asks her to pick up her toys or help around the house and always reasons with Theresa about acceptable standards of behavior. What parenting style does Theresa's mother use?
   a. permissive
   b. authoritative
   c. harmonious
   d. authoritarian

6. Yan has been raised in a harmonious parenting household. She has just started kindergarten. Which behavior is she most likely to exhibit at school?
   a. She runs to the teacher often to "tattle" on what other children are doing.
   b. She is regimented and obedient in her behavior, doing everything she is told to do immediately.
   c. She is almost oblivious to oral directives, doing very much as she pleases whenever she wants.
   d. She is not fearful of the classroom environment or the teacher and readily consoles other children if they become upset.

7. In your house, the children are all given rules and responsibilities. However, they negotiate with each other for who does what tasks (e.g., dishes) if there is a special event (e.g., a school play). Based on Baumrind's research, we could predict that
   a. your sons will be very permissive
   b. your children will be self-reliant
   c. your daughters will not be very self-reliant
   d. your children will be withdrawn

Chapter 8 Early Childhood: Emotional and Social Development

8. Warren is about to become a stepfather. He is most likely to be successful if he
   a. allows the children's mother to continue being the authority figure
   b. is authoritarian and warm
   c. is not demanding but is permissive
   d. is authoritative and warm

9. Martha's 3-year-old son Cory has thrown his toys all over his room. Which statement demonstrates scaffolding?
   a. "Please pick up the toys, honey?"
   b. "Pick up those toys right now!"
   c. "It's time to pick up your toys, and I'll show you how to put them away."
   d. "You can pick up the mess whenever you want to."

10. McClelland's Harvard Child-Rearing Study is to _____ as White's Harvard Preschool Project is to _____.
    a. child abuse; competence
    b. parenting techniques; aggressive behavior
    c. parenting techniques; spanking
    d. personality development; competence

11. Billy's parents have been divorced for one year, and he now lives with his mother. His mother is unsuccessful in her efforts to decrease his acting-out behavior and she spanks him. Billy tells her, "You can't make me stop." She hits him harder. Psychologists could predict that
    a. as time goes by, Billy's mother will give up on him and make fewer demands for mature behavior
    b. as time goes by, Billy's mother will start ignoring him more and showing him less attention
    c. Billy's school grades will decrease, and he will become more abusive and demanding
    d. Billy would be more obedient for his mother if his father was more psychologically available to him

12. Sue is the artificially inseminated child of a lesbian couple. She is a third grader, age appropriate in all developmental domains, and is a well-adjusted girl. School officials are concerned, however, that being raised in this environment will influence her sexual orientation later. According to the chapter, which response is most accurate in this case?
    a. Sue will grow up to be a lesbian.
    b. It will be very difficult for Sue to ever be attracted to members of the opposite sex.
    c. There is no clear evidence as to whether homosexual parents produce homosexual children.
    d. Sue will unlikely be a "tomboy" because of her infrequent association with males.

13. Monique is a very social teenager — many phone calls, invitations to parties, a constant stream of friends in her home, and she was just voted "Most Popular" in her graduating class. Based on birth-order research, she is likely to be
    a. the "baby" in her family
    b. the middle child in her family
    c. the firstborn in her family
    d. the only child in her family

Chapter 8   Early Childhood: Emotional and Social Development

14. As a preschool teacher, what type of peer interaction would you expect when you walk into a play area?
    a. boys and girls playing together
    b. boys playing with boys; girls playing with girls
    c. both boys and girls involved in rough-and-tumble play
    d. girls playing in larger groups; boys playing in more solitary situations

15. Your husband is always telling the children, "Quit playing around and do something useful with your time." Your best advice to your husband might be that
    a. although play is a poor use of time, children need to expend energy
    b. although most play is a waste of time, middle-class children generally use playtime efficiently
    c. telling this to the children will decrease their enjoyment of play
    d. play is children's work; it has vital social, cognitive, and physical benefits

16. A pair of young parents is seeking a preschool for their 4-year-old child. There are several options available to them in their community. They have, however, heard conflicting reports about the educational quality of these preschools and are now confused. Which advice would you supply these parents?
    a. Go to the school and meet the director, teacher, and aides.
    b. Inquire about the academic qualifications of staff, and ask to see verifications, if possible.
    c. Determine the goals of the preschool and their policies.
    d. All of the above.

17. Your city's mayor is threatening to cut the funding for the local Head Start program. You decide to write a letter to support the continuance of this program based on the findings of more recent research that states
    a. socioeconomically disadvantaged children perform as well as or better than their peers in regular schools and have fewer grade retentions or special education placements because of this program.
    b. socioeconomically disadvantaged children have been provided with essential health care through this program
    c. the Head Start program gives parents access to community resources that provide parenting skills and support for the entire family
    d. all of the above

18. Ivan is a 12-year-old child who has grown up in a single-parent home with his mother. He has recently been getting detentions in school for misbehavior, which his mother doesn't understand. The school psychologist suggests that Ivan's mother enroll Ivan in the Big Brother program at the local YMCA. Why?
    a. Ivan is just naturally mischievous — you know, "Boys will be boys."
    b. Ivan needs the influence of an older male role model to develop his athletic skills.
    c. An older male role model will probably help Ivan gain some self-control.
    d. Ivan's gender identity might become more feminine if he doesn't have a male role model.

19. Mr. Jones refers to his child as "strong, alert, and well-coordinated." Studies show he's most likely referring to his
    a. son
    b. daughter
    c. either his son or daughter
    d. his oldest daughter

Chapter 8   Early Childhood: Emotional and Social Development

20. Which of the following concepts provides social (cultural) guidelines that define for us our obligations and expectations?
    a. roles
    b. egocentric perspective
    c. self
    d. construct perspective

21. Mom is acting as if she has just declared war on the world and Dad is treating every day as if it's Christmas. What is likely to be going on in this family?
    a. They have gone through a divorce
    b. They have a child entering puberty
    c. They are having their first child
    d. They are becoming stepparents

Essay Questions

1. How much of your sense of gender identification comes from external factors? How much from biological factors?

2. What are the implications of family and different parenting styles on self-concept and self-esteem?

3. Examine the implications of peer relationships and media influence on emotional development. If possible, ask a 10-year-old and a 75-year-old where their sense of self originated from, and what most influenced their concepts of gender and emotional expression.

Chapter 8 Early Childhood: Emotional and Social Development

ANSWERS FOR SELF-TESTS

Matching

1. f
2. t
3. h
4. l
5. b
6. a
7. j
8. m
9. i
10. c
11. n
12. p
13. q
14. g
15. s
16. u
17. e
18. k
19. r
20. d
21. o

Multiple Choice

Factual

1. b
2. a
3. d
4. a
5. b
6. c
7. c
8. a
9. b
10. d
11. a
12. d
13. a
14. b
15. a
16. d
17. b
18. b
19. d
20. d
21. a
22. a
23. b
24. d
25. d
26. c
27. a
28. b
29. d
30. d

Conceptual

1. b
2. b
3. b
4. b
5. c
6. d
7. b
8. d
9. c
10. d
11. c
12. c
13. a
14. b
15. d
16. d
17. d
18. c
19. a
20. a
21. a

Chapter 9

Middle Childhood:
Physical and Cognitive Development

INTRODUCTION

Chapter 9 presents an overview of the advances in cognitive and moral development that occur during middle childhood. These changes are discussed within the context of the developing child during his or her elementary school years – ages 7 to 12. Several topics are covered, including:

- Physical Development. We look at growth and body changes, motor and brain development, health and fitness. Issues of bulimia, anorexia, giftedness, play and the role of exercise are all examined.

- Cognitive Development. This is a discussion of children's emerging cognitive capabilities, which permit them to organize and process environmental stimuli. Piaget's stage of concrete operations is presented as characterizing the elementary school child. An analysis of how children acquire socialization skills is also presented. Suggestions for recognizing and fostering creativity in children are highlighted

- Language Development. We further explore the mechanics of language as well as bilingual education in schools. Forms of bilingual education include English as a second language, bilingualism, and immersion.

- Learning Disabilities. Learning disabilities are covered, including ADHD, and educational responses are presented.

- Moral Development. The text presents the major theories used to understand children's moral development: psychoanalytic, cognitive learning, and cognitive-developmental theories. Also included is a review of the inconsistency of children's moral behavior, as well as the various personal and situational factors most closely associated with moral behavior.

- Prosocial Behavior. The chapter concludes with an overview of the ways in which children acquire prosocial behaviors.

Chapter 9 Middle Childhood: Physical and Cognitive Development

LEARNING OBJECTIVES

After completing Chapter 9, you should be able to:

1. State and briefly explain the typical health and fitness issues of middle childhood.

2. Describe how children's cognitive abilities begin to advance when they are around 6 and 7 years old, and define *metacognition* and *executive strategies*.

3. Summarize what is known about creativity and discuss the following:

relationship between intelligence and creativity

role of formal education

Institute of Personality Assessment and Research studies

Vera John-Steiner's findings

Dr. Luria's suggestions

Chapter 9   Middle Childhood: Physical and Cognitive Development

4. Define what Piaget meant by the *period of concrete operations* when referring to middle childhood, and contrast some advances with those of the earlier preoperational stage abilities.

5. Compare concrete operational thought with preoperational thought by explaining the concepts of conservation, decentering, and transformations.

conservation

decentering

transformations

horizontal decalage

6. Summarize cross-cultural research on conservation ability, and draw a conclusion about the administration of cognitive tests to children from various cultures.

7. Identify the changes that occur in children's person-perception abilities, and tell how we activate stereotyping.

8. Describe the qualitative, age-related differences in regard to children's descriptive statements about other people, and developmental changes in the ways children see and describe people.

9. Discuss the issue of bilingual education the United States and define:

English as a second language approach (ESL)

bilingualism

total immersion

10. Explain the term learning disabilities (LDs).

Chapter 9 Middle Childhood: Physical and Cognitive Development

11. Explain an Individual Education Plan (IEP) and the concept of inclusion.

12. Explain important aspects of effective schools.

13. Describe the concept of *morality* and its significance for society, and define *moral development*.

14. Describe the following concepts and studies in cognitive/social learning theory :

imitation

study results on temptation and models

dishonest or deviant behavior

Chapter 9 Middle Childhood: Physical and Cognitive Development

15. Summarize the major premise on *moral development* by cognitive-developmental theorists.

16. Explain Jean Piaget's theory of *moral development* and its stages.

active participation

heteronomous morality (morality of constraint)

autonomous morality (morality of cooperation)

acquiring a sense of justice

17. Explain Lawrence Kohlberg's theory of development of values and moral judgments.

moral judgment

ethical dilemma

Stages:
Preconventional,
    Level 1, Stage 1

    Level 1, Stage 2

Conventional
> Level 2, Stage 3

> Level 2, Stage 4

Postconventional
> Level 3, Stage 5

> Level 3, Stage 6

universal morality

Carol Gilligan's criticism of Kohlberg's theory

18. Describe how the following factors may have an association with moral behavior:

intelligence

age

sex

group norms

motivation

19. Explain the following concepts related to *prosocial behavior*.

helping

altruism

egocentrism

parenting style

parental guidelines

empathy

Chapter 9   Middle Childhood: Physical and Cognitive Development

WEB SITES

The following web sites deal with some of the major concepts and issues presented in Chapter 9. Additional resources can be found on the text's web site at http://www.mhhe.com/crandell7.

EDINFO: An Index of the Pediatric Internet
http://www.pedinfo.org/

The Center for Eating Disorders
http://www.eating-disorders.com/

Dyslexia
http://www.dyslexia.com/

Speech and Language Disorders
http://www.kidsource.com/NICHCY/speech.html

The Council for Exceptional Children
http://www.cec.sped.org/

How Can Schools Help Prevent Children from Using Drugs?
http://ericps.crc.uiuc.edu/npin/respar/texts/preteen/druguse.html

Key Characteristics of Middle Level Schools
http://ericae.net/edo/ED401050.HTM

Discipline: A Parent's Guide
http://ericps.crc.uiuc.edu/npin/respar/texts/preteen/discipli.html

Gangs in the Schools
http://ericae.net/edo/ED372175.HTM

The Debate Over Spanking
http://ericps.crc.uiuc.edu/eece/pubs/digests/1997/ramsbu97.html

Research on the Effects of Television Viewing
http://netletter.com/GMWS/unTV/research.htm
http://ericps.crc.uiuc.edu/npin/respar/texts/preteen/tvview.html

Chapter 9 Middle Childhood: Physical and Cognitive Development

SELF-TESTS

Matching

Match the key terms with their definitions:

a. bilingualism
b. cognitive styles
c. conservation
d. dyslexia
e. empathy
f. executive strategies
g. horizontal décalage
h. inclusion
i. individualized education plan
j. learning disabilities
k. limited English proficiency
l. moral development
m. obesity
n. period of concrete operations
o. prosocial behaviors
p. stereotypes
q. total immersion

1. ____ when a child develops the ability to apply logical thought to concrete problems

2. ____ a legal document which ensures that the child with special learning needs will be provided with the needed educational support services in the least restrictive environment

3. ____ certain exaggerated cultural understandings which influence the mutual set of expectations that will govern the social exchange

4. ____ differences in how individuals organize and process information

5. ____ difficulty with school-related material, despite the fact that students appear to have normal intelligence and lack a demonstrable physical, emotional, or social impairment

6. ____ extreme difficulty in learning to read in an otherwise normally intelligent, healthy child or adult

7. ____ implies that repetition takes place within a single period of development such as the period of concrete operations

8. ____ provides instruction in both first languages by teachers proficient in both

9. ____ the ability to integrate and orchestrate lower-level cognitive skills

10. ____ the concept that the quantity or amount of something stays the same regardless of changes in its shape or position

11. ____ the excess accumulation of body fat, considered an increase of 20 pounds over typical weight for height

12. ____ the feelings of emotional arousal that lead an individual to take another perspective and to experience an event as the other person experiences it

13. ____ the instructional approach of placing children with limited English proficiency in regular classrooms (with or without support in their first language) and using English for all instruction

14. ____ the integration of students with special needs within the regular classroom programs of the school

15. ____ the legal term for students who were not born in the United States or whose native language is not English and who cannot participate effectively in the regular school curriculum because they have difficulty speaking, understanding, reading, and writing English

16. ____ the process by which children adopt principles that lead them to evaluate given behaviors as "right" and others as "wrong" and to govern their own actions in terms of these principles

17. ____ ways of responding to other people through sympathetic, cooperative, helpful, rescuing, comforting, and giving acts

Chapter 9 Middle Childhood: Physical and Cognitive Development

Multiple Choice

Circle the letter of the response which <u>best</u> completes or answers each of the following statements and questions.

Factual Questions

1. A disorder in which one has difficulty in reading, and has no other cognitive difficulties is called
   a. hyperlexia
   b. dyslexia
   c. ADHD
   d. paralexia

2. According to Jean Piaget, children in the concrete operational stage are able to recognize that an original state can be regained. They recognize that water poured from one container into another can be poured back into the original container. This is called
   a. decentering
   b. transformations
   c. reversibility
   d. horizontal décalage

3. During the period of concrete operations, children acquire and develop specific skills in a sequential manner. This type of development, with each skill dependent on the acquisition of earlier skills, is called
   a. conservation
   b. transformations
   c. executive development
   d. horizontal décalage

4. Cross-cultural research on the acquisition of conservation skills indicates that
   a. these skills may not occur in the invariant sequence postulated by Piaget
   b. non-Western children are ahead of their Western counterparts in developing conservation skills
   c. conservation skills develop only in children who achieve formal mental operations
   d. Western children are more likely than children from nonindustrialized cultures to attribute magical action to the experimenter

5. Which of the following is <u>not</u> a characteristic of a person considered to be creative?
   a. a strong, forceful personality
   b. self-confidence
   c. preference of dealing with people rather than things
   d. independence

6. Children under 8 years of age tend to describe other people in
   a. terms of external, readily observable attributes
   b. terms of unchanging qualities and inner dispositions
   c. specific, precise, and concrete ways
   d. a straightforward, non-stereotypical way

Chapter 9   Middle Childhood: Physical and Cognitive Development

7. The 1983 federal law that ensures children with disabilities the right to a free, appropriate public education is called
    a. Bilingual Education Act
    b. Individuals with Disabilities Education Act
    c. Education for All Handicapped Children Act
    d. Limited English Proficiency Act

8. Which of the following is not a method of teaching English to non-English speakers in school?
    a. bilingualism
    b. English as a second language
    c. total immersion
    d. English language acquisition device

9. A person's preferred way of perceiving, remembering, and using information is referred to as
    a. a portfolio assessment
    b. a learning abilizer
    c. a cognitive style
    d. emotional intelligence

10. Between 1977 and 1995 the percentage of children with specific learning disabilities as a percentage of total public school K-12 enrollment
    a. rose from 6 percent to 15 percent
    b. dropped from 15 percent to 6 percent
    c. rose from 2 percent to 6 percent
    d. dropped from 6 percent to 2 percent

11. Which of the following statements is not true concerning ADHD?
    a. There is little consensus on what causes ADHD.
    b. There are probably multiple routes to the development of ADHD in childhood.
    c. The most recent variation of ADHD involves lethargy and inability to remain awake.
    d. ADHD is probably the most common behavioral disorder among children today.

12. Which of the following is usually not included in the creation of an Individual Education Plan (IEP)
    a. parents
    b. child
    c. psychologist
    d. teachers

13. Jean Piaget indicated that heteronomous morality is characterized by which of the following?
    a. mutual respect
    b. morality of cooperation
    c. an egalitarian attitude
    d. conception of moral rules as absolute

14. At which level of Kohlberg's theory of moral development are individuals capable of stating that Heinz is a lawbreaker?
    a. conventional level
    b. postconventional level
    c. heteronomous morality level
    d. autonomous morality level

15. Gilligan's research on Kohlberg's moral dilemmas suggests that women have a morality of _____ whereas men have a morality of _____.
    a. justice; care
    b. equality; loyalty
    c. care; justice
    d. loyalty; equality

16. The average 8-year-old will probably still have difficulty
    a. riding a bike
    b. jumping rope
    c. judging speed
    d. aiming a ball

17. The most common childhood illness during the ages 7 to 12 is
    a. AIDS
    b. mononucleosis
    c. upper respiratory infection
    d. lower intestinal infection

18. Executive strategies are used to
    a. revise behavior
    b. evaluate behavior
    c. monitor behavior
    d. all to the above

19. Concrete operations includes all of the following except
    a. decentering
    b. transformations
    c. reversibility
    d. abstraction

20. Effective schools exhibit all of the following except
    a. high achievement expectation
    b. homework is considered important
    c. students have as much autonomy as teachers
    d. students are encouraged to use the library

21. Research undertaken by Hugh Hartshorne and Mark A. May involving the moral behavior of some 11,000 children revealed that children's moral behavior was
    a. linked to gender
    b. linked to group social norms
    c. linked to parenting style
    d. linked to subject matter

22. Research reveals that age, sex, and IQ variables are _____ correlated with moral behavior.
    a. very highly
    b. highly
    c. moderately
    d. minimally

23. Behavior that is carried out to benefit the other person without the expectation of an external reward is termed
    a. altruism
    b. prosocial behavior
    c. empathy
    d. autonomous morality

24. A feeling of emotional arousal that leads an individual to take another perspective and to experience an event as the other person experiences it is referred to as
    a. prosocial behavior
    b. internalization
    c. empathy
    d. repression

Chapter 9   Middle Childhood: Physical and Cognitive Development

Conceptual Questions

1. Robert's teacher was discussing the various parts of a river system with his class. Robert immediately drew a picture to represent his teacher's oral lesson because he has realized that he learns things more quickly this way. Psychologists refer to Robert's understanding of his own mental processes as
   a. conservation
   b. executive strategy
   c. decentering
   d. metacognition

2. Margaret watches her mother pour water from a short, wide container into a long, narrow flower vase. She realizes that the initial state of the water can be regained by pouring it back into the original container. Piaget would say Margaret has attained which of the following?
   a. reversibility
   b. transformation
   c. decentration
   d. internal locus of control

3. Kara observes that her son has developed the various conservation skills in a sequential manner. According to Piaget, this type of successive skill development is referred to as
   a. locus of control
   b. conventional development
   c. horizontal décalage
   d. decentration

4. You are a third grade teacher preparing your lesson plans for the second half of the year. If you have just taught the lesson on conservation of <u>area</u>, which conservation skill is next?
   a. substance
   b. length
   c. weight
   d. volume

5. A 5-year-old child suffers a stroke, how could you expect language development to progress?
   a. normally, because of the existence of "backups" in the brain
   b. normally, because of faster neurological response time
   c. abnormally, due to loss of oxygen to the brain
   d. abnormally, due to slower neurological response time

6. Suzanne, a fifth grade teacher, wants to instill in her students a sense of originality and the willingness to think creatively. Psychologists would offer all of the following as tips to foster creativity in children except
   a. using provocative and thought-producing questions
   b. discouraging children from questioning the rules established for their own safety
   c. giving youngsters an opportunity to communicate what they have learned and accomplished
   d. encouraging children's awareness and sensitivity regarding environmental stimuli

Chapter 9 Middle Childhood: Physical and Cognitive Development

7. Muriel's father, Vincent, has noticed that his daughter uses very simplistic words such as "good" and "nice" when describing the characters in her stories. According to researchers, Muriel's tendency to categorize people in such a moralistic manner shows that she is how old?
   a. 7 years old
   b. 8 years old
   c. 9 years old
   d. 10 years old

8. After her parents were divorced, 10-year-old Jennifer remarked, "Even though Mom and Dad act like they like each other, I don't really think they do." This statement indicates
   a. the use of simple moralistic social categories
   b. insightful person-perception ability
   c. an inability to activate social stereotypes
   d. that Jennifer has internalized moral prohibitions

9. Which of the following is most likely to be the cause of death in middle childhood ?
   a. cancer
   b. a car accident
   c. a snake bite
   d. drowning

10. Francine is an average 8-year-old girl. She spends approximately 23 a week _____. Knowing how she spends her time, you ask her to give a report on the value of _____.
   a. doing homework, education
   b. shopping, consumerism
   c. playing with imaginary friends, creativity
   d. watching television, distance learning through media

11. Larry is a child in your classroom who is having trouble learning math. Which approach should work best in helping him learn the subject?
   a. examples using induction
   b. examples using deduction
   c. examples using decalage
   d. examples using conservation

12. While waiting for her dinner at the restaurant, Lauren tries to get her father's attention by making various animal sounds. Lauren's father reprimands her and tells her that such behavior is inappropriate in public. Lauren is at first angry, but then she behaves nicely and tells her little brother not to "make funny noises in public." Lauren's internalization of her father's social standard in this situation most clearly exemplifies which approach toward moral development?
   a. cognitive-developmental theory
   b. psychoanalytic theory
   c. cognitive learning theory
   d. behaviorism

Chapter 9   Middle Childhood: Physical and Cognitive Development

13. You moved to the United States from a foreign country and do not speak English. You find yourself in a classroom where the teachers are speaking to you in English and your first language. This approach to learning English is called
    a. English as a Second Language
    b. bilingualism
    c. total immersion
    d. code switching

14. A sixth grade student displays a willingness to cooperate with his fellow classmates. Piaget would state that this child's egalitarian relationship with his peers will lead to which type of moral development?
    a. autonomous morality
    b. heteronomous morality
    c. conventional level
    d. preconventional level

15. According to Kohlberg, which of the following children is demonstrating the highest level of moral development?
    a. Billy, who treats his sister nicely when Mom and Dad are around so that he won't get yelled at.
    b. Jimmy, who tells his mother that he got good grades because he knows his mother will like hearing this.
    c. Don, who cleans the blackboards for his teacher so he might get a better grade.
    d. Mary, who refuses to dissect a frog in biology class even though her grade will suffer.

16. Donny tells his older brother, "I won't tell Mom that you were kissing your girlfriend in the living room if you don't tell her I was eating cheese and crackers in the bedroom." Donny is displaying
    a. autonomous morality
    b. concrete operational reasoning
    c. conventional morality
    d. preconventional morality

17. Missy is a 14-year-old girl who has grown up in an inner-city environment. She's been a gang member for two years now, and last night she helped "initiate" another girl into the gang by assisting in "beating up" the new girl. Missy does not feel guilty over her actions — as a matter of fact, she's proud of what she's done. How does the text explain Missy's thinking and actions?
    a. Missy is a delinquent who has never learned right from wrong.
    b. Missy has internalized her standards of improper behavior in accordance with the standards of the group.
    c. Missy felt she had to do these terrible things to another person or else she would lose face in front of her peers and get kicked out of the gang.
    d. Missy would be classified as a "sociopath" – someone who cares only for herself and her own needs.

18. Sam is an Eagle Scout and has been praised for his honesty and trustworthiness. However, yesterday Sam got caught stealing a pen from the store. On the basis of research, the most logical conclusion one can reach is that
    a. Sam's stealing is motivated by a universal ethical orientation
    b. Sam's honesty is specific to particular situations and not a trait of his character
    c. Sam is morally immature because his moral attitudes are inconsistent with his behavior
    d. if Sam were more intelligent, he would have avoided being caught

Chapter 9   Middle Childhood: Physical and Cognitive Development

19. After shoveling his own driveway, 11-year-old Alex decided to shovel the driveway of his elderly neighbor, Mr. Hogan. As Alex was leaving to go home, Mr. Hogan said he wanted to pay him for his work. Alex refused the offer and said, "I didn't do it for the money, I just wanted to help you out." Alex's behavior clearly represents
   a. coping
   b. empathy
   c. altruism
   d. autonomy

20. According to research, parents who wish to foster helping and altruistic behaviors in their children should do all of the following except
   a. make the child feel guilty if they do something wrong
   b. convey a certain intensity about their own concern for living things
   c. describe to the child how the other person feels if the child hurts someone else
   d. provide guidelines and set limits on what youngsters can get away with

Essay Questions

1. Discuss the different approaches to moral development and link prosocial behavior to moral cognition.

2. Make an argument for both inclusion and non-inclusion of learning disabled children in public schools.

3. Give an argument for or against a proposal in your school district that all children, not just disabled children, should be given an Individualized Education Plan (IEP).

Chapter 9   Middle Childhood: Physical and Cognitive Development

ANSWERS FOR SELF-TESTS

Matching

1. n
2. i
3. p
4. b
5. j
6. d
7. g
8. a
9. f
10. c
11. m
12. e
13. q
14. h
15. k
16. l
17. o

Multiple Choice

Factual

1. b
2. c
3. d
4. a
5. c
6. a
7. b
8. d
9. c
10. c
11. c
12. b
13. d
14. a
15. c
16. c
17. c
18. d
19. d
20. c
21. b
22. d
23. a
24. c

Conceptual

1. d
2. a
3. c
4. c
5. a
6. b
7. a
8. b
9. b
10. d
11. a
12. c
13. b
14. a
15. d
16. d
17. b
18. b
19. c
20. a

Chapter 10

Middle Childhood:
Emotional and Social Development

INTRODUCTION

Chapter 10 describes a variety of ways in which the school environment influences children's development. More specifically, this chapter illustrates how the school setting affects the development of a child's personality, cognitive capabilities, interpersonal skills, and school behavior. Several important issues are discussed, including:

- The Quest for Self-Understanding. Topics covered include self-image, self-esteem and the manner in which children deal with fears and stress.

- Family Influences. The section examines maternal, paternal and sibling influences on behavior as well as the makeup of the family – divorced, single parent or stepfamily.

- The World of Peer Relationships. Several areas are covered within this context: functions of the peer group, gender cleavage, the consequences of social acceptance and rejection, development of children's self-esteem and the factors that contribute to a healthy self-concept, the processes by which children conform to a peer group, and children's awareness of and experience with members of different social and ethnic groups.

- The World of School. The areas examined include the direct functions of the school, characteristics of effective schools, identification and placement of children with learning disabilities, factors associated with improving student motivation, and the close relationship between school performance and socioeconomic status.

LEARNING OBJECTIVES

After completing Chapter 10, you should be able to:

1. Define Erikson's fourth stage of industry vs. inferiority

Chapter 10 Middle Childhood: Emotional and Social Development

2. Discuss the meaning, origins, and factors associated with the development of self-esteem in children.

emerging self-conception

self-appraisal/reflected appraisal

3. Explain research on parental attitudes and practices associated with high levels of self-esteem.

4. Explain why children experience changes in their abilities to understand emotion.

5. Explain the role that fear plays in the lives of children.

6. Define *locus of control* and *coping* and explain the role these play in assuaging stress.

7. Summarize the influence of mothers and fathers on the emotional stability of a child.

Chapter 10   Middle Childhood: Emotional and Social Development

8. Explain the important tasks that children who are dealing with a divorce must complete.

9. Summarize the differences between two-parent families and single-parent families and their effects on children's emotional development.

10. Summarize the significant functions of children's peer relationships and peer groups.

independence from adults

effects on school motivation, performance, and adjustment

relationship as equals

Piaget's autonomous morality

solidarity

Chapter 10   Middle Childhood: Emotional and Social Development

transmission of information and secrets

peers as a form of "control" of unwanted behaviors

11. Define gender cleavage, and describe the changes that occur as children pass from a gender cleavage orientation to a heterosexual orientation to social behavior.

gender cleavage

gender separation

two factors that give rise to gender segregation

boys' typical behavior

girls' typical behavior

Freud's latency period and the contemporary view

12. Define the following terms as they relate to social acceptance or rejection in peer relationships.

group

values

sociometry

Chapter 10 Middle Childhood: Emotional and Social Development

13. Discuss what researchers have found regarding the physical qualities which make children attractive or unattractive in the eyes of their peers.

14. Discuss the behavioral characteristics which seem to be related to children's social acceptance by their peers.

popular traits

unpopular traits

cross-cultural findings

consequences of rejection

15. Illustrate the effects of children's social maturity on their social desirability by their peers.

16. Discuss children's development of racial awareness, prejudice, and ways to promote positive interracial contact.

Chapter 10 Middle Childhood: Emotional and Social Development

17. List the developmental functions that schools serve.

18. Discuss the following factors that impact student motivation.

motivation

extrinsic motivation

intrinsic motivation

attributions of causality

high attainment

low attainment

locus of control and school achievement

external control

internal control

19. Describe the results of research on the relationship between school performance and socioeconomic status.

middle-class bias

subcultural differences

English language as a barrier

educational self-fulfilling prophecy

bias toward white students

effect on African-American and Hispanic students

WEB SITES

The following web sites deal with some of the major concepts and issues presented in Chapter 10. Additional resources can be found on the text's web site, at http://www.mhhe.com/crandell7.

Developmental Psychology Links
http://www.wesleyan.edu/spn/develop.htm

Girl Power
http://www.health.org/gpower/

Panel Study of Income Dynamics, Child Development Supplement
http://www.isr.umich.edu/src/child-development/fullrep.html

National Adoption Institute
http://www.adoptioninstitute.org

Youth Information, Department of Health and Human Services
http://youth.os.dhhs.gov/

Chapter 10   Middle Childhood: Emotional and Social Development

SELF-TESTS

Matching

Match the key terms with their definitions:

a. coping
b. educational self-fulfilling prophecies
c. emotion-focused coping
d. extrinsic motivation
e. fear
f. gender cleavage
g. group
h. industry vs. inferiority
i. intrinsic motivation
j. locus of control
k. motivation
l. phobia
m. post-traumatic stress disorder
n. prejudice
o. problem-focused coping
p. self-image
q. sociogram
r. values

1. ____ a disorder that may exhibit a variety of symptoms including numbing and helplessness, increased irritability and aggressiveness, extreme anxiety, panic and fears, exaggerated startle response, sleep disturbances, and bed wetting

2. ____ a system of negative conceptions, feelings, and action orientations regarding the members of a particular religious, racial, or nationality group

3. ____ a type of coping which changes one's appraisal of the situation

4. ____ a type of coping which changes the troubling situation

5. ____ activity that is undertaken for its own sake

6. ____ activity that is undertaken for some purpose other than its own sake

7. ____ an excessive, persistent, and maladaptive fear response – usually to benign or ill-defined stimuli

8. ____ an important moderator of an individual's experience of stress — people's perception of who or what is responsible for the outcome of events and behaviors in their lives

9. ____ an unpleasant emotion aroused by impending danger, pain, or misfortune

10. ____ depicts the patterns of choice existing among members of a group at a given time

11. ____ inner states and processes that prompt, direct, and sustain activity

12. ____ teacher expectation effects whereby some children fail to learn because those who are charged with teaching them do not believe that they will learn

13. ____ the criteria used in deciding the relative merit and desirability of things

14. ____ the fourth stage of the life cycle when children in middle childhood become interested in how things were made or how they work

15. ____ the overall view that children have of themselves

16. ____ the responses we make in order to master, tolerate, or reduce stress

17. ____ the tendency for boys to associate with boys and girls with girls

18. ____ two or more people who share a feeling of unity and are bound together in relatively stable patterns of social interaction

Multiple Choice

Circle the letter of the response that <u>best</u> completes or answers each of the following statements and questions.

Factual Questions

1. Erikson's fourth stage, industry vs. inferiority, suggests that children must
    a. learn a skill or trade
    b. begin doing activities by themselves
    c. reject parents' help
    d. all of the above

2. A major cognitive and social change occurs as children go through their elementary school years, as compared to their preschool years. They are most likely to
    a. be best friends with the child next door rather than classmates
    b. select friends from their own age group who have similar interests and personality traits similar to their own
    c. play with the children their parents select
    d. make friends with the kids who have the nicest homes and toys

3. Which of the following functions is performed by peer groups?
    a. Peer groups give children experience with relationships in which they are on an equal footing with others.
    b. Peer groups help teach children that they must subordinate group goals to their own interests.
    c. Peer groups provide an arena in which children cannot be independent of adult control.
    d. Peer groups provide children with marginal stress.

4. The tendency for elementary school boys to associate with boys and elementary school girls with girls is called
    a. gender consciousness
    b. peer groups
    c. gender cleavage
    d. gender experimentation

Chapter 10 Middle Childhood: Emotional and Social Development

5. According to your text, gender segregation tends to reach its peak in
    a. third grade
    b. fourth grade
    c. fifth grade
    d. sixth grade

6. According to Eleanor Maccoby's findings on gender segregation, which of the following statements is not true?
    a. Children systematically frustrate adult efforts to diffuse their preferences for interacting with same-sex peers.
    b. Children segregate themselves into same-sex groups because they find play partners of the same sex more compatible.
    c. Girls find it difficult to establish reciprocity with boys.
    d. Boys in their own groups are more likely to engage in "collaborative speech acts."

7. "I am a good girl" is an example of
    a. self-image
    b. self-concept
    c. self-esteem
    d. all of the above

8. When asked, the majority of children ages 8 to 12 listed which of the following as the most important for self-esteem?
    a. scholastic ability
    b. athletic competence
    c. physical appearance
    d. social acceptance

9. Which of the following is not put forth in the text as one of three factors researchers use in studying stress?
    a. characteristics of the child
    b. developmental factors
    c. situation specific factors
    d. societal factors

10. Boys are more likely than girls to do all of the following except
    a. interrupt one another
    b. use commands and threats
    c. tell jokes or suspenseful stories
    d. provide nonverbal signals of attentiveness

11. Members of a group
    a. are bound together in relatively stable patterns of social interaction
    b. are attracted to each other as a result of sociometry
    c. share a temporary feeling of unity until a sociogram is developed
    d. join together to preserve a sense of independence

Chapter 10 Middle Childhood: Emotional and Social Development

12. The criteria that people use in deciding the relative merit and desirability of things is termed
    a. gender cleavage
    b. sociometrics
    c. values
    d. morals

13. Sociometry is a
    a. meter instrument for counting social interactions
    b. measure used for assessing patterns of attraction, rejection, or indifference
    c. direct measure of the desirability of one's name
    d. measure of physical attractiveness

14. In a sociogram, a person who is not part of any group is called
    a. a mesomorph
    b. an athlete
    c. an isolate
    d. an introvert

15. Researchers have conducted several studies using many different methods and have found a significant relationship exists between children's physical attractiveness and their level of
    a. athleticism
    b. popularity
    c. intelligence
    d. extroversion

16. Evidence suggests that, by the age of six, boys have already developed a favorable stereotype of which type of body configuration?
    a. ectomorph
    b. endomorph
    c. mesomorph
    d. mectomorph

17. Popular children tend to be described by their peers as
    a. noisy, rebellious, and peppy
    b. alert, self-assured, and helpful
    c. confident, aggressive, and attention-seeking
    d. active, egocentric, and strong

18. Children with high self-esteem are likely to have parents who
    a. have low self-esteem
    b. set vaguely defined limits
    c. show respect for their children's opinions
    d. abuse their children

19. The system of negative conceptions, feelings, and action orientations regarding the members of a particular religion, race, or nationality is referred to as
    a. stereotyping
    b. prejudice
    c. group norms
    d. values

Chapter 10 Middle Childhood: Emotional and Social Development

20. During the preschool period, white children
    a. show consistent prejudice toward non-white children
    b. attend less to differences among non-white children than they do to differences among white children
    c. use hair and eye characteristics to distinguish between African-American and Caucasian children
    d. perceive and think about African-Americans in stereotyped ways

21. Which of the following is not described as a developmental function of schools?
    a. teaching specific cognitive skills
    b. transmitting society's goals and values
    c. preparing for higher education and technical skills
    d. transmitting religious morals

22. Which of the following is the most closely associated with intrinsic motivation?
    a. praise
    b. an increase in allowance
    c. rewards that are part of the activity
    d. achievement of honor roll for money

23. Studies have shown that the higher the social class of children's families
    a. the lower the number of elective offices they hold in school life
    b. the lower their participation in extracurricular activities
    c. the higher their rate of truancy and suspensions from school
    d. the greater number of formal grades the children complete

24. Regarding research on motivation and learning, which statement is accurate?
    a. Punishment (staying in at lunchtime or after school) is shown to be an effective motivator to get children to do their homework.
    b. Extrinsic rewards, such as candy and stars, are effective in getting students to read more.
    c. With less motivated students, teachers should lavish praise on their every good deed.
    d. Extrinsic rewards should be used sparingly and only when necessary.

25. Poor school achievement seems to be related to
    a. low motivation or effort
    b. external locus of control
    c. socioeconomic status
    d. all of the above

26. When children fail to learn because those who are charged with teaching them do not believe that they will learn, do not expect that they can learn, and do not act toward them in ways that help them to learn, psychologists say that they are the victims of
    a. a learning disability
    b. educational self-fulfilling prophecies
    c. cultural bias
    d. gender cleavage

Chapter 10 Middle Childhood: Emotional and Social Development

Conceptual Questions

1. Connie decides to allow her class of fifth-grade children to decide for themselves where they should sit in the classroom. Connie's only provision is that the children arrange the desks in groups of three. When the children finalize their new desk arrangement, she is surprised to find that each group consists of same-gender peers. Psychologists refer to this phenomenon as
    a. mainstreaming
    b. educational self-fulfilling prophecy
    c. locus of control
    d. gender cleavage

2. Your child is in the industry vs. inferiority stage of psychosocial development. Which adult would Erikson probably advise you to talk to concerning helping your child resolve this crisis positively?
    a. religious leader
    b. teacher
    c. police officer
    d. grandparent

3. You are babysitting a typical 9-year-old. Of the following, she is most likely to be afraid of
    a. a dark room
    b. a ghost
    c. failing an exam
    d. a troll under the bridge

4. Marcus' father doesn't really want to spend a lot of time with him and he is never home to eat with Marcus. His father is most likely to be
    a. a biological parent
    b. a stepparent
    c. single
    d. Hispanic and educated

5. Regardless of gender, class, or ethnicity children are most likely to fear
    a. war
    b. nuclear weapons
    c. drive-by shootings
    d. drugs abuse

6. Jamie was anxious about her upcoming spelling test. She started showing some signs of stress. You tell her that failing one test will not affect her chances of getting into college. She listens, agrees, and begins to relax. You have relied on an appeal to
    a. problem-focused coping
    b. emotional-focused coping
    c. external locus of control
    d. internal locus of control

Chapter 10 Middle Childhood: Emotional and Social Development

7. You are a sixth grade teacher. Around November, a new teacher at your school seems distressed in the faculty lounge because she states that the girls and boys in her fifth grade class just don't get along. There's a lot of teasing, name calling, and sometimes loud disagreements over nearly everything between the boys and girls in your class. The girls blame the boys. The boys blame the girls. What should she do? As the teacher with more experience, you are likely to tell her
    a. the class needs discipline and order; provide more structure and less opportunity for discussion – and they'll get along just fine
    b. the class is acting normally for their ages – gender segregation seems to be a part of normal development
    c. the class needs to be punished, so make arrangements for the culprits to stay after school
    d. to call in the parents; she'll need their cooperation to straighten out the problem

8. Karen, the psychologist in an elementary school, is conducting a behavioral observation on a fourth-grader. Karen enters the classroom during "snack time" and observes the child talking to a group of girls at her desk. According to Maccoby's research depicting the characteristic ways in which girls behave in same-gender groups, Karen would most likely witness the girls engage in which of the following behaviors?
    a. interrupting one another
    b. calling each other names
    c. using commands and threats when responding to each other
    d. pausing to give each other a chance to speak

9. Midway though the school year, Kirsten decides that she wants to modify the seating chart in her fifth grade classroom to achieve an optimal level of compatibility between her students. In order to assess the patterns of attraction, rejection, and indifference among the children in her class, psychologists would recommend that she conduct a
    a. social skills rating
    b. sociometry exercise
    c. home visit
    d. family history analysis

10. A sixth grade student is described by his peers as noisy, attention-seeking, and arrogant. According to behavioral research, he would most likely be labeled as which of the following?
    a. social isolate
    b. mesomorph
    c. hyperactive
    d. introverted

11. Sociologists such as Cooley and Mead would maintain that other people serve the role of a(n) _____ in affecting self-esteem.
    a. magnifying glass
    b. mirror
    c. microscope
    d. amplifier

Chapter 10 Middle Childhood: Emotional and Social Development

12. Your neighbor's 8 year old son is always putting himself down when he speaks, and he relies on other children to tell him what to do. On the basis of the research on self-esteem, you might conclude that his
    a. father does not allow him to engage in give-and-take discussions concerning how the house chores are decided
    b. father treats him in a matter-of-fact, neutral manner while praising good behavior
    c. mother is a loving parent who allows him to break rules occasionally
    d. father lets him do everything for himself and then praises him liberally

13. The Wilsons recently divorced, and they are concerned about the impact their separation will have on the emotional development of their 11 year old daughter, Leslie. According to Coopersmith's analysis of the kinds of parental practices that are associated with the development of high levels of self-esteem in children, the Wilsons should do all of the following except
    a. maintain a high level of self-esteem for themselves
    b. set and enforce clearly defined limits for Leslie's behavior
    c. show respect for Leslie's rights and opinions
    d. set no limitations on Leslie's behavior

14. You work in a shelter for run-away, homeless youth in a large city. Your clients tell you stories of beatings, neglect, and alcohol, drug, and sex abuse – behavior they've experienced in their own homes from their own parents. From your background in adolescent psychology, you come to the conclusion that none of the teenagers have good self-esteem. You can also reach the conclusion from Coopersmith's research that their parents
    a. wanted to set strong limits for their children, but their children fell in with a "bad crowd" and became rebellious
    b. had tried to show approval and acceptance of their children up to the onset of the turbulent adolescent years
    c. could have been warm, responsive people, but their children were born belligerent and difficult and this affected the parents' psychological well-being
    d. probably have low self-esteem themselves and are unlikely to be able to listen to and respect their own children

15. Which implementation would be most effective in promoting a sense of interracial friendliness in a school district?
    a. an interracial high school basketball league
    b. an interracial middle school chess club
    c. an interracial soccer league for upper elementary school students
    d. an interracial learning team made up of kindergarten and first grade children

16. James is a new third grade teacher, and he wishes to establish a reward system in his classroom that facilitates children's intrinsic interest in activities. According to the research conducted by Lepper and Greene, in deciding on a type of reinforcement schedule, James should adhere most closely to which of the following guidelines?
    a. Reward the children in a highly unpredictable manner.
    b. Use rewards only when necessary to draw children into activities that do not at first attract their interest.
    c. Consistently reward children for good behavior by offering lavish praise, gold stars, and other extrinsic rewards.
    d. Never give the children any reward, regardless of their interest level in a specific activity.

17. Margaret is concerned about how her son, Michael, will respond to the results of his recent unit test in social studies. Research on the attributions of causality suggests that she should be most concerned if Michael reacts with which of the following explanations of his test performance?
    a. "I failed because I did not put much effort into studying."
    b. "I failed because I was not lucky."
    c. "I was successful because I am smart."
    d. "I was successful because I got lucky."

18. Roberta believes she has done a great deal of diligent work in her seventh grade science class and feels that she is solely responsible for determining her final grade. According to research on the attributions of causality, Roberta is most likely to have
    a. an external locus of control
    b. a need to be intrinsically motivated
    c. an internal locus of control
    d. a need to be extrinsically motivated

19. Maria's family is considered to be in the upper class in socioeconomic status (SES). Psychologists would be the least likely to attribute the positive relationship between Maria's high educational achievement and her SES to which of the following?
    a. bias of teachers toward middle-and upper-class youngsters
    b. subcultural differences in regard to their expectations about academics
    c. educational self-fulfilling prophecies
    d. the low value assigned. to education by parents of middle- and upper-class children

20. Your son is an average "C" student, and your daughter is an "A" student. Your daughter's teacher gets your son in a class and assumes that he will be an "A" student, too. Your son's grades improve. This demonstrates
    a. gender cleavage
    b. the middle-class bias effect
    c. the effects of excellent teaching
    d. an educational self-fulfilling prophecy

Chapter 10 Middle Childhood: Emotional and Social Development

Essay Questions

1. Pat's family is stable, with two parents and two siblings, and is middle class. Sam's family is not stable, divorce is imminent, he has five stepsiblings and the household is of lower socioeconomic status. How popular would you expect each child to be in school? What factors might counteract the expected social outcome for Pat and Sam?

2. Marcia went to school in the first grade with a positive self-image; now in the sixth grade she has a sense of inferiority and low self-esteem. She hates her classmates and no longer wants to go to school. What might have happened?

3. Your friend is trying to decide whether to homeschool her son or to send him to a public school with a diverse population. Give arguments for both sides.

Chapter 10 Middle Childhood: Emotional and Social Development

ANSWERS FOR SELF-TESTS

Matching

1. m
2. n
3. c
4. o
5. i
6. d

7. l
8. j
9. e
10. q
11. k
12. b

13. r
14. h
15. p
16. a
17. f
18. g

Multiple Choice

Factual

1. b
2. b
3. a
4. c
5. c
6. d
7. a
8. c
9. d

10. d
11. a
12. c
13. b
14. c
15. b
16. c
17. b
18. c

19. b
20. c
21. d
22. c
23. d
24. d
25. d
26. b

Conceptual

1. d
2. b
3. b
4. b
5. c
6. b
7. b

8. d
9. b
10. c
11. b
12. a
13. d
14. d

15. d
16. b
17. d
18. c
19. d
20. d

Chapter 11

Adolescence:
Physical and Cognitive Development

INTRODUCTION

In adolescence, one's biological, social, and moral foundations all go through rapid changes. The complete transition to physical and reproductive maturity occurs, with accompanying adjustments in identity, social interactions, cognitive abilities, and moral values. The following areas are specifically examined in Chapter 11:

- Puberty. The physical development and maturity issues that accompany the adolescent growth spurt for both boys and girls are presented. The implications of growth variations and sexual maturation on adolescent personality and behavior are also discussed.

- Health Issues. The effects of smoking, drugs, alcohol, STDs, and stress are examined.

- The Development of Identities and Self-Concepts. Adolescence is a time of egocentricity and needing to be like others. Anyone who is perceived as "different" may have difficult experiences. Within this context, the development of individual differences in identity, the impact of the timing of maturation, the nature of obesity, and the body-image disorders of anorexia and bulimia are examined. Some recent studies are presented which suggest that girls emerge from adolescence with a poorer self-image than boys.

- Cognitive Development. By older adolescence, most teenagers acquire the ability for logical reasoning and abstract thought, known as the period of formal operations.

- Moral Development. During adolescent transition, most teenagers also attain Kohlberg's postconventional stage of morality. Their political thinking becomes more abstract and idealistic.

Chapter 11 Adolescence: Physical and Cognitive Development

LEARNING OBJECTIVES

After completing Chapter 11, you should be able to:

1. Explain the role of the pituitary gland and gonadotropic system in activating growth-stimulating hormones leading to sexual maturation.

2. Describe how one's cognitive processes are affected by these biological changes.

3. Describe recent theories addressing why large numbers of young women in their early teens are becoming pregnant or having babies.

ethological (sociobiological) theory (Belsky, Steinberg, & Draper)

alternative theory (Maccoby)

sociological theory (Anderson)

4. Explain what is meant by the *adolescent growth spurt* and *asynchrony*.

Chapter 11 Adolescence: Physical and Cognitive Development

5. Describe the changes that accompany the maturity of the female reproductive system, including *menarche*.

9-10 years old

12-13 years old

12-13 *months* later

self-image

6. Describe the changes that accompany the maturity of the male reproductive system.

11-11.5 years old

13-14 years old

14-15 years old

15-18 years old

7. Discuss the research findings on the timing of maturation and its effects on self-image and behavior of boys.

early maturation

late maturation

Chapter 11   Adolescence: Physical and Cognitive Development

8. Discuss the research findings on the timing of maturation and its effects on self-image and behavior of girls.

early maturation

late maturation

9. Explain why a teenager's physical appearance is related to popularity and gender-related expectations.

10. Describe the following factors that relate to obesity.

demographic data

causes of obesity

consequences of dieting

long-term health effects

long-term social consequences

social prejudice and discrimination

Chapter 11 Adolescence: Physical and Cognitive Development

11. Describe the reasons for and demographics of adolescent risky behaviors.

smoking

alcohol and drugs

STDs

HIV/AIDS

teen pregnancy

body art/tattooing

12. Complete the following information about anorexia and bulimia.

describe anorexia and the person's self-perception

cite reasons why anorexia occurs

describe personality characteristics associated with anorexia

describe bulimia and the person's self-perception

cite reasons why bulimia occurs

describe personality characteristics associated with bulimia

Chapter 11   Adolescence: Physical and Cognitive Development

13. Describe why Piaget called adolescence the *period of formal operations*. Cite some contradictory views.

14. Cite some findings from the University of Chicago study (1984) on mood swings.

mood swings

time with family

sibling conflicts

solitude

sports and hobbies

15. Define what is meant by adolescent egocentrism proposed by Elkind.

the personal fable

imaginary audience

Chapter 11   Adolescence: Physical and Cognitive Development

16. Describe Even Start and discuss its goals

17. Give reasons why high school seniors in the United States have overall lower science and math scores than students in many other countries.

18. Tell how adolescents' political thinking develops as they make the transition through adolescence.

WEB SITES

The following web sites deal with some of the concepts and issues presented in Chapter 11. Additional resources can be found on the text's web site, at http://www.mhhe.com/crandell7.

Adolescent Health from the American Medical Association
http://www.ama-assn.org/adolhlth/adolhlth.htm

AIDS Prevention Education
http://www.siecus.org/progs/prog0004.html

Survey of the Health of Adolescent Girls
http://www.cmwf.org/programs/women/factshet.asp

TIMSS International Study Center at Boston College
http://timss.enc.org/

Chapter 11 Adolescence: Physical and Cognitive Development

SELF-TESTS

Matching

Match the key terms with their definitions:

a. adolescent growth spurt
b. anorexia nervosa
c. asynchrony
d. bulimia
e. egocentrism
f. imaginary audience
g. menarche
h. obesity
i. period of formal operations
j. personal fable
k. puberty
l. sexually transmitted diseases
m. substance abuse

1. ____ a lack of awareness that there are viewpoints other than one's own

2. ____ a romantic imagery in which adolescents tend to view themselves as somehow unique and even heroic – as destined for unusual fame and fortune

3. ____ an eating disorder characterized by repeated episodes of bingeing, particularly on high-calorie foods, such as candy bars, cakes, pies, and ice cream

4. ____ an eating disorder that primarily affects females, causing some to become obsessed with looking thin and terrified of becoming fat

5. ____ diseases – including gonorrhea, syphilis, chlamydia, AIDS – transmitted by engaging in sexual intercourse while not using condoms

6. ____ refers to the final and highest stage in the development of cognitive functioning from infancy to adulthood

7. ____ the belief of an adolescent that everyone in the local environment is primarily concerned with the appearance and behavior of the adolescent

8. ____ the excess accumulation of body fat, considered to be an increase of twenty pounds over typical weight for height

9. ____ the first menstrual period

10. ____ the harmful use of drugs or alcohol, lasting over a prolonged period, which self or others are placed in hazardous situations

11. ____ the period of the life cycle when sexual and reproductive maturation becomes evident

12. ____ the rapid increase in height and weight that occurs during the early adolescent years

13. ____ the term used to describe this dissimilarity in the growth rates of different parts of the body

Chapter 11   Adolescence: Physical and Cognitive Development

Multiple Choice

Circle the letter of the response that best completes or answers each of the following statements and questions.

Factual Questions

1. The period of the life cycle when sexual and reproductive maturation becomes evident defines
    a. adolescence
    b. puberty
    c. adulthood
    d. psychological maturation

2. Which gland in the body (also known as the "master gland") secretes the hormones into the bloodstream that trigger the changes at puberty?
    a. endocrine
    b. adrenal
    c. thyroid
    d. pituitary

3. Which of the following statements is inaccurate about biological changes that influence cognitive development?
    a. Adult brains use twice as much energy as children's brains.
    b. From 11 to 14, metabolic activity falls to the adult level.
    c. Children experience twice as much deep sleep as adults.
    d. Unused synapses are depleted.

4. Researchers at the National Institute of Mental Health have found supportive evidence that lower levels of testosterone and higher levels of an adrenal androgen are linked to
    a. feelings of sadness and confusion
    b. good adjustment behaviors
    c. behavioral problems, including rebelliousness and fighting
    d. early menarche

5. Belsky has recently advanced a controversial sociobiological theory suggesting that
    a. some young mothers are responding to an evolutionary pattern to bear children early and often
    b. boys are more likely to exhibit behavioral problems than girls
    c. youngsters growing up in affluence are likely to have more children
    d. girls reared in homes where there is a great deal of emotional stress typically enter puberty later than other girls

6. Which organ almost doubles in weight during adolescence?
    a. brain
    b. heart
    c. pituitary gland
    d. all of the above

7. Which of the following about the adolescent growth spurt is true?
    a. Boys' growth spurt occurs about two years earlier than girls'.
    b. Children grow at a rate they last experienced when 2 years old.
    c. It lasts about six months.
    d. By age 16, 98 percent of adolescents reach their final height.

8. During puberty, different parts of the body grow at different rates, sometimes causing awkwardness. This is called
    a. clumsiness
    b. adolescent growth spurt
    c. acceleration
    d. asynchrony

9. The release of a woman's mature egg, which occurs 12 to 18 months after the first menstruation, is called
    a. menarche
    b. menses
    c. ovulation
    d. fertilization

10. An earlier onset of the first menstruation over the past century in Western nations appears to have resulted from
    a. genetic predispositions
    b. an improvement in overall nutrition
    c. hormone replacement therapy
    d. less strenuous lives for women

11. Menarche can be delayed because of
    a. strenuous physical exercise
    b. a very thin body type with little fat reserve
    c. poor nutrition
    d. all of the above

12. American girls' attitudes toward menarche include all of the following except
    a. it gives girls a sense of identity as women
    b. most girls are happy about their first menses
    c. most girls begin to think about having babies
    d. most girls are concerned about physical discomfort, moodiness, hygiene, and disruption of activities

13. Mature sperm, which can fertilize a woman's egg, appear in the semen about when?
    a. in the first ejaculate fluid during orgasm
    b. in the first nocturnal emissions called "wet dreams"
    c. in the semen about one year after the first ejaculation
    d. in the semen about a month after the first ejaculation

Chapter 11   Adolescence: Physical and Cognitive Development

14. Children show enormous variation in growth and sexual maturation. Some do not begin their growth spurt and development of secondary sexual characteristics until many of their peers have virtually completed these stages. The most logical conclusion that can be arrived at from these facts is
    a. the larger the body frame, the earlier the maturation
    b. there is no "set pattern" that is applicable for all children
    c. good nutrition ensures "on time" physical maturation
    d. females always reach maturation before males

15. Early-maturing adolescent boys tend to
    a. possess feelings of adequacy in comparison with peers
    b. possess feelings of inadequacy in comparison with peers
    c. be born leaders
    d. be more aggressive and rebellious than their peers

16. Early-maturing adolescent girls are more likely to
    a. develop symptoms such as depression
    b. have a negatively affected prestige status
    c. develop eating disorders
    d. all of the above

17. Which of the following statements pertaining to adolescent self-image is true?
    a. Teenagers are preoccupied with the issue of who is the most intelligent.
    b. Popularity and peer approval are major issues.
    c. Preteens are more concerned with developing intimate friendships than teenagers.
    d. Concern with weight is not an issue to an adolescent.

18. Female models are 9 percent taller and 16 percent thinner than are average American women. Based on this fact and the studies discussed in the chapter, one can conclude
    a. this is the primary cause of anorexia among adolescent girls
    b. girls' self-esteem develops more slowly than males
    c. the majority of adolescent females are unhappy with their physical appearance
    d. advertisements present an unrealistic ideal of beauty for females to emulate

19. Obesity is
    a. the second most common eating disorder in the United States.
    b. the most common eating disorder in the United States.
    c. ten pounds over your desired weight
    d. twenty pounds more fat than muscle

20. Obese adults are at greater risk of
    a. diabetes
    b. all cancers
    c. liver disorders
    d. all of the above

21. Substance abuse is defined as
    a. beating someone while intoxicated
    b. using drugs for more than three months
    c. prolonged use of drugs that endangers self or others
    d. taking more of a drug than weight/height ratio dictates

Chapter 11 Adolescence: Physical and Cognitive Development

22. Sexually active U.S. teens have _____ of the sexually active U.S. population
    a. the lowest rates of gonorrhea, syphilis, and chlamydia
    b. the lowest rates of gonorrhea, syphilis, and AIDS
    c. the highest rates of gonorrhea, syphilis and chlamydia
    d. the highest rates of gonorrhea, syphilis and AIDS

23. Although victims of bulimia are typically female, the disorder also manifests itself in males, particularly those who are participating in contact sports. Studies show that a male bulimic would most likely be a
    a. football player
    b. jogger
    c. soccer player
    d. wrestler

24. A common reason for body piercing is
    a. to find one's true self
    b. to win a bet
    c. to fit in with a group
    d. to commemorate an event

25. Jean Piaget called adolescence the period of formal operations because
    a. adolescents are able to argue persuasively in both formal and informal discussion
    b. adolescents are formally out of the required educational system
    c. adolescents gain the ability to think in logical, abstract terms to solve complex problems
    d. adolescents can think in immediate terms

26. According to Elkind, the two dimensions of egocentrism are
    a. abstract fable and imaginary audience
    b. abstract audience and imaginary fable
    c. personal fable and imaginary audience
    d. personal abstraction and imaginary fable

27. On the basis of information presented in the chapter on adolescent egocentricity, it would be fair to conclude that
    a. most adolescents are not concerned with what their peers think
    b. most adolescents are less self-conscious at this stage
    c. most adolescents believe other people are as admiring or critical of them as they are of themselves
    d. most adolescents are concerned with observing others rather than being observed

28. A finding from Kohlberg's work on moral development is that
    a. by early adolescence, children are generally more liberal in their outlook
    b. adolescents are often idealistic and think they have to reform the world
    c. adolescents are often unconcerned with the adult world and its issues
    d. moral development in adolescence doesn't develop in an orderly sequence

Chapter 11   Adolescence: Physical and Cognitive Development

Conceptual Questions

1. You are asked to evaluate the reasons why many adolescent boys are being rebellious, talking back to teachers, and fighting. Based on your knowledge of biology, you suggest
    a. that boys will be boys
    b. that the cause might be low levels of testosterone and high levels of androstenedione
    c. that the cause might be low levels of androstenedione and high levels of testosterone
    d. the pituitary gland has not caught up with the boys' psychological changes

2. Jennifer's home is stressful and unpredictable, and no father is present. She had her first child at 13, her second at 15, and her third at 17. Belsky would argue that
    a. this happened because of a lack of parental supervision
    b. she had no prospect for a job and was poor so decided to have children
    c. she adjusted her reproductive strategies to take into account her precarious situation and began having children early in order to ensure the next generation
    d. her lack of self-actualized identity formation caused her to confuse sex for love and therefore to have children early

3. You enter your daughter's room and find a pamphlet with the title "STDs and You." You might think
    a. it is about a rock band that she likes
    b. she is part of a new religious cult
    c. she is having sex or thinking about it
    d. it is a new television channel

4. You are asked to draw a graph of all teenage birth rates over the past 30 years. You graph will
    a. show a moderate increase
    b. show a moderate decrease
    c. show no change
    d. show no discernible pattern

5. Your son is disturbed because his nose seems to have grown too large and his feet and hands seem out of proportion to his legs and arms. Your best advice to him would be which of the following?
    a. Don't worry; your body dimensions aren't awkward; you're just being self-conscious and egocentric.
    b. Don't worry; early maturers like you tend to be more awkward and gangly than late maturers.
    c. Don't be alarmed; everyone in our family had big feet when they were younger, and we'll just have bigger feet when we're older.
    d. Don't worry; in kids your age the head, hands, and feet complete their growth before the legs, arms, and trunk.

6. Your 11 year old daughter is concerned because many of her friends have started menstruating, and she hasn't. Your best response to her would be which of the following?
    a. Don't be concerned; you've already started to grow much taller and heavier, and you'll soon be a young woman.
    b. The average girl doesn't have her period until age 13, therefore most of the girls in her class have probably not started yet.
    c. Be happy you haven't started because menstruating only produces discomfort.
    d. Be glad you're not menstruating because you're too young to be a woman.

Chapter 11   Adolescence: Physical and Cognitive Development

7. Your 15 year old daughter is an athlete, exercises strenuously every day, and eats a very lean diet to prepare for competition. She has not started menstruating. She is anxious about this, but your best advice to her would be which of the following?
   a. Let's get you to the doctor immediately; there's a possibility that something is wrong.
   b. Don't worry about it; it is common for menstruation to begin later in female athletes, but I'll take you for a checkup to be safe.
   c. Don't worry about it; just start eating more foods with fat.
   d. It doesn't matter because there'll be plenty of time for that in the future.

8. Stout physique in girls is linked to
   a. anorexia nervosa
   b. athletic behavior
   c. early menarche
   d. feelings of adequacy

9. As an adult, Jason has been an attention seeker, defies authority, has lost several jobs, and, in general, asserts unconventional adult behavior. We can infer from this description that Jason
   a. was a late maturer and hasn't made a successful transition from adolescence to adulthood
   b. was an early maturer and hasn't made a successful transition from adolescence to adulthood
   c. is more likely to have a tall, large physique
   d. is more likely to have a small physique

10. Your adolescent seems to have an obsession with her weight. She has reacted to her small weight gain by going on crash diets and still thinks she is overweight. Which of the following would be the most reasonable, considering that she is 5'3" and 115 pounds?
    a. You should be somewhat concerned because your daughter may be at risk for developing anorexia nervosa.
    b. Ignore the problem because her dieting is a self-conscious effort to deal with her newfound sexuality.
    c. You should advise your daughter to exercise more to burn off excessive calories.
    d. You should advise your daughter that it's healthy to put on a few pounds at this stage of her life; she has a great personality anyway.

11. Bill was always a heavy child and weighed 280 pounds at his high school graduation. With the assistance of a trained professional, Bill engaged in a vigorous diet and exercise regimen that resulted in a 100-pound weight reduction over a year. Even though he continued his workout regimen faithfully, he could never reduce his weight below 180 pounds. According to Bennett and Gurin,
    a. Joe had no more excess body fat to lose
    b. Joe must have become less stringent with his program
    c. some of Joe's fat cells had become metabolically "permanent"
    d. Joe had reached the metabolic regulator, or "set point" in his natural body weight

12. Mr. and Mrs. Jones are amazed at how their 14-year-old daughter has suddenly emerged with definitive opinions about the activities at her school. She speaks to them of the pros and cons of the school district's stand on student discipline, prayer in the schools, dress code, and drug use. From reading this chapter, you can see that young Miss Jones
    a. is asserting her individual identity
    b. is echoing her peer comments from school
    c. has begun to think in logical and abstract terms
    d. has begun to seek adult parallelism from her parents

13. Your adolescent daughter frequently becomes moody, requests to be left alone, and then seems to bounce back from a low mood within a relatively short period of time. Should you be concerned about her mood swings?
    a. Yes, these are warning signs that she is experiencing PMS.
    b. Yes, these mood swings are early warning signs of manic depression.
    c. No, she just needs to keep her mind and hands more active by doing more household chores.
    d. No, these mood swings are a normal part of adolescent life.

14. A boy is presented with the following problem: "All ants that can fly are as big as zebras. This ant can fly. Is this ant as big as a zebra?" He responds by saying, "Yeah, sure." We can conclude from Piaget's findings that this boy is
    a. in the period of concrete operations
    b. not paying attention enough to analyze the problem
    c. in the period of formal operations
    d. understanding the question but doesn't like to respond with a ridiculous answer

15. Your teenage son stands in his closet entrance for a half hour imagining how his friends will admire him if he wears the right name-brand shirt to the school dance. Psychologists would explain this behavior as indicative of
    a. personal fable
    b. imaginary audience
    c. stage of self-centered preoccupation
    d. phenomenon called adolescent attention-seeking

16. Your brother and his teenage daughter are continually getting into disagreements about how his generation has made such a mess of the world. She says that her generation is going to clean up the environment, feed the homeless, and pay back the federal deficit. Your brother doesn't understand that she
    a. is learning in school that those people who grew up in the sixties and early seventies dropped out of society, and that's why it's in such a mess
    b. is naturally concerned with moral values and principles as a part of adolescent idealism
    c. is naturally going to oppose her parents because adolescents shouldn't trust anyone over 30 years of age
    d. is trying to manipulate him to get what she wants

17. Two students meet at the International Math and Science Achievement Contest. Student A scores a top score in both math and physics. Student B scores about 150 points lower on both tests and attributes this to her part-time employment and the fact that she only has one hour of math per week in school. Student A is most likely from _____ and student B is most likely from _____.
    a. the United States; Brazil
    b. Sweden; the United States
    c. Japan; France
    d. Norway; Sweden

18. You read a paper on punishment by a student which contains the following: "He was a bad guy and deserved to be punished. The king was right to throw him in the shark pool to show the other people he was not a weak king." The author of this paper is probably
   a. 8 years old
   b. 15 years old
   c. 20 years old
   d. 32 years old

Chapter 11   Adolescence: Physical and Cognitive Development

Essay Questions

1. Discuss the differences between an early and a late maturer that might be taken into account when deciding whether to choose a traditional or an alternative high school.

2. Pat is an adolescent deciding whether to engage in some risky behaviors. Discuss how physical development and cognitive development might affect the decision making process, what sort of issues will arise for Pat, and how these issues will differ depending on whether Pat is a girl or a boy.

3. Discuss the connections between physical and cognitive changes in adolescence and how the tensions might lead to certain eating disorders.

Chapter 11 Adolescence: Physical and Cognitive Development

ANSWERS FOR SELF-TESTS

Matching

1. e
2. j
3. d
4. b
5. l
6. i
7. f
8. h
9. g
10. m
11. k
12. a
13. c

Multiple Choice

Factual

1. b
2. d
3. a
4. c
5. a
6. b
7. b
8. d
9. c
10. b
11. d
12. c
13. c
14. b
15. a
16. d
17. b
18. d
19. b
20. a
21. c
22. c
23. d
24. d
25. c
26. c
27. c
28. b

Conceptual

1. b
2. c
3. c
4. b
5. d
6. b
7. b
8. c
9. b
10. a
11. d
12. c
13. d
14. c
15. b
16. b
17. b
18. a

Chapter 12

Adolescence:
Emotional and Social Development

INTRODUCTION

Chapter 12 discusses the stage of adolescence in the context of society's need to facilitate young people's quest for autonomy and a positive self-identity. Several significant issues are explored, including the following:

- Development of Identity. Several theories of adolescent emotional and social development are introduced, including those of Hall, Sullivan, Erikson, Bandura, and Gilligan.

- Peers and Family. The unique developmental role of the adolescent peer group is discussed, as well as the importance of adolescents' relationships with their families.

- Teenage Courtship, Love, and Sexuality. The difficult adjustment by young people in regard to their experiences with dating, love, and sexuality is examined. The typical patterns and functions of dating are presented; the indefinable notion of love, as well as a possible physiological basis for this romantic attraction, is discussed. The chapter reviews the dynamic state of adolescent sexual expression, recent changes in sexual behavior, and (within this context) problems associated with teenage pregnancy.

- Vocational Choices. The importance of adolescent decisions regarding vocational options is presented, as well as the issue of working teens. Special attention is given to the topic of whether or not teenagers should work.

- Risky Behaviors. Other important issues relevant to teenagers are examined, such as drug abuse, teenage suicide, antisocial behavior, juvenile delinquency, and high school attrition. Special emphasis is given to suicide warning signals among adolescents.

Chapter 12   Adolescence: Emotional and Social Development

LEARNING OBJECTIVES

After completing Chapter 12, you should be able to:

1. Briefly define the notion of *storm and stress*.

2. State the three periods of Sullivan's interpersonal theory of development and briefly define each.

   -

   -

   -

3. Explain Erikson's view of the importance of a crisis in adolescence.

4. Explain the following concepts.

identity diffusion

identity foreclosure

Chapter 12   Adolescence: Emotional and Social Development

identity moratorium

identity achievement

5. Discuss the different approaches to reducing unsafe sex amongst teens.

6. Describe the things that influence adolescent values.

selection of friends

parental control

"right to choose"

7. Explain some of the differing patterns of behavior that impact on adolescent sexuality.

female sexual exposure

hormonal basis

early onset of intercourse and relationship to other behaviors

virginity

Aspects of family life:
   mother's sexual experience

   older sibling's behavior

   living in poverty

single-parent families

community social context

social factors that may encourage teenage pregnancy

8. Cite several descriptions of "love" from the research studies.

media and myth

multicultural view of love

romantic love

agitated state

neurochemical reaction

9. Explain what is known about the development of sexual behavior.

infants

boys

girls

10. Critically appraise the incidence and implications of teenage pregnancy.

current statistics and historical view

long-term consequences of early childbearing

Chapter 12   Adolescence: Emotional and Social Development

implications for family life and the children

11. List the factors that influence adolescent vocational choice.

12. Define *drug* and describe the prevalence and consequences of *drug abuse*.

drug

drug abuse

statistics

binge drinking and consequences

casual drug experimentation

factors contributing to illicit drug use

13. Discuss the following aspects of teenage suicide.

worldwide suicide rates

statistics

depression

at-risk factors for suicidal behavior

treatment options

Chapter 12   Adolescence: Emotional and Social Development

14. List some of the warning signals for teenage drug or alcohol problems.

15. Explain what is meant by antisocial behaviors, and cite some related statistics.

16. Discuss the problem of juvenile crime and the juvenile-justice system in the United States.

statistics

Chapter 12   Adolescence: Emotional and Social Development

WEB SITES

The following web sites deal with some of the concepts and issues presented in Chapter 12. Additional resources can be found on the text's web site, at http://www.mhhe.com/crandell7.

Teen Pregnancy
http://www.teenpregnancy.org/

Risk Behaviors for Adolescents
http://education.indiana.edu/cas/adol/risk.html

Understanding Depression and Suicide
http://www.execpc.com/~corbeau/suicide.html

Chapter 12 Adolescence: Emotional and Social Development

SELF-TESTS

Matching

Match the key terms with their definitions:

a. binge drinking
b. consciousness of oneness
c. depression
d. deviant identity
e. drug abuse
f. generation gap
g. identity
h. identity achievement
i. identity diffusion
j. identity foreclosure
k. identity moratorium
l. negative identity
m. puberty rites
n. storm and stress
o. youth culture

1. ____ a debased self-image and social role
2. ____ a feeling of being at home in one's body, a sense of "knowing where one is going," and an inner assuredness of anticipated recognition from those who count
3. ____ a lack of ability to commit oneself to an occupational or ideological position and to assume a recognizable station in life
4. ____ a lifestyle that is at odds with, or at least not supported by, the values and expectations of society
5. ____ a period of delay, during which adolescents can experiment with or "try on" various roles, ideologies, and commitments
6. ____ a stage of turmoil, maladjustment, tension, rebellion, dependency conflicts, and exaggerated peer-group conformity that some believe to be inevitable in adolescence
7. ____ five or more drinks in a row for men, or four or more in a row for women
8. ____ implies the existence of mutual antagonism, misunderstanding, and separation between youth and adults
9. ____ initiation ceremonies that socially symbolize the transition from childhood to adulthood
10. ____ standardized ways of thinking, feeling, and acting that are characteristic of a large body of young people
11. ____ sympathetic identification in which group members come to feel that their inner experiences and emotional reactions are similar
12. ____ the avoidance of autonomous choice
13. ____ the excessive or compulsive use of chemical agents to an extent that interferes with people's health, their social or vocational functioning, or the functioning of the rest of society
14. ____ when the individual is able to achieve inner stability that corresponds to what others perceive that person to be
15. ____ prolonged feelings of gloom, despair, and futility, profound pessimism, and a tendency toward excessive guilt and self-reproach

Chapter 12 Adolescence: Emotional and Social Development

Multiple Choice

Circle the letter of the response that best completes or answers each of the following statements and questions.

Factual Questions

1. In Sullivan's theory, the period of early adolescence should fulfill three separate needs. Which is not a need according to Sullivan?
    a. need for personal diffusion
    b. need for sexual satisfaction
    c. need for personal intimacy
    d. need for personal security

2. Which type of identity formation, according to Marcia, describes an adolescent's acceptance of someone else's values and goals without exploring alternatives?
    a. identity diffusion
    b. identity foreclosure
    c. identity moratorium
    d. identity achievement

3. The function of puberty rites is
    a. to acknowledge the right to enter puberty
    b. to symbolize the transition from childhood to adulthood
    c. to announce the onset of menarche
    d. to form a psychological pact with others in the community

4. According to Gilligan, girls in adolescence tend to
    a. be rather outspoken
    b. be autonomous
    c. be angry
    d. be inauthentic

5. When social scientists talk about a generation gap, they are referring to
    a. mutual antagonism and separation between young people and adults
    b. the youth-oriented and age-fearing culture we live in
    c. the age-segregated nature of most family activities
    d. a youth-culture idea that the past is irrelevant and the future is uncertain

6. Boys scored higher than girls in all categories of self esteem except_____
    a. personal security
    b. academics
    c. home/parents
    d. attractiveness

7. Social scientists have concluded that the
    a. youth culture is a monolithic group for all adolescents
    b. youth culture is composed of several distinct crowds
    c. peer group has a greater influence on the adolescent than the family
    d. differences among young people are not so great

8. Adolescents are most influenced by their parents when the issues pertain to
    a. career plans
    b. personal adornment
    c. autonomy
    d. communication

9. The extent and intimacy of peer relationships increases dramatically in which age range?
    a. early and late adulthood
    b. middle childhood and adolescence
    c. young adulthood and middle age
    d. middle age and old age

10. Which of the following situations is related to a <u>less likely</u> incidence of teenage pregnancy?
    a. older sexually active siblings
    b. daughters from a single-parent home
    c. high academic achievement and close ties with family
    d. living in poverty

11. Generally speaking, the earlier the _____ first sexual experience and first birth, the earlier the _____ first sexual experience.
    a. father's; daughter's
    b. mother's; daughter's
    c. mother's; son's
    d. father's; son's

12. Research on the origin of the emotion "love," suggests that love is
    a. a unique chemical reaction in the brain
    b. diffuse physiological reactions
    c. a perceptual tendency
    d. a myth promoted by the media

13. According to your text, the nature of courtship behavior in the United States
    a. has not changed
    b. has rapidly changed
    c. has become more patriarchal
    d. has become more formal

14. Research on adolescent sexual expression indicates that
    a. boys first experience nocturnal orgasms in their late teens
    b. group masturbation is uncommon among preteen boys
    c. teenage masturbation is often accompanied by erotic fantasies
    d. sex play with other children begins in adolescence

Chapter 12 Adolescence: Emotional and Social Development

15. Most boys experience nocturnal emissions, or "wet dreams," between _____ years old.
   a. 8-10
   b. 11-12
   c. 13-15
   d. 16-17

16. Which of the following statements regarding adolescent sexuality is least accurate?
   a. Rates of teenage sexual experience have plateaued.
   b. More girls than boys have had sexual experience at every age level.
   c. Men from lower socioeconomic backgrounds appear to have had a higher rate of premarital sexual experience.
   d. Growing numbers of teenagers are having multiple sexual partners.

17. In the United States, approximately what percent of teenagers have had multiple sex partners before high school?
   a. 2 percent
   b. 20 percent
   c. 38 percent
   d. 12 percent

18. A decade or so ago, teenage pregnancy and childbearing were seen primarily as what type of problem?
   a. economic
   b. social
   c. health
   d. not viewed as a problem

19. The teenage pregnancy rate is highest in which of the following countries?
   a. Canada
   b. France
   c. United States
   d. Saudi Arabia

20. In the United States the rate of all unintended pregnancies ending in abortion is
   a. increasing
   b. decreasing
   c. stable
   d. unreported

21. Given the importance of the job entry process, how prepared are American teenagers for making vocational decisions?
   a. highly prepared through high school guidance offices and home and careers classes
   b. ill prepared
   c. more prepared than their parents were during adolescence
   d. more prepared than their European counterparts

22. It is estimated that _____ percent of college graduates will be "underemployed" between 1990 and 2005.
    a. 10
    b. 20
    c. 30
    d. 40

23. What percentage of high school students work more than one-half time during the school year?
    a. 16 percent
    b. 18 percent
    c. 22 percent
    d. 40 percent

24. Labor Department economists calculate that while skill levels in the workplace rose over the past decade,
    a. fewer adolescents can afford to go to college to prepare for those jobs
    b. many adolescents aren't motivated to strive for success
    c. the supply of college graduates rose even more rapidly, which may contribute to "underemployment"
    d. fewer colleges can afford to train students in these technical skills

25. Among adolescents in the United States, the most frequently abused drug is
    a. alcohol
    b. marijuana
    c. cocaine
    d. heroin

26. Sixty percent of college women who were diagnosed with a sexually transmitted disease such as herpes reported that at the time they became infected they were under the influence of which drug?
    a. LSD
    b. alcohol
    c. amphetamines
    d. cocaine

27. Data on suicide reveal that
    a. suicide is not a leading cause of death among adolescents in the United States
    b. suicide is the third leading cause of death among adolescents in the United States
    c. suicide is the first leading cause of death among adolescents in the United States
    d. suicide is the second leading cause of death among adolescents in the United States

28. Which term best describes America's juvenile-justice system?
    a. effective but slow
    b. antiquated
    c. adequate
    d. underfinanced

Chapter 12 Adolescence: Emotional and Social Development

29. The leading cause of death among African American youth is
    a. suicide
    b. homicide
    c. motor vehicle accidents
    d. cancer

30. Lesbian, gay, and bisexual youth are at a particularly high risk of
    a. suicide
    b. dropping out of school
    c. losing friends
    d. remaining inhibited

Chapter 12 Adolescence: Emotional and Social Development

Conceptual Questions

1. Your child is having a very stressful adolescence. You go to the library to find out what is going on. You will be most likely to check out a book by
    a. Bandura
    b. Offer
    c. Hall
    d. VanderZanden

2. Although you want him to go to college, your teenage son expresses a desire to go into the military so that he can decide what he would really like to do with his adult life. Erikson would consider his choice an example of
    a. role confusion
    b. identity diffusion
    c. negative identity
    d. adolescent moratorium

3. Charlotte was a rebellious teenager who began self-destructive habits early and carried them on into her 30's. She never sets goals for herself or makes commitments. She has always been irresponsible and has never held a job for very long. According to Erikson, Charlotte is suffering from long-term
    a. role confusion
    b. negative identity
    c. identity diffusion
    d. deviant identity

4. John is 15, has a severe reading disability, and has been in trouble with the law for disorderly conduct and truancy from school. Erikson would suggest that John is
    a. trying to be a leader for his peers
    b. trying to fit in with a particular peer group
    c. taking on a negative identity role
    d. having difficulty adjusting to late adolescence expectations

5. Most modern high schools have groups of students referred to as "jocks," "nerds," "burnouts," and "brains." This provides evidence of
    a. a youth culture
    b. a monolithic peer group
    c. heterogeneous peer groups
    d. heterosexual cliques

6. Your adolescent son started to wear an earring in one ear like some sports celebrities on television. You should conclude that his behavior indicates a(n)
    a. deviant identity
    b. effort to renounce your values
    c. conformist trend he'll overcome in high school
    d. normal peer-group identification

Chapter 12 Adolescence: Emotional and Social Development

7. Aaron, who is in the ninth grade, feels that his mother is overly restrictive and does not provide him with sufficient "space." Who would Aaron most likely turn to if he needed advice?
   a. his peer group
   b. his father
   c. the school guidance counselor
   d. one of his teachers

8. When you ask your 14-year-old son to attend a family reunion, he refuses, saying, "They're just a bunch of old fogies; I'm going to stay here with my friends." The most reasonable conclusion you can reach is that
   a. he loves his friends more than his family
   b. if your son had another group of friends, he would be more likely to respect your wishes
   c. your son still loves and respects you, but he'd rather do things he chooses to do
   d. by tenth grade, his friends will have less influence on him

9. You are a female high school guidance counselor. One of your female students approaches you and verbalizes a concern about not being normal because she is 16 years old, is still a virgin, and has not yet begun dating. Your best advice to her would be which of the following?
   a. Virgins like yourself are psychologically healthier than other girls because you believe that romantic love should precede rather than follow sex.
   b. Being a virgin isn't abnormal; maybe you're setting your standards higher for achievement for yourself at this time.
   c. Dating is just game playing; people like yourself concentrate on your studies and are better off in the long run.
   d. Consider masturbation while imagining erotic scenes.

10. An eleven year old boy in your health class asks, "If someone masturbates, does that make that person a homosexual?" Your best response to him would be
    a. yes
    b. I don't know
    c. no
    d. it can lead to becoming a homosexual

11. You are asked to write a research paper on adolescent sexual orientation for your Developmental Psychology professor. After reviewing the literature on teenage homosexuality, what conclusion would you reach concerning causes of sexual orientation in adolescence?
    a. Homosexuality is inherited.
    b. Lesbianism occurs most frequently among members of sororities and the military.
    c. Homosexuality is more frequently found among those who are not in sports.
    d. No conclusion can be reached because research on teenage homosexuality and lesbianism is limited.

12. A teenage girl comes into a federally funded birth control clinic for her first visit. Which of the following assumptions would be the most valid?
    a. She has probably never used any form of contraception.
    b. She started using contraception months after she became sexually active.
    c. She thinks that if she does not want to become pregnant, she won't.
    d. She is probably using withdrawal as a contraceptive technique.

Chapter 12 Adolescence: Emotional and Social Development

13. Of the following, which activity is more likely to build character in your teenage son who is a junior in high school?
    a. working 20 hours per week after school at a store in the mall
    b. engaging in after-school activities, such as sports or clubs
    c. giving your son $20 per week allowance for his help around the house
    d. becoming an expert at a computer simulation game

14. You caught your son smoking pot in his bedroom. You can legitimately conclude that
    a. your use of sleeping pills did not influence his decision to smoke pot
    b. he perceives a consciousness of oneness with you because you drink cocktails when you get home from work
    c. his pot smoking makes him feel "cool" in competitive situations and increases his status
    d. regular use of pot may adversely affect his future school performance

15. Your daughter informs you that she sometimes drinks alcohol and smokes pot at parties. According to recent research on casual drug experimentation, what is the most valid conclusion you can draw about your daughter's disclosure?
    a. It will lead to addiction.
    b. It is associated with poor social adjustment.
    c. It will lead to pathological functioning.
    d. It is frequently associated with good social and personal adjustment.

16. A teenage relative of yours has just made a suicide attempt. Which of the following conclusions would be least valid?
    a. The relative is more likely to be male than female.
    b. Feelings of helplessness and boredom preceded the attempt.
    c. The relative was ambivalent about his or her willingness to die.
    d. The relative had an increased number of psychosomatic complaints.

17. Which of the following adolescents would you be most concerned about? A boy who
    a. normally has a B+ overall average but is now failing three of his classes
    b. considers school a waste of time and likes hanging around with jobless dropouts
    c. is not interested in grades and cares only about extracurricular activities
    d. is emotionally immature and enjoys playing the class clown

18. Jimmy is in the ninth grade at Mulberry High School. He has sixth grade equivalent scores in reading and math, has a long truancy record, and resents his teachers for hassling him. We are likely to infer that Jimmy will
    a. go to a vocational school and gain employment skills
    b. impulsively attempt suicide to escape his helpless situation
    c. stay out of mischief if he is retained in school
    d. drop out of high school

Chapter 12 Adolescence: Emotional and Social Development

Essay Questions

1. Discuss how changing sexual attitudes and behavior in teens might impact theories of identity development.

2. Discuss connections between risky behaviors and career development.

3. Why should peers become more influential at this time in an adolescent's life?

Chapter 12 Adolescence: Emotional and Social Development

ANSWERS FOR SELF-TESTS

Matching

1. l
2. g
3. i
4. c
5. k
6. n
7. a
8. e
9. m
10. o
11. b
12. j
13. d
14. h
15. c

Multiple Choice

Factual

1. a
2. b
3. b
4. d
5. a
6. b
7. b
8. a
9. b
10. c
11. b
12. a
13. b
14. c
15. c
16. b
17. d
18. c
19. c
20. b
21. b
22. c
23. b
24. c
25. a
26. b
27. b
28. b
29. b
30. a

Conceptual

1. c
2. d
3. d
4. b
5. c
6. d
7. a
8. c
9. b
10. c
11. d
12. b
13. b
14. d
15. b
16. a
17. a
18. d

Chapter 13

Early Adulthood:
Physical and Cognitive Development

INTRODUCTION

Chapter 13 focuses on the dynamic life stage of young adulthood. Developmental perspectives of adulthood are introduced – illustrating that this period of life is a process of "becoming," as opposed to a static state of being. Several relevant topics are emphasized, including:

- Developmental Perspectives. Demographic features of this age group are revealed, and conceptions of the various age periods are discussed.

- Social Changes that Accompany Adulthood. The functions of age-grade systems are presented, along with an explanation of how these serve to prepare individuals for the various roles associated with each distinct life stage. Finally, life events – those critical turning points at which people change direction in the course of their lives – are examined.

- Physical Changes and Health. The implications of the typical changes in adult physical performance and mental health are highlighted. In addition, this chapter addresses the issue of stress and explores the ways in which individuals deal with their stress.

- Changes in Cognitive Development. A brief discussion explores the possibility of a "post-formal stage" of cognitive development. Sternberg's information processing approach explains how adults conceptualize their complex world. Finally, adult moral reasoning capacity is discussed.

LEARNING OBJECTIVES

After completing Chapter 13, you should be able to:

1. List the contemporary demographic features of early adulthood.

baby-boom generation

effect on popular culture

labor force

effect on baby-busters, generation X, twentysomethings

2. Discuss perceptions of getting old.

3. Define the following and identify the relationships among each.

aging

biological aging

social aging

social norms

age norms

social clock

Chapter 13   Early Adulthood: Physical and Cognitive Development

4. Discuss concept of the "young-old" category and the "blurring" of the distinction between middle age and old age.

5. Describe the functions that *age-grade* systems provide for adults across different cultures.

6. Discuss the role that *life events* play in helping people locate themselves across the life span, and list some examples of life events.

7. Explain what is known about rape as a stressful life event.

prevalence

resulting health problems

marital rape

myths and misperceptions

8. Summarize the effects of age on

diet

obesity

crosscultural statistics on physical performance and health

9. Discuss briefly how different strategies are used to deal with mental health problems.

10. List the changes that occur in each of the following areas of adulthood.

physical performance

physical health

mental health

11. Define *stress* and briefly explain current demographics, its physiology, and hardiness.

survey results

Chapter 13   Early Adulthood: Physical and Cognitive Development

younger adults vs. older adults

women vs. men

Rumination theory:
   gender role perspective

   traditional and non-traditional student

Stages of stress

12. Define post-formal mental operations, and give some examples.

13. Explain Sternberg's adult *information processing* model.

14. Compare Kohlberg's cognitive-developmental theory with Gilligan's adult moral reasoning.

15. Discuss sexuality and identity in young adulthood.

Chapter 13   Early Adulthood: Physical and Cognitive Development

heterosexuals

lesbian, gay, and bisexual

WEB SITES

The following web sites deal with some of the concepts and issues presented in Chapter 13. Additional resources can be found on the text's web site, at http://www.mhhe.com/crandell7.

Women of the World: Reproduction and Contraception
htp://www.crlp.org/searchworld.html

National Institutes of Health: Adult Health
http://www.nih.gov/

World Wide Web Virtual Library — Social Sciences
http://www.clas.ufl.edu/users/gthursby/socsci/index.htm

Psychology Virtual Library
http://www.clas.ufl.edu/users/gthursby/psi

Chapter 13 Early Adulthood: Physical and Cognitive Development

SELF-TESTS

Matching

Match the key terms with their definitions:

a. age grading
b. age norms
c. aging
d. biological aging
e. information processing
f. life events
g. post-formal operational thought
h. social aging
i. social clock
j. social norms
k. transition points

1. ____ a set of internalized concepts that regulate our progression through the age-related milestones of the adult years

2. ____ adults come to realize that knowledge is not absolute but relativistic; adults come to accept the contradictions contained in life and the existence of mutually incompatible systems of knowledge; because they recognize that contradiction is inherent in life, adults must find some encompassing whole by which to organize their experience

3. ____ changes in an individual's assumption and relinquishment of roles through time

4. ____ changes in the structure and functioning of the human organism through time

5. ____ social norms that define what is appropriate for people to be and to do at various ages

6. ____ standards of behavior that members of a group share and to which they are expected to conform

7. ____ the arranging of people in social layers that are based on periods in the life cycle

8. ____ the biological and social change across the life span

9. ____ the relinquishment of familiar roles and the assumption of new ones

10. ____ the step-by-step mental operations that we use in tackling intellectual tasks

11. ____ turning points at which individuals change direction in the course of their lives

Chapter 13   Early Adulthood: Physical and Cognitive Development

Multiple Choice

Circle the letter of the response that best completes or answers each of the following statements and questions.

Factual Questions

1. Which researcher assumed that no additional cognitive changes occur after adolescence?
    a. Sigmund Freud
    b. Jean Piaget
    c. Lawrence Kohlberg
    d. Charlotte Bühler

2. The beginning of adulthood is not defined as when one
    a. leaves school
    b. starts work (full-time)
    c. gets married
    d. has children

3. Because of the size of the baby-boom generation
    a. the nation's labor force has rapidly expanded
    b. competition for professional jobs has decreased
    c. the number of teenagers has increased
    d. these individuals now make up one-half of the American population

4. Today's young adults (ages 18-27) are called
    a. the independent generation
    b. generation X
    c. generation Z
    d. the sandwich generation

5. An important part of the aging transition for young adults of all generations is
    a. graduating from high school
    b. getting a job
    c. moving out of the parental home
    d. getting married

6. Younger adults view older adults as being
    a. more desirable to be around than younger adults
    b. equally desirable to be around as younger adults
    c. less desirable to be around than younger adults
    d. sources of authority

7. Which adults are more likely to have a positive attitude toward older people?
    a. adult women in middle age who are responsible for their aging parents
    b. young adults who aspire to have careers in psychology
    c. people in the clergy, who are trained to work with the elderly
    d. people who have had a more formal education and experience with a range of adults

Chapter 13   Early Adulthood: Physical and Cognitive Development

8. Today, fewer people say that part of their American Dream includes _____ than previously
    a. becoming wealthy
    b. being a winner
    c. having children
    d. college education

9. Changes in the structure and functioning of the human organism through time best defines
    a. a social clock
    b. biological aging
    c. the BOOM phenomenon
    d. cultural adaptation

10. An adult's passing through a socially regulated cycle in his or her assumption and relinquishment of roles through time is called
    a. biological aging
    b. social aging
    c. the BOOM phenomenon
    d. resettlement

11. Compulsory school attendance, minimum voting age, and the age at which one gets Social Security benefits are examples of
    a. social norms
    b. age norms
    c. social clock periods
    d. informal expectations

12. Although the members of a society tend to share similar expectations about the life cycle, some variations do occur. The social clock in your text indicates
    a. that there has been virtually no change in attitudes over the last 30 years
    b. that there has been a lot of change in attitudes over the last 30 years
    c. that ages have generally gone up
    d. that ages have generally gone down

13. Bernice Neugarten's concept of the "young-old" is exemplified by all of the following except
    a. some retirees and their spouses are healthy and vigorous
    b. the line between middle age and old age is no longer clear – it is "blurring"
    c. an 18-year-old is married and supporting a family
    d. a 30-year-old woman has her first child

14. The arrangement of people in social layers that are based on periods in the life cycle best defines
    a. an age-grade system
    b. the empty nest
    c. biological aging
    d. the BOOM phenomenon

15. Turning points at which individuals change direction in the course of their lives are called
    a. life stages
    b. life events
    c. developmental stressors
    d. constructed realities

16. What percent of rapes are committed by an acquaintance of the victim
    a. 50
    b. 80
    c. 20
    d. 60

17. Peak years for speed and agility are ages
    a. 15-25
    b. 17-40
    c. 18-30
    d. 20-25

18. For all adults concerned with physical and mental health, _____ affords benefits in both domains.
    a. dieting
    b. exercise
    c. metacognition
    d. less television viewing

19. Regarding physical performance, which sense is the one most individuals in early and middle adulthood are most likely to notice changes in?
    a. hearing
    b. touch
    c. smell
    d. vision

20. The most common explanation for women's longer life expectancy is
    a. women smoke less
    b. women have two X chromosomes and more estrogen
    c. women are less prone to depression
    d. women keep close ties to children

21. Overall, a variety of surveys reveal that mental illness becomes more prevalent as
    a. people approach retirement age
    b. income levels drop
    c. education levels drop
    d. income and education levels drop

22. People have found a comfortable fit between themselves and the world – that they "have it all together" if they
    a. are only depressed over aging
    b. have a positive social and psychological perspective
    c. suffer minor role conflicts but have good jobs
    d. have a higher IQ than their parents

23. Research has found a positive relationship between stress and
    a. sleep
    b. gender
    c. older students
    d. All of the above

24. Stress-resistant individuals display an openness to change, feelings of involvement in what they are doing, and
    a. lowered psychological arousal
    b. heightened sensitivity to other people
    c. more life events experience
    d. a sense of control over events

25. Post-formal operational thought is <u>not</u> characterized by an understanding that
    a. knowledge is relativistic
    b. life is full of contradictions and incompatible systems of knowing
    c. information must be processed in smaller rather than larger chunks
    d. information must be integrated

26. Sternberg has found that the best problem solvers
    a. execute the steps of encoding, inferring, mapping, applying, and justifying an answer more quickly than poor problem solvers
    b. execute the steps of encoding, inferring, mapping, applying, and justifying more slowly than poor problem solvers
    c. skip steps in the problem-solving process
    d. spend more time on the encoding phase of problem solving than poor problem solvers

27. Gilligan, in contrast to Kohlberg's views of moral development, asserts all of the following <u>except</u>
    a. men deem autonomy and competition to be central in life — thus, they regard morality as a system of rules
    b. women deem relationships to play a central role in life; therefore, morality is meant to protect the integrity of relationships
    c. men perceive morality as an obligation to exercise care and to avoid hurting others
    d. men define moral problems in terms of rules and rights, the "justice" approach

Conceptual Questions

1. Which of the following descriptions best includes Phoebe, who was born in 1950, and Phil, who was born in 1960?
    a. thirtysomethings
    b. baby-busters
    c. baby-boomers
    d. generation Xers

2. Roxanne grew up with her mother working full time to support the family, and she has two stepbrothers who joined the family when her mother remarried. Her hometown in upstate New York has become ethnically diverse, and her roommate from college was a refugee from Vietnam. Roxanne has been described by her mother as "too liberal and accepting of others." Roxanne, in turn, has accused her mother's generation of partying and showing no concern for the environment. Roxanne is most likely to be from what generation?
    a. the "rock-n-roll" generation
    b. baby boomers
    c. generation X
    d. the "me" generation

Chapter 13   Early Adulthood: Physical and Cognitive Development

3. Mr. and Mrs. Robilotti are very concerned about their 18-year-old son, Anthony. He is arguing with them more, contradicting their traditional opinions, staying out later at night with his friends after his part-time job at the local mall. They love him and just want what's best for him, and they wish they could just get their son Tony back — the way he was just six months ago! Tony loves his parents, but he resents their trying to enforce all those rules! If his parents approach you, as the high school counselor, your best advice would be to tell them:
    a. Tony needs to see you and "settle down" a little if he wants to be successful in college.
    b. Tony needs the discipline that the military offers – they'll "make a man out of him!"
    c. Tony's behavior is typical of young people when they desire to be independent and is starting the move out of the parental home.
    d. Relax. He'll appreciate you more and be more like his old self after spring vacation.

4. On April 10, 1996, the nation was shocked and then angry about the death of Jessica Dubroff, a 7-year-old pilot on a mission to become the youngest pilot to cross the United States. Her story was in every major newspaper, magazine, and television talk show for at least a week. Jessica's parents spoke of her passion for flying, but *Boston Globe* columnist Ellen Goodman wrote what seemed to sum up the feelings of a nation in her editorial "Why not let children have their childhood?" According to your text, why did our nation react so strongly to Jessica's death?
    a. The majority of the population in this country is aging and is more conservative in their child-rearing views.
    b. Americans hold the belief that there are appropriate ages for experiencing various life events, and Jessica was too young for this.
    c. Americans, on the whole, react very strongly to tragedies involving children.
    d. Americans dislike permissive parenting.

5. All of the following statements are accurate except
    a. Younger Americans are more likely to indicate they wish to live to be 100.
    b. Older Americans believe they will live to old age.
    c. The average age the respondents said someone is considered "old" was 65.
    d. Younger people look at the late sixties as being "old," whereas older respondents viewed middle seventies as being "old."

6. Shirley MacLaine, Lynn Redgrave, Marsha Mason, and Jane Fonda used to be prominent actors but are seldom seen in major "blockbuster" movies anymore, most likely because
    a. there are fewer roles for women in the popular action-packed thrillers that sell
    b. our society really perceives middle age as more like "over the hill"
    c. women are perceived to age more quickly than men in our society
    d. these women are now peaking by becoming producers and directors

7. You always joke around with your 25-year-old, unmarried sister and tell her she's two-and-a-half decades old. She is likely to
    a. take you seriously and feel older than she actually is
    b. ignore your joking and be happy with her age
    c. speed up her social clock by getting married
    d. employ a double standard of aging when viewing her own age

8. A year after your father died, your elderly mother started living with an elderly gentleman in her senior citizens' apartment complex. Now, no one in your mother's building talks to her. This example demonstrates the effect of

a. violating the social clock
b. violating age norms
c. ageism and sexism directed at women
d. conflict between age grades

9. Many people are against the practice that older women in their fifties and sixties who have gone through menopause can now reverse the aging process and become pregnant (using a donated egg and husband's sperm and the process of in vitro fertilization). There is opposition mainly because
   a. the social clock sets standards that individuals use in assessing conformity to age-related expectations
   b. people have expectations about what kinds of roles are appropriate for people of various ages
   c. people believe that technology is outpacing the human experience
   d. both a and b

10. Shirley grew up in a poor coal-mining town in Appalachia. She got married at the age of 15 and had three children by the time she was 20. We can infer that
    a. she will feel younger because she'll still be fairly young when her children are all grown
    b. Shirley's social clock has been slowed down by her early introduction to adulthood
    c. she will feel older than she is because her social clock has been accelerated
    d. Shirley will experience role confusion because there was no clear transition between her childhood and adulthood

11. A 98-year-old ex-Olympian medalist in gymnastics was introduced at the 1996 Olympics opening ceremonies in Atlanta. He still exercises daily, doing chin ups on a pull-up bar. His "youthful" activity supports Neugarten's theory about the
    a. old-old
    b. young-young
    c. old-young
    d. young-old

12. Which of the following is an example of a life event?
    a. playing basketball when you are 12 years old
    b. attending family reunions each year
    c. learning to play the piano
    d. becoming paralyzed after a motorcycle accident at 19 years old

13. Gloria, a college sophomore, was date-raped during her first semester at school. Which of the following statements is least likely to be her reaction to this life event?
    a. Gloria quickly reported the rape to campus police and authorities.
    b. Gloria blamed herself for the rape and chose not to talk about it.
    c. Gloria suffered an increase in health-related problems during the year following the rape.
    d. Gloria has tried to forget the rape.

14. You are arm wrestling with your 20-year-old son. Which of the following conclusions would be the most valid?
    a. He will win because his arm strength is at its maximum.
    b. You will win because you are a construction worker, and he is a sedentary student.
    c. He will win: quickness and agility can overcome your greater strength.
    d. Although his physical strength should be at its peak, we still cannot predict a clear winner because of the minimal changes in physical performance which accompany adult development.

Chapter 13   Early Adulthood: Physical and Cognitive Development

15. Which of the following statements is <u>not</u> a finding regarding adult mental health?
    a. It involves the ability of people to function effectively in their social roles.
    b. It is a subjective sense of well-being.
    c. It is enhanced when people remain static throughout life's challenges.
    d. It requires that people continually change and adapt to life's fortunes.

16. A group of students is taking their final exam. Which of the following students is likely to perform best in this situation?
    a. a student who has elevated levels of the hormone ACTH throughout the exam
    b. a student who says to himself, "Boy, I could flunk this test, but why think of that? I'll do the best I can."
    c. a student who says to herself, "I don't know what I'll do if I don't pass this exam."
    d. a student who has recently dealt with other stressful events

17. A biologist accepts the principle of determinism, assuming that events have causes which can be established experimentally. Yet the same biologist believes in God, a belief that cannot be proven experimentally. This biologist is demonstrating one of the aspects of
    a. post-formal mental operations
    b. mental rigidity
    c. dialectical reasoning
    d. information encoding

18. A college senior is asked by his math teacher to compute a calculus problem. As he takes in the information presented to him step-by-step, he is demonstrating
    a. moral reasoning
    b. information processing
    c. irrational thought
    d. post-formal operations

Chapter 13 Early Adulthood: Physical and Cognitive Development

Essay Questions

1. Discuss the changes in physical and cognitive development that distinguish early adulthood from adolescence. What issues are young adults dealing with that adolescents do not confront?

2. Why do people identify with certain generations? What do they hope to secure for themselves by being part of a bigger group?

3. Would you consider someone an adult if they still lived at home, had no job, were unmarried, and had no children at the age of 40? Does the fact that the poet Emily Dickinson fit this description suggest that she was not an adult? Explain your answer, taking into account historical changes in the conception of adulthood.

Chapter 13 Early Adulthood: Physical and Cognitive Development

---

ANSWERS FOR SELF-TESTS

Matching

1. i
2. g
3. h
4. d

5. b
6. j
7. a
8. c

9. k
10. e
11. f

Multiple Choice

Factual

1. b
2. d
3. a
4. b
5. c
6. c
7. d
8. c
9. b

10. b
11. b
12. a
13. d
14. a
15. b
16. b
17. c
18. b

19. d
20. b
21. d
22. b
23. d
24. d
25. c
26. d
27. c

Conceptual

1. c
2. c
3. c
4. b
5. c
6. c

7. a
8. b
9. d
10. c
11. d
12. d

13. a
14. d
15. c
16. b
17. a
18. b

Chapter 14

Early Adulthood:
Emotional and Social Development

INTRODUCTION

Chapter 14 continues the exploration of early adulthood with the primary focus on love and work – the central themes of adult life. The chapter is subdivided into three main categories:

- Theories of Emotional and Social Development. A variety of relationships are examined.

- Options in Lifestyles. A variety of lifestyle patterns are examined, including leaving home, living at home, being single, living together, and being married. Homosexuality and bisexuality are discussed as well, and several theories are presented regarding the sources and causes of these behaviors.

- Stages of Development. Erikson, Levinson, and Gilligan are reviewed, and a critique of the stage approach is presented.

- Family Transitions. Sociologist Reuben Hill's nine stages in the family life cycle are outlined and critically evaluated. Pregnancy and the beginning of parenthood are discussed, with emphasis on the changes parents and families face during these transitional periods. Various current lifestyle patterns are examined as well, including those of employed mothers, single-parent mothers, and single-parent fathers.

- Relationships in Early Adulthood. Friendships and love are explored.

- Work. The significance of work for adults is discussed, including the social, emotional, and economic functions of work. The socioeconomic life cycle technique for studying the course of an individual's occupational status attainment is presented according to the studies of both sociologists and psychologists.

Chapter 14 Early Adulthood: Emotional and Social Development

LEARNING OBJECTIVES

After completing Chapter 14, you should be able to:

1. Define the following terms central to adult life.

social relationships

expressive tie

primary relationship

instrumental tie

secondary relationship

2. Briefly explain each of the following terms or concepts that pertain to patterns of living.

Erikson's *intimacy vs. isolation*

intimacy

historical pattern of lifestyle changes in the United States over the past forty years

cultural dislocation

Chapter 14 Early Adulthood: Emotional and Social Development

3. Describe the phases of adult *male* development according to Levinson.

leaving family

entering adult work

settling down

becoming one's own man

4. Describe the phases of adult *female* development according to Levinson.

work and family

re-entering work force

stocktaking

5. Explain the factors that deter young adults from leaving home.

Chapter 14 Early Adulthood: Emotional and Social Development

6. Compare and contrast some of the features of nonmarital cohabitation with marriage.

historical perspective

current perspective

demographics

research on duration of relationships

subtle differences from marriage

likelihood and consequences of "splitting up"

7. Explain each of the following expressions that pertain to sexual orientation.

sexual orientation

heterosexual orientation

homosexual orientation

bisexual orientation

sexual orientation as a continuum

aging and gender differences

"behavior"

8. Referring to anthropologist Murdock's research, define marriage, explain its overall function, and describe the ways in which societies differ in how they structure marriage relationships.

marriage and its functions

monogamy

polygyny

polyandry

group marriage

9. Cite the most common marriage lifestyle in the United States, and explain serial monogamy.

10. Explain the two types of nuclear families that most Americans are a part of in their lifetime.

Chapter 14 Early Adulthood: Emotional and Social Development

11. Briefly give an historical account of United States families throughout history.

seventeenth century England and New England

pre-industrial revolution families (prior to 1890s)

early 1900s

WWII years and pre-1950s

today's state of families

12. Cite some shortcomings of Hill's family life cycle model as articulated by Elder.

13. Describe the significance of pregnancy, particularly a first pregnancy, for both a woman and a man, and cite several changes that can be expected in a couple's life.

14. Cite Belsky's findings on insights about the transition to parenthood, with a special emphasis on what makes for a healthier transition.

Chapter 14 Early Adulthood: Emotional and Social Development

15. Describe the following factors which affect employed mothers.

historical trends

statistics

impact on children

impact as role models

16. Describe the variety of explanations for postpartum blues.

17. Explain the following factors that have an impact on single-parent mothers.

historical trends

current statistics

time

economic resources

stress

child support

juvenile delinquency

social isolation

18. Explain the significance of work for adults.

why people work

relationship between childhood characteristics and willingness to work

19. Describe the challenges women encounter when trying to reenter the labor force.

WEB SITES

The following web sites deal with some of the concepts and issues addressed in Chapter 14. Additional resources can be found on the text's web site, at http://www.mhhe.com/crandell7.

Single Parent Resource Center
http://www.singleparentresources.com/

Single Fathers
http://www.singleparentresources.com/singlefathers_548.html

Unmarried Couples and the Law
http://www.palimony.com/

Chapter 14   Early Adulthood: Emotional and Social Development

SELF-TESTS

Matching

Match the key terms with their definitions:

a. companionate love
b. consummate love
c. cultural dislocation
d. expressive tie
e. family life cycle
f. instrumental tie
g. intimacy
h. intimacy vs. isolation
i. lifestyle
j. marriage
k. mentor
l. pregnancy
m. primary relationship
n. role conflict
o. role overload
p. romantic love
q. secondary relationship
r. social relationship
s. triangular theory of love

1. _____ the ability to experience a trusting, supportive, and tender relationship with another person

2. _____ a period characterized by physical and emotional change that precedes the birth of a baby

3. _____ the theory that companionate love consists of two other types of love: intimacy and commitment

4. _____ a social link that is formed when we cooperate with another person to achieve a limited goal

5. _____ a socially and/or religiously sanctioned union between a woman and a man with the expectation that they will perform the mutually supportive roles of wife and husband

6. _____ a teacher, experienced co-worker, or boss who provides guidance

7. _____ an alienation from a traditional way of life

8. _____ occurs when a person has too many role demands and too little time to fill them

9. _____ social interactions that rest on expressive ties

10. _____ social interactions that rest on instrumental ties

11. _____ social link formed when we invest ourselves in and commit ourselves to another person

12. _____ the emotional bond when all aspects of triangular love exist in a relationship

13. _____ the experience of pressures within one role that are incompatible with the pressures that arise within another role

14. _____ the kind of love that you have for a very close friend

15. _____ the overall pattern of living whereby we attempt to meet our biological, social, and emotional needs

16. _____ the sequential changes and realignments that occur in the structure and relationships of family life between the time of marriage and the death of one or both spouses

17. _____ the stage of reaching out and making connections with other people

18. _____ typically what we think of when we say we are "in love" with someone

Chapter 14 Early Adulthood: Emotional and Social Development

Multiple Choice

Circle the letter of the response that best completes or answers each of the following statements and questions.

Factual Questions

1. A couple that has just made a commitment to getting married is an example of a(n)
    a. expressive tie
    b. personal tie
    c. life relationship
    d. instrumental tie

2. A social link formed when we cooperate with another person to achieve a limited goal best describes a(n)
    a. expressive tie
    b. primary relationship
    c. life cycle
    d. instrumental tie

3. What issue did Erik Erikson propose is being worked out by individuals in early adulthood?
    a. identity vs. identity confusion
    b. intimacy vs. isolation
    c. integrity vs. despair
    d. separation vs. separation anxiety

4. While the timing of marriage typically rests on _____, leaving the parental home for a nonmarital situation usually involves _____.
    a. the sole decision of the young adult; a joint decision of child and parents
    b. the sole decision of the young adult; the sole decision of the parents
    c. a joint decision of child and parents; the sole decision of the young adult
    d. the sole decision of the parents; the sole decision of the young adult

5. Levinson's "transition periods" refer to
    a. significant birthdays (20th, 30th, 40th, 50th)
    b. distinct breaks in roles (child, adult, parent)
    c. significant changes in career (student, worker, retiree)
    d. all of the above

6. Role conflict occurs when
    a. there are too many role demands and too little time
    b. one questions gender orientation
    c. one experiences pressures form one role that are incompatible with another
    d. women and men argue over who will work and who will stay home

Chapter 14   Early Adulthood: Emotional and Social Development

7. What sort of love has intimacy and commitment but lacks passion?
   a. fatuous
   b. empty
   c. companionate
   d. romantic

8. Which of the following ethnic groups is least likely to remain in the parental home until marriage?
   a. Hispanic Americans
   b. Asian Americans
   c. Americans with strong religious affiliations
   d. African Americans

9. Approximately what percentage of today's young adults (ages 18 to 24) are living at home with their parents?
   a. less than one-third
   b. more than one-half
   c. more than three-quarters
   d. less than one-half

10. There are several disadvantages in returning to the parental home to live. What represents the most common complaint voiced by members of both generations?
    a. increased drug abuse by children
    b. over dependence on parents
    c. lack of privacy
    d. financial problems

11. Which of the following statements regarding singles is the least accurate?
    a. Single status among both men and women under 35 years of age has decreased in recent years.
    b. A growing proportion of Americans will never marry.
    c. The population remaining single today is smaller than it was at the turn of the century.
    d. Most single men and women were ridiculed and treated with disapproval until more recent times.

12. One of the major advantages of being single is
    a. achieving maximum happiness
    b. greater freedom of choice
    c. the lessening of social stigma
    d. the impersonal nature of relationships

13. The number of adults who are sharing living quarters with an unrelated adult of the opposite sex has
    a. decreased substantially over the past thirty years
    b. increased substantially over the past thirty years
    c. stabilized over the past thirty years
    d. increased minimally over the past thirty years

14. Living together as an alternative to marriage
    a. is not radically different from marriage
    b. allows for the elimination of traditional gender roles
    c. eliminates many of the problems found among married couples
    d. reduces the level of interpersonal violence in a couple

Chapter 14   Early Adulthood: Emotional and Social Development

15. Whether one is more strongly aroused sexually by members of one's own sex, opposite (cross) sex, or both sexes is referred to as one's
    a. sexual libido
    b. sexual orientation
    c. sexual drive
    d. sexual arousal

16. When discussing human sexuality, it is always important to distinguish between _____ (an individual's erotic attraction) and _____ (how an individual acts).
    a. orientation; sexuality
    b. behavior; sexuality
    c. affection; behavior
    d. orientation; behavior

17. The National Research Council, between 1970 and 1988, surveyed U.S. males and found that approximately what percentage of men were willing to admit that they had had at least one homosexual experience, and what percentage of men admit willingly to homosexuality as frequent behavior?
    a. 10 percent; none
    b. 20 percent; 3-4 percent
    c. 30 percent; 9-10 percent
    d. 40 percent; 14-15 percent

18. Which of the following statements is the least accurate regarding homosexual and lesbian relationships?
    a. Gays and lesbians are a varied group, reflecting all occupational fields, political outlooks, and races.
    b. "One-night stands" are much less common among lesbians than among gay men.
    c. Gay men tend to form more lasting relationships than lesbians.
    d. On the whole, homosexual adults resemble heterosexual adults in their physical health and feelings of happiness or unhappiness.

19. Polyandry is a form of marriage characterized by
    a. two or more husbands and two or more wives
    b. one husband and two or more wives
    c. one wife and two or more husbands
    d. one wife and one husband

20. Currently, approximately what percentage of marriages end in divorce in the United States?
    a. 5 out of 10 percent
    b. 9 out of 10 percent
    c. 1 out of 10 percent
    d. 7 out of 10 percent

21. Currently, approximately what percentage of divorced people remarry?
    a. 40 percent
    b. 60 percent
    c. 80 percent
    d. 100 percent

Chapter 14   Early Adulthood: Emotional and Social Development

22. In sociologist Reuben Hill's nine stages in the family life cycle, the period from departure of the first child to departure of the last child is termed the stage of the
    a. school-age family
    b. aging family
    c. preschool family
    d. family as a launching center

23. Recent research on the health of the American family indicates that
    a. we are returning to the more orderly family life we had prior to 1950
    b. today's adults marry younger
    c. in general, the U.S. family is a dying institution
    d. for most Americans, the family remains a vital, adaptive, resilient human institution

24. All of the following are developmental tasks facing a pregnant woman and her partner during pregnancy except
    a. fatigue and morning sickness
    b. changes in identity and life plans
    c. frequent suggestions from concerned parents and in-laws
    d. changes in the couple's sexual behavior

25. The accomplishment of the developmental tasks accompanying pregnancy might best be expedited by the woman's
    a. taking childbirth training classes
    b. fusing her identity with that of the fetus
    c. defining herself as a parent through her mother's influence
    d. having a husband do housework

26. Researchers have found that having a first baby may
    a. lead to an increased divorce rate
    b. have a stabilizing effect on marriages
    c. lead to increased romantic intimacy among married couples
    d. cause fathers to become more heavily immersed in their jobs

27. In 1960 _____ percent of mothers with children under 6 years old were in the labor force; by 1991, _____ percent were in the labor force?
    a. 5; 18
    b. 10; 28
    c. 20; 58
    d. 30; 78

28. Which of the following explanations has not been advanced to explain the postpartum blues occurring in some new mothers?
    a. hormonal changes after childbirth
    b. feelings of being overwhelmed by the responsibility of caring for another human being
    c. psychological depression stemming from a mother's love-hate conflict with herself
    d. psychological depression stemming from a mother's inability to return to her pre-pregnancy weight

Chapter 14 Early Adulthood: Emotional and Social Development

29. According to your text, the most recent statistic for births to unmarried women in the United States is
    a. 15 percent
    b. 30 percent
    c. 45 percent
    d. 60 percent

30. Women who head single-parent families are most likely to experience
    a. time pressure to get everything done
    b. being isolated from others
    c. difficulty meeting their child's social, physical, and psychological needs
    d. all of the above

31. Which of the following does not pose a particular problem for single-parent mothers?
    a. lack of free time
    b. increasing child care costs
    c. loneliness
    d. pessimism regarding the future

32. Which of the following statements regarding single-parent fathers is least accurate?
    a. Single fathers who care for their children may be seen as less "manly" because they are performing a traditionally female role.
    b. In general, single fathers seem better prepared for dealing with their children's emotional needs than for the physical aspects of parenting, such as cooking and cleaning.
    c. Compared with single mothers, single fathers tend to have more money and greater job flexibility.
    d. Many single working fathers favor the professional commitment of nurseries and childcare centers over live-in babysitters.

33. A 1995 survey confirmed that
    a. Americans are happier and better able to support their families
    b. over half of the respondents indicated they have less time to spend on family, friends, and leisure
    c. 50 percent said they would work more hours for more income
    d. real wages have actually been slightly increasing since the 1970's

34. Over the past fifteen years, the trend in college enrollment to improve one's employability has been
    a. a 25 percent increase in students enrolling right out of high school
    b. a 25 percent decline in the number of older students returning to college on a part-time basis
    c. a 70 percent increase in the number of non-traditional students
    d. nearly 25 percent of all college enrollment is part-time students

35. Which of the following statements is least accurate about the significance of work?
    a. Work structures one's time and provides a context in which to relate to other people.
    b. Work offers an escape from boredom and helps the workers sustain a sense of identity and worth.
    c. College-educated workers not only seek jobs that are intellectually challenging, they often seek out intellectually demanding leisure pursuits.
    d. When posed with a hypothetical large inheritance, about 20 percent surveyed said they would continue working.

Chapter 14 Early Adulthood: Emotional and Social Development

Conceptual Questions

1. Sheila and Antonio have been married for five years. They are the best of friends and very much in love with one another. Sociologists refer to the bond between Sheila and Antonio as a
    a. cohabitation
    b. primary relationship
    c. lifestyle orientation
    d. secondary relationship

2. _____ are to expressive ties as _____ are to instrumental ties.
    a. primary relationships; secondary relationships
    b. social relationships; lifestyles
    c. secondary relationships; primary relationships
    d. homosexual relationships; heterosexual relationships

3. You have joined the local PTA at your son's high school because you are concerned about combating the growing drug problems. Your participation in the PTA
    a. is an example of a conventional morality
    b. helps to provide you with primary relationships
    c. is an example of an instrumental tie
    d. is an example of an expressive tie

4. Rashad, a 19-year-old, has been sharing an apartment with a friend for three months. Based on the information in your text, what is Rashad most likely discovering?
    a. he has gained respect for his parents now that he is away from them
    b. he has not been prepared for the economic reality of living on his own
    c. he has the resources to continue his college education
    d. he has good employment opportunities because he's strong, has graduated from high school, and is willing to work

5. Kurt, a 23-year-old college student, lives at home with his parents. He has been considering moving into an apartment of his own near school. The most likely reason for Kurt's wanting to leave home is
    a. to improve his social life
    b. to maintain his privacy
    c. to be where it's quieter to improve his grades
    d. to make it more convenient for himself by being closer to school

6. Dwayne, age 25, is single and lives alone. Which of the following predictions about Dwayne's behavior is most likely to be accurate?
    a. He is likely to never marry.
    b. He is not like other single people because he lives alone.
    c. He lives alone to avoid getting married.
    d. He can be placed in the same category with young women and elderly widows.

7. Although two of her sisters got married in their early twenties, Kathy decides to wait until she is finished with graduate school before she ties the knot. It appears as if her decision
   a. was a wise one because she avoided the marriage squeeze
   b. was ill-advised, and she will probably have to forgo marriage
   c. will not hurt her, and her chances for getting married are quite good
   d. was ill-advised because she will now have fewer men to choose from

8. Aretha and her husband have two sets of twin boys: James and Richard (who are identical twins) and Clyde and Jeremy (who are fraternal twins). According to recent research on homosexuality, which of the following predictions is the most legitimate?
   a. It is more likely that both James and Richard are gay than both Clyde and Jeremy.
   b. The two sets of twins have equally likely chances of both members becoming gay.
   c. If at least one of the twins is gay, then the chances of Aretha having a lesbian daughter are increased.
   d. Clyde and Jeremy have higher levels of testosterone than James and Richard.

9. According to the Old Testament, King David had not one, but several, wives. This type of marriage relationship, which stills exists in some parts of the world, is called
   a. monogamy
   b. group marriage
   c. polygyny
   d. polyandry

10. Rebecca, who is 19 years old, lives at home with her parents and two younger brothers. This exemplifies which type of family group?
    a. family of orientation
    b. family of procreation
    c. family of establishment
    d. family of conformity

11. The idea that best describes research on the disintegration of the American family would be which of the following?
    a. "The early reports of my death were greatly exaggerated."
    b. "The family that prays together stays together."
    c. "Ring out the old, and bring in the new."
    d. "The road to Hell is paved with good intentions."

12. Julianne is pregnant with her first child. Which of the following behaviors is Julianne least likely to exhibit before the birth of her child?
    a. She will grow more preoccupied with the fetus inside of her and begin to define herself as a parent-to-be.
    b. She will attempt to reconcile with her own mother, from whom she has remained distant for a few years.
    c. She will experience some anxiety concerning the loss of independence which accompanies motherhood.
    d. She will view her fetus as a part of herself.

Chapter 14 Early Adulthood: Emotional and Social Development

13. Sheila and Stewart are about to have their first baby. Which of the following predictions would be the most reasonable upon the birth of their child?
    a. Sheila and Stewart will experience a short-lived, renewed romantic interest in each another.
    b. Sheila will feel more satisfied with the quality of their marital life than Stewart.
    c. Sheila and Stewart will initially show each other less affection and spend less time sharing leisure activities.
    d. The likelihood of Sheila and Stewart divorcing will dramatically increase.

14. Faith, a 32-year-old married woman, just gave birth to her first child. With a Ph.D. and several years work experience at a local university, what could one predict Faith is likely to do now?
    a. She is likely to stay at home full-time with her new child until he's school age.
    b. She is most likely going to return to work full-time after the allowed 3-month maternity leave and put her child into the university day care.
    c. She is most likely going to hire a full-time, live-in nanny to take care of her baby.
    d. She is most likely going to take a year's leave of absence and then ask her widowed mother to live in and help her for the next few years while she goes back to work.

15. Shortly after the birth of their first child, Rob comes home and finds his wife crying at the kitchen table. We can reasonably infer that she
    a. is acting normally because she's very tired from being up at night
    b. is displaying a manic-depressive episode
    c. feels overwhelmed and upset over her loss of independence
    d. was abused by her mother as a youngster

16. For the first ten years of her marriage, Marlene has been a traditional homemaker. Now she wants to return to the work force, but her husband says that the children will be adversely affected by being deprived of their mother. In her defense, Marlene's most legitimate argument would be which of the following?
    a. If I stay at home frustrated as I am now, the kids will be more adversely affected.
    b. We'll be OK; you and the children can learn to help out more.
    c. Our children are too old to be affected by my returning to work.
    d. My return to work will improve the children's school grades.

17. Paula, 48, is recently divorced after having been married for thirty years. She is the mother of two boys and maintains full custody, in addition to working. We can reasonably infer that Paula
    a. will experience a dramatic downward change in her standard of living and lifestyle
    b. will experience minimal disruptions the first year after divorce
    c. will not be discriminated against as a single parent, head of household
    d. will be viewed by her friends as a "heroic," extraordinary person

Essay Questions

1. Discuss the similarities and differences between Erikson's theory of intimacy vs. isolation and both of Levinson's theories of men's and women's adult development.

Chapter 14   Early Adulthood: Emotional and Social Development

2. Discuss the problems with the following statements: only same sex relationships can produce love; only opposite sex relationships can produce love; there can be no love between married couples; friends cannot remain friends if they live together.

3. Discuss different transitions such as having a child, entering the workforce, or divorcing. Discuss how these would be different depending on when they occurred in one's stage of adult development

---

ANSWERS FOR SELF-TESTS

Matching

1. g	7. c	13. n
2. l	8. o	14. a
3. s	9. m	15. i
4. f	10. q	16. e
5. j	11. d	17. h
6. k	12. b	18. p

Multiple Choice

Factual

1. a	13. b	25. a
2. d	14. a	26. b
3. b	15. b	27. c
4. a	16. d	28. d
5. a	17. b	29. b
6. c	18. c	30. d
7. c	19. c	31. d
8. d	20. a	32. b
9. b	21. c	33. b
10. c	22. d	34. c
11. a	23. d	35. d
12. b	24. c	

Conceptual

1. b	7. c	13. c
2. a	8. a	14. b
3. c	9. c	15. c
4. b	10. a	16. a
5. b	11. a	17. a
6. d	12. d	

Chapter 15

Middle Adulthood: Physical and Cognitive Development

INTRODUCTION

Chapter 15 focuses on the middle adulthood years. The major emphasis is on the changes, both physical and cognitive, experienced by middle-aged individuals. The chapter covers three main areas:

- Physical Changes. Some common changes in vision and hearing during middle adulthood are presented. Female mid-life change, including menopause, and male mid-life change are examined in detail.

- Health Changes. The sexuality and overall health of middle-aged individuals are discussed, with special attention to why many individuals resist changing unhealthy habits. Risks that begin to surface at this time are also examined, including cancer and cardiovascular problems.

- Cognitive Functioning. Cognitive abilities are presented that only seem to appear during middle adulthood. These abilities include dialectical thinking and moral commitment.

LEARNING OBJECTIVES

After completing Chapter 15, you should be able to:

1. Describe the contemporary view of middle age.

Chapter 15   Middle Adulthood: Physical and Cognitive Development

2. Describe several vision-related changes and/or disorders that often are evident in middle age, and cite medical interventions that are available to improve quality of vision.

3. Explain when hearing changes usually begin to occur, how these changes affect one's daily living, and who is most at risk for hearing loss.

4. Describe each of the following physical changes of middle age.

changes in skin, teeth, and hair

muscle atrophy, weight gain, osteoporosis, rheumatoid arthritis

menopause

climacteric

reported psychological consequences of menopause

Chapter 15   Middle Adulthood: Physical and Cognitive Development

5. Describe several common male mid-life changes and the treatments which improve the quality of a man's life.

prostate gland

drop in testosterone and accompanying changes

circadian rhythm

impotence

factors that impact a man's virility on a temporary basis

male menopause

6. Discuss findings concerning changes in sexual functioning in middle age.

frequency of sexual activity

frequency of orgasm

number of sex partners

faithfulness or extramarital sex

inability to achieve orgasm

7. Describe several medical conditions that have an impact on sexual functioning as one ages.

Chapter 15 Middle Adulthood: Physical and Cognitive Development

8. Discuss cardiovascular health problems, including risk factors, the course of the disease, and treatments.

9. Discuss different diseases connected with the brain: stroke, Parkinson's, Alzheimer's.

10. Discuss several risk factors related to cancer.

11. Explain the relationship between social support and health.

12. Explain the terms *fluid intelligence* and *crystallized intelligence.*

Chapter 15 Middle Adulthood: Physical and Cognitive Development

13. Discuss the differences between *cognition* and *intelligence*.

dialectical thinking

Schaie's four stages

convergent

divergent

14. Discuss the research by Colby and Damon on moral exemplars.

WEB SITES

The following web sites deal with some of the concepts and issues introduced in Chapter 15. Additional resources can be found on the text's web site, at http://www.mhhe.com/crandell7.

Health Touch Online
http://www.healthtouch.com/

National Cancer Institute
http://www.nci.nih.gov/

National Institutes of Health — Alphabetical Index
http://www.nih.gov/news/96index/pubincov.htm

Elderhostel
http://www.elderhostel.org/

SELF-TESTS

Chapter 15   Middle Adulthood: Physical and Cognitive Development

Matching

Match the key terms with their definitions:

a. amenorrhea
b. cataract
c. cholesterol
d. climacteric
e. convergent thinking
f. crystallized intelligence
g. dialectical thinking
h. divergent thinking
i. dry eye
j. floaters
k. fluid intelligence
l. glaucoma
m. human growth hormone
n. hormone replacement therapy
o. hypertension
p. impotence
q. macular degeneration
r. menopause
s. osteoporosis
t. perimenopause
u. presbycusis
v. presbyopia
w. prostate gland
x. rheumatoid arthritis
y. stroke

1. ____ a blockage of blood flow to the brain
2. ____ a condition associated with a slow, insidious loss of calcium, producing porous bones
3. ____ a normal condition in which the lens of the eye starts to harden, losing its ability to accommodate as quickly as it did in youth
4. ____ a powerful hormone which was developed to treat children afflicted by dwarfism, and has become a trendy anti-aging potion
5. ____ a regime often recommended by physicians to maintain cardiovascular fitness, slow bone loss, and slow memory loss
6. ____ a vision impairment condition caused by clouding of the lens
7. ____ a walnut-sized male gland at the base of the urethra
8. ____ a white, waxy fat found naturally in the body and used to build the cell walls and make certain hormones
9. ____ an inflammatory disease that causes pain, swelling, stiffness, and loss of function of the joints
10. ____ an open-ended way of thinking: multiple solutions are sought, examined, and probed, thereby leading to what are deemed creative responses on measures of creativity
11. ____ an organized approach to analyzing and making sense of the world one experiences that differs fundamentally from formal analysis
12. ____ changes in the ovaries and the various biological processes associated with these changes
13. ____ diminished tear production
14. ____ evidenced by faded, distorted, or blurred central vision
15. ____ floating spots that actually are particles suspended in the jell-like fluid that fill the eyeball but generally do not impair vision
16. ____ high blood pressure
17. ____ increased pressure caused by fluid buildup within the eye that can damage the optic nerve if left untreated
18. ____ the ability to hear high-pitched sounds
19. ____ the ability to make original adaptations in novel situations

Chapter 15   Middle Adulthood: Physical and Cognitive Development

20. ____ the ability to reuse earlier adaptations on later occasions

21. ____ the absence of a menstrual cycle

22. ____ the application of logic and reasoning to arrive at a single correct answer to a problem

23. ____ the cessation of menstruation, typically over a period of two to four years, with an intermittent missing of periods and the extension of intervals between periods

24. ____ the inability for a male to have or sustain an erection

25. ____ the process culminating in the cessation of menstrual activity

Multiple Choice

Circle the letter of the response that best completes or answers each of the following statements and questions.

Factual Questions

1. Explaining the research on HGH, it is hypothesized that around age 35 changes in body composition are linked to decreasing
    a. brain activity
    b. fat deposits
    c. muscle tissue
    d. hormone levels

2. Women are at greater risk for osteoporosis after age 35 than are men because
    a. men have 30 percent more bone mass than women
    b. men's higher levels of testosterone prevent bone deterioration
    c. men lose old bone tissue more quickly than do women
    d. all of the above

3. Which of the following disorders does not affect persons in middle adulthood?
    a. cataracts
    b. glaucoma
    c. retinal detachment
    d. macular degeneration

Chapter 15 Middle Adulthood: Physical and Cognitive Development

4. By age 50, one should eat how many fewer calories a day in order to maintain the same weight as at age 30?
   a. 170
   b. 240
   c. 300
   d. 1200

5. In terms of physical changes and health, at age 50-60
   a. most individuals report a dramatic loss in their quality of life
   b. vital organs are functioning as they were at age 30
   c. the kidneys, lungs, and heart are less efficient than they were at age 20
   d. approximately 30 percent of this population suffers from substantial hearing problems

6. Which of the following mid-life change in vision explains why most people in their forties require glasses, especially to see near objects?
   a. myopia
   b. loss of the eye's ability to adapt to darkness
   c. increased pressure in the eye
   d. loss of the eye's ability to accommodate

7. By the age of 50, what percent of our population typically has difficulty hearing a whisper?
   a. 7 percent
   b. 17 percent
   c. 27 percent
   d. 33 percent

8. The end of menstrual activity is called
   a. androgyny
   b. maturity
   c. menopause
   d. menarche

9. Which of the following statements is an accurate description of the cessation of menstrual activity?
   a. cessation occurs, for most women, within a very short time period, usually within two to three months
   b. cessation is more gradual, often over two to four years, with intervals between symptoms
   c. most women have ceased menstruation by the time they are 45 years old
   d. the symptoms typically attributed to menopause are really related to the stress of a woman's working, taking care of a family, and taking care of parents at this time in her life

10. Which of the following statements regarding estrogen-replacement therapy (ERT) is the most accurate?
    a. Estrogen increases the development of osteoporosis.
    b. Estrogen therapy is recommended for all postmenopausal women.
    c. Estrogen therapy is the leading cause of breast cancer in women.
    d. Estrogen therapy, by itself, has been linked with uterine cancer.

11. Which of the following statements regarding hormone-replacement therapy (HRT) is least accurate?
    a. HRT improves the quality of life for many women going through the transition of menopause, relieving some symptoms of hot flashes, headaches, depression, etc.
    b. HRT while seemingly protecting the uterus does not afford protection against breast cancer, particularly if the women has been on HRT for 5 or more years.
    c. HRT seems to reduce a woman's risk of osteoporosis and heart disease.
    d. HRT is the "wonder drug" of the 1990s and has support and approval by most medical practitioners and about 75 percent of their patients.

12. During the male mid-life change, men experience
    a. a rapid plunge in hormonal levels
    b. increased levels of testosterone and human growth hormone
    c. increased incidence of prostate enlargement and its accompanying symptoms
    d. markedly decreased virility

13. Several symptoms that middle-aged males experience which may be related to the decline in testosterone are all of the following except
    a. increased susceptibility to diabetes and heart disease
    b. decline in muscle mass and strength
    c. build up of body fat and loss of bone density
    d. loss of energy and lowered sperm output

14. About 50 percent of American males over age 40 experience a higher incidence of impotence, most likely because of
    a. preexisting medical conditions that warrant drug consumption
    b. stress in the workplace and lack of exercise
    c. smoking, alcohol consumption, and general depression
    d. all of the above

15. You take your blood pressure reading and it is 140/70. You immediately
    a. call the doctor
    b. lie down and rest
    c. take it again to be sure
    d. relax because this is in the normal range

16. Each of the following is considered to reduce hypertension except
    a. eating foods high in starch
    b. eating foods low in salt
    c. drinking alcohol in moderation
    d. sleeping more

17. Which of the following is not designated as a risk factor for cancer?
    a. race
    b. weight
    c. poverty
    d. gender

Chapter 15   Middle Adulthood: Physical and Cognitive Development

18. In female to female transmission of AIDS/HIV, 97 percent of the surveyed women also had which other risk?
    a. receipt of blood products
    b. sex with high risk men
    c. injected drug use
    d. body piercing and tattoos

19. According to the National Health and Social Life Survey (1992), which of the following is not true?
    a. 20 percent of men and 31 percent of women have had 1 sex partner since age 18
    b. 21 percent of men and 36 percent of women have had 2-4 sex partners since age 18
    c. 45 percent of men and 30 percent of women have had 5-10 sex partners since age 18
    d. 17 percent of men and 3 percent of women have had 21 or more sex partners since age 18

20. Tests that measure verbal ability show _____ after the age of 60.
    a. little or no decline
    b. substantial decline
    c. moderate increase
    d. moderate decrease

21. The ability to reuse earlier adaptations on later occasions is called
    a. fluid intelligence
    b. crystallized intelligence
    c. culture-free intelligence
    d. multiple intelligence

22. One reason cited for older individuals displaying more post-formal thought is
    a. higher creativity
    b. lower creativity
    c. life experience
    d. life satisfaction

23. Which of Schaie's four stages would the middle-aged adult most likely use?
    a. acquisitive
    b. achieving
    c. responsible/executive
    d. reintegrative

24. Colby and Damon's research implies that moral exemplars
    a. are highly educated
    b. are spiritual
    c. are politically liberal
    d. are all involved in charity work

25. According to Guilford, the application of logic and reasoning is called
    a. creativity
    b. divergent thinking
    c. convergent thinking
    d. productive thinking

Chapter 15 Middle Adulthood: Physical and Cognitive Development

Conceptual Questions

1. You like to invest in the stock market for long-term growth and know that millions of people, the baby boomers, are now entering middle age. Based on your text's information about physical changes and health in mid-life, of the following companies and products, which would you be least likely to invest in?
   a. RJR Tobacco – produces cigarettes
   b. Bausch and Lomb – produces eye glasses and lenses
   c. Nike – produces footwear and clothing for recreational activities
   d. Revlon – produces anti-wrinkling creams, concealers for skin imperfections, and dyes for hair color

2. In which of the following situations will a 50-year-old driver be the most adversely affected?
   a. driving down a dark highway toward a car that is approaching with its bright lights on
   b. trying to judge the distance necessary to stop the car when driving at high speed
   c. trying to carry on a conversation, listen to the radio, and simultaneously drive in rush hour traffic
   d. trying to accelerate and merge with traffic when entering a busy expressway

3. You are going through menopause and are concerned because your mother told you about unpleasant hot flashes. Your gynecologist should advise you that
   a. symptoms such as hot flashes occur only if your ovaries are removed
   b. ERT can eliminate hot flashes and profuse sweating
   c. women who report hot flashes are merely psychosomatic complainers
   d. most women who go through this perceive the "bark" of menopause to be worse than the "bite"

4. If you suffer presbycusis you will probably have trouble hearing which instrument?
   a. bass
   b. voice
   c. cello
   d. saxophone

5. Andre is at his first wine tasting, at the age of 60. Which aspect of the wine will he probably not appreciate?
   a. the color
   b. the temperature
   c. the bouquet
   d. all of the above

6. Recently Duane, 52, is having difficulty trying to urinate, is waking up at night to go to the bathroom, and is urinating more frequently during the day. This is an obvious change in his urinary habits, and he is concerned. As his physician, you are most likely to tell Duane there is
   a. a strong likelihood of cancer of the bladder, and he must be hospitalized immediately
   b. nothing unusual about his symptoms because there is no blood in the urine
   c. probably some type of calcium deposit obstruction at the beginning of the urethra
   d. a typical enlargement of his prostate gland

7. When Stephen was in his late twenties, he was in a motorcycle accident which left him in the hospital for nearly two months recuperating. For most of his adult life he has taken pain medications to help alleviate the aches and pains associated with the aftereffects of this accident. He also hasn't been able to exercise and play sports like he did prior to the accident. Now that Stephen is approaching 50 years old, he's finding that the quality of his sex life seems to be diminishing also, and he has serious self-doubts about his virility. As a sex therapist, you are most likely to tell Stephen that
   a. he's going through the typical hormonal mid-life change for men, similar to menopause
   b. it's the self-fulfilling prophecy at work — it's all a matter of a positive attitude when it comes to adapting to aging — and the "big 5-0" is probably a precipitating factor
   c. in his particular case, a combination of physical trauma, overmedication, and lack of exercise have probably contributed to what will probably turn out to be temporary impotence
   d. he's a likely candidate for the new medical treatment for impotence

8. You are an average person of 60. How much has your muscle mass probably declined?
   a. it hasn't
   b. 20 percent
   c. 45 percent
   d. 85 percent

9. You and your wife have been married for thirty years. While she is still interested in having sex regularly, you are increasingly less interested. A sex therapist would probably tell you that
   a. too much sexual interest in people your age is perverse
   b. your loss of interest may be caused by fear of failure rather than lack of physical ability
   c. your loss of interest is being caused by your wife's persistence and sexual aggressiveness
   d. your loss of interest is predictable because people with active sex lives in their twenties have more difficulty becoming aroused in their fifties

10. Based on the National Health and Social Life Survey, who of the following are most likely to have a frequent, healthy sex life?
    a. John and Charlotte, a cohabiting couple
    b. Charlie and Theresa, a couple who have been married for fifteen years
    c. Fred and Linette, who frequently view X-rated videos
    d. Peter, a single man in his thirties

11. Karen has been married to Bradley for twenty-five years. Recently, Karen has begun having an extramarital affair. Karen's behavior
    a. typifies nearly 75 percent of American married men, who say they have been unfaithful at least once
    b. typifies nearly 85 percent of American married women, who say they have been unfaithful at least once
    c. is atypical of American married men and women, of whom the majority report they have never been unfaithful
    d. is a common occurrence for American couples who have been married longer than twenty years

12. You are interested in becoming an anti-aging consultant. What product might you be promoting?
    a. video on tai-chi
    b. perimenopausal tablets
    c. human growth hormones
    d. ERT treatment

Chapter 15 Middle Adulthood: Physical and Cognitive Development

13. Juan is 50 years old, with a history of coronary artery disease in his family. The initial advice his doctor might give him to prolong his life expectancy might be to
    a. receive injections of estrogen
    b. have coronary bypass surgery
    c. exercise more and eat fewer fatty foods
    d. limit his exposure to carcinogens

14. Which of the following individuals is the least likely to die of heart disease?
    a. Mark, a competitive 45-year-old businessman who smokes and drinks
    b. Joshua, a 50-year-old Mormon who watches his diet, exercises regularly, and finds time to relax
    c. Julianne, an aggressive 42-year-old stockbroker who avoids eating red meat to monitor her high cholesterol
    d. Tanya, a 45-year-old fitness instructor with a family history of high blood pressure

15. You have just read an article on the climacteric. What will this article cover?
    a. the male multi-orgasm
    b. the drop in female hormone production
    c. the change in body temperature in old age
    d. cardiovascular disease

16. Joann seemingly changes her personality style during menopause, becoming more cold, anxious, and depressed. Which of the following conclusions seems to be the most legitimate?
    a. Menopause is an inner biological event that is commonly associated with major personality change.
    b. The woman's husband experienced similar personality changes when he went through male climacteric.
    c. The woman possessed all these personality predispositions earlier in adult life.
    d. The woman has probably displayed major changes in intellectual and cognitive functioning as well.

17. Statistically, you are more likely to suffer from depression if you are
    a. going through menopause
    b. past menopause
    c. 20-30 years old
    d. 10-19 years old

18. You are very good at test taking and vocabulary but find you are not very creative. Which type of intelligence do you have more of?
    a. fluid
    b. crystallized
    c. multiple
    d. performance

19. You are able to take many different perspectives in settling an argument. You are using
    a. dialectical thinking
    b. convergent thinking
    c. divergent thinking
    d. metacognitive thinking

20. You find yourself asking the following question: "How can I use the things I've learned to help my family, community, and society?" Which stage are you in?
    a. acquisitive
    b. achieving
    c. executive
    d. reintegrative

21. Someone has suggested that you are a moral exemplar. What trait would you not have?
    a. commitment to moral ideals
    b. willingness to risk your self-interest for your moral values
    c. letting others know you are right
    d. inspiring others

Essay Questions

1. It would seem as if everything is settled by middle adulthood – why then do men and women go through lifestyle changes in this period?

2. Do you agree with the argument, made by some, that graduate studies should really be reserved for those in middle adulthood? Why or why not?

3. Discuss why moral exemplars would tend to be middle and older adults instead of young adults. How do mid-life changes affect moral development?

ANSWERS FOR SELF-TESTS

Matching

1. y	10. h	19. k
2. s	11. g	20. f
3. v	12. d	21. a
4. m	13. i	22. e
5. n	14. q	23. t
6. b	15. j	24. p
7. w	16. o	25. r
8. c	17. l	
9. x	18. u	

Multiple Choice

Factual

1. d	10. d	19. c
2. a	11. d	20. a
3. c	12. c	21. b
4. b	13. a	22. c
5. c	14. d	23. c
6. d	15. d	24. b
7. d	16. d	25. c
8. c	17. b	
9. b	18. c	

Conceptual

1. a	8. c	15. b
2. a	9. b	16. c
3. d	10. a	17. c
4. b	11. c	18. b
5. c	12. c	19. a
6. d	13. c	20. c
7. c	14. b	21. c

Chapter 16

Middle Adulthood:
Emotional and Social Development

INTRODUCTION

Chapter 16 focuses on some of the changing aspects of mid-life associated with the family life cycle and the workplace. Two main topics are addressed:

- Social Relationships. The importance of developing friendships and becoming part of a couple during adulthood are examined. Issues such as the battering of women, extramarital sexual relationships, divorce, and remarriage are all covered in detail. The difficulties as well as the opportunities encountered by stepfamilies as a result of remarriage are considered. The empty-nest period – when children have grown up and left home – is discussed, along with the topic of adults caring for their elderly parents.

- The Workplace. Individual satisfaction derived from work and the factors associated with job burnout are discussed. Mid-life career changes are also examined. The impact of unemployment and the four stages commonly resulting from job loss are outlined. Also addressed are female work force expansion and its effects on women and traditional gender roles. Finally, the significance of dual-career couples is presented.

- Theories of Self. Life-span perspectives, stage models, trait models, situational models, and interactionist models are discussed.

Chapter 16 Middle Adulthood: Emotional and Social Development

---
LEARNING OBJECTIVES

After completing Chapter 16, you should be able to:

1. Define and discuss different aspects of *maturity*.

2. Explain various models of development in mid-life

Erikson: *generativity vs. stagnation*

Peck: four aspects

trait models

Mischel's situational model

interactionist model studies of personality continuity/discontinuity

Chapter 16 Middle Adulthood: Emotional and Social Development

3. Discuss Levinson's stages of male and female development in mid-life

male mid-life transition to late adulthood

female transitions

4. Explain findings from research on continuity and discontinuity in gender characteristics as one ages.

active vs. passive mastery

androgyny

5. Cite findings from the study on the first baby boom generation to turn 50.

percent married

number of children still at home

role of religion

change in attitude (liberal or conservative)

private time

sexual behavior (quantity/quality)

tenderness and aggressiveness

caretaking

6. Cite some statistics about the nature of American friendships.

close friends

expectations about friends

Chapter 16   Middle Adulthood: Emotional and Social Development

seeking different friends as we change

fulfilling friendships

quality of women's friendships

quality of men's friendships

7. Describe from the Lauer and Lauer study how couples' marriages survive.

8. Explain Americans' attitudes toward extramarital sexual relations.

beliefs

survey results

impact of AIDS

husbands' affairs

wives' affairs

reason for affairs

9. Briefly describe current information about these divorce-related topics.

divorce rates

historical trends

views of women now in their thirties and forties

emotional and psychological toll

10. Describe a typical household of a divorced mother and father.

mother's household

father's household

11. Explain the special consequences of divorce for a *displaced homemaker*.

12. Cite some findings regarding the influence and attitude of stepfathers.

13. Briefly describe factors that affect a child's adjustment to a remarriage.

mother-custody household

half-siblings

apprehension/resentment

Chapter 16 Middle Adulthood: Emotional and Social Development

14. Describe the following factors associated with caring for elderly parents.

the *sandwich generation*

Who takes responsibility for the elderly?

demographics

independent living arrangements vs. living with family

the "enhancement" hypothesis

15. Describe the significance of each of the following topics regarding job satisfaction in the workplace.

alienation

burnout symptoms

statistics of job satisfaction

job satisfaction and control

effects on family

occupational self-direction

older workers vs. younger workers

16. Explain mid-life career change.

one career vs. job shifting

statistics

reasons for career change

17. Briefly describe each of these unemployment-related topics.

reasons for unemployment

health effects

financial and family effects

Kaufman's stages

long-term unemployment

women as the main support

18. Discuss the circumstances of women in the workplace.

19. Briefly summarize the information on dual-earner couples.

Chapter 16 Middle Adulthood: Emotional and Social Development

WEB SITES

The following web sites deal with some of the concepts and issues presented in Chapter 16. Additional resources are available on the text's web site, at http://www.mhhe.com/crandell7.

MacArthur Foundation Research Network on Successful Midlife Devleopment (MIDMAC)
http://midmac.med.harvard.edu/midmac.html

Institute on Aging and Love
http://www.ssc.wisc.edu/aging/love.htm

Midlife Mommies
http://www.midlifemommies.com/

The Sandwich Generation
http://www.ianr.unl.edu/pubs/family/g1117.htm

The Riley Guide: Employment Opportunities and Job Resources on the Internet
http://www.dbm.com/jobguide/

Chapter 16 Middle Adulthood: Emotional and Social Development

SELF-TESTS

Matching

Match the key terms with their definitions:

a. alienation
b. androgyny
c. displaced homemaker
d. empty nest
e. empty-nest syndrome
f. generativity
g. generativity vs. stagnation
h. job burnout
i. maturity
j. sandwich generation
k. self-concept
l. social convoy
m. traditional marriage

1. ____ the presence of both male-typed and female-typed characteristics

2. ____ the "crisis" that, according to Erikson, the mid-life years are devoted to resolving through guiding the next generation

3. ____ the company of other people who travel with us from birth to death

4. ____ people caring for both growing children and aging parents

5. ____ a pervasive sense of powerlessness, meaninglessness, normlessness, isolation, and self-estrangement

6. ____ a social arrangement in which a woman lives the life of a homemaker and the man lives as the provisioner

7. ____ a term used when work that once was fulfilling and satisfying may over time become unfulfilling and unsatisfying

8. ____ a woman whose primary activity has been homemaking and who has lost her main source of income because of divorce or widowhood

9. ____ the capacity of individuals to undergo continual change in order to adapt successfully and cope flexibly with the demands and responsibilities of life

10. ____ the concern in establishing and guiding the next generation

11. ____ the emotional difficulties that women face when their children leave home

12. ____ the image one has of oneself

13. ____ the term applied to that period of life when children have grown up and left home

Chapter 16 Middle Adulthood: Emotional and Social Development

Multiple Choice

Circle the letter of the response that best completes or answers each of the following statements and questions.

Factual Questions

1. David Levinson and colleagues at Yale University researched the stages of male adult development and concluded that
   a. there is a stage of "male menopause"
   b. men have a pathological fear of aging and dying
   c. men at middle age often become keenly aware of how much more time is left to accomplish life goals
   d. most men actually do go through a mid-life crisis, and many are likely to make drastic changes in their lives at this time

2. Many men at age 50 begin to realize that
   a. their lives are over and they begin to plan their retirement from the labor force
   b. they are likely to go downhill physically and sexually from this point on
   c. this is a time to introspect and take stock of the priorities in life
   d. it's now or never for the big promotions and attack their work with zeal

3. The middle years can also be referred to as a "crisis point" for some couples
   a. as they realize their sexual desire is waning because of physical changes
   b. as the wife desires to resume her career, while the husband is readying for exiting the work world
   c. because the husband is likely to be seeking younger sex partners to reaffirm his masculinity
   d. as the woman typically settles into the "grandmothering" stage and is probably less interested in regular sexual activity

4. Erik Erikson deems the central task of middle age to be resolving the issue of
   a. identity vs. identity diffusion
   b. intimacy vs. isolation
   c. generativity vs. stagnation
   d. maturity vs. immaturity

5. Developmentalists McAdams and de St. Aubin see _____ as springing from two deeply rooted desires: the communal need to be nurturant and the personal desire to do something or be something that transcends death.
   a. empathy
   b. personality
   c. maturity
   d. generativity

6. Robert Peck's aspect of mid-life which concerns the ability to become emotionally flexible is called
   a. socializing vs. sexualizing
   b. mental flexibility vs. mental rigidity
   c. cathectic flexibility vs. cathectic impoverishment
   d. valuing wisdom vs. physical powers

7. According to Peck, individuals cultivate greater understanding and compassion when they confront the mid-life task of
   a. mental flexibility vs. mental rigidity
   b. cathectic flexibility vs. cathectic impoverishment
   c. valuing wisdom vs. valuing physical powers
   d. socializing vs. sexualizing in human relationships

8. Until recently, most psychologists believed that personality patterns are established during early childhood and then remained relatively stable throughout life. Which model is being described?
   a. situational model
   b. trait model
   c. interactionist model
   d. psychoanalytic model

9. According to the _____ model of adult personality development, people seek out congenial environments that reinforce their preexisting bents.
   a. situational
   b. interactionist
   c. dynamic
   d. trait

10. Neugarten suggests that middle age typically brings a(n)
    a. concern with one's legacy or psychological survivorship
    b. renunciation of life's losses
    c. awareness of oneself as the "breadwinner"
    d. different reactions depending on socioeconomic status

11. Gutmann has compared individuals in a number of cultures and finds that with advancing age
    a. both men and women tend to move toward more passive mastery
    b. both men and women tend to move toward more active mastery
    c. men tend to move toward passive mastery, and women tend to move toward more active mastery
    d. men tend to move toward more active mastery, and women tend to move toward passive mastery

12. According to Gutmann, in later life those people who age successfully tend towards *androgyny*, which is
    a. incorporating both male-typed and female-typed characteristics within a single personality
    b. having the same view of themselves over time
    c. having mental pictures of themselves that are relatively temporary
    d. moving from passive mastery to active mastery

13. The capacity of individuals to undergo continual change in order to adapt successfully and cope flexibly with the demands and responsibilities of life best defines
    a. maturity
    b. sanity
    c. stability
    d. satisfaction

14. The view we have of ourselves through time as "the real me" is referred to as
    a. self-image
    b. self-concept
    c. personality
    d. maturity

15. The mature personality will have which of the following traits?
    a. relate warmly to others
    b. possess emotional security
    c. wide sense of self
    d. all of the above

16. Which substage of Levinson's model of male development includes reappraisal and exploration of one's self
    a. mid-life transition
    b. age 50 transition
    c. late adult transition
    d. all of the above

17. Women in Levinson's model constituted three groups. Which is not one of these groups?
    a. women in academia
    b. homemakers
    c. athletes
    d. women in the corporate world

18. Sociologists Blumstein and Schwartz, investigating the experiences of different types of couples, found that
    a. straight and homosexual women emphasize power and dominance in their relationships
    b. even when wives had full-time jobs, they did most of the housework
    c. married couples measured their financial success in terms of total earned income
    d. quantity and quality of sex were more important for homosexual couples than for heterosexual couples

19. Heterosexual men take the most pleasure in their partner's success when
    a. it is nearly equal to their own
    b. it is superior to their own
    c. it is inferior to their own
    d. it is in an area vastly outside of their own

20. Married couples measured their financial success by looking at
    a. the wife's income
    b. the husband's income
    c. their joint income
    d. a variety of factors including income, benefits, flextime, childcare, pension, etc.

21. Women's prime of life, according to Mills Longitudinal Study, is at
    a. 30, the world is my oyster, no responsibilities
    b. 40, the kids are in school, I can start my life
    c. 50, family and work are past, I have accomplished one thing so I'll begin another
    d. 60, I can see the world with a clear eye, time to make up for lost time

22. Being simultaneously responsible for children and parents is a task of the
    a. baby boom generation
    b. sandwich generation
    c. interactionist generation
    d. alienated generation

23. What is a major reason for successful marriage listed by both men and women?
    a. when women tend to think sex will bring tenderness and emotional expressiveness
    b. when men tend to express their love through sex rather than through emotional expressiveness and tenderness
    c. having a positive attitude towards one's spouse
    d. all of the above

24. Which of the following statements regarding sexual relations is accurate?
    a. Extramarital affairs tend to decrease at age 50.
    b. 20 year old women are as likely as 40 year old women to enter extramarital relations.
    c. Extramarital transgressions usually indicate loneliness or lack of excitement.
    d. The incidence of marital infidelity has declined as couples realize that sexual activity is their marital obligation.

25. In a study of couples who have had extramarital affairs, researchers did not find
    a. husbands are more likely than wives to engage in and repeat extramarital affairs
    b. men are more likely than women to let an extramarital affair blossom into an full-fledged love affair
    c. most people transgress the marital relationship because they are very dissatisfied with their spouse
    d. sex is the major lure for extramarital love affairs

26. According to 1998 statistics, a married woman has a greater risk of going through a divorce
    a. if she doesn't have a high school diploma
    b. if she marries young
    c. if she has no children
    d. all of the above

27. The overall divorce rate now seems to be
    a. slowly increasing
    b. dramatically increasing
    c. slowly decreasing
    d. about the same as the past twenty years

28. The displaced homemaker is likely to be devastated by divorce because
    a. divorce is more uncommon in this group of people
    b. she has a more difficult time forming new sexual relationships
    c. she is ill-equipped to deal with the financial consequences of divorce
    d. she is more likely than the working wife to have positive feelings toward her husband

Chapter 16 Middle Adulthood: Emotional and Social Development

29. Men who do not remarry are more likely to suffer from
    a. more care accidents
    b. drug abuse
    c. alcoholism
    d. all of the above

30. Studies show that men are likely to seek a mate who is
    a. physically and emotionally at odds with them
    b. younger than they are
    c. financially on a par with them
    d. more educated than they are

31. Middle-aged couples whose children left home have been found to experience
    a. the empty-nest syndrome
    b. feelings of new freedom
    c. marital discord and discontent
    d. the desire to go to college or start a business

32. For members of the sandwich generation
    a. responsibility for the elderly falls most commonly on daughters and daughters-in-law
    b. men are most likely to experience role overload
    c. elderly parents are considered a burden and are rarely taken care of
    d. elderly parents are more likely to be taken care of if the parents live far away

33. The best defenses against job burnout are
    a. good pay and job security
    b. apathy and fatalism
    c. self-respect and a chance to perform well
    d. idealism and high expectations

34. According to a recent survey, what percentage of Americans polled switched careers last year?
    a. more than 75 percent
    b. over 50 percent
    c. 12 percent
    d. 25 percent

35. Job insecurity in the United States has been rising because of all of the following except
    a. automation and technological advances
    b. corporate downsizing
    c. globalization of the economy
    d. underskilled labor force

36. Kaufman's fourth stage of unemployment is
    a. resignation, withdrawal, settling for other work
    b. high levels of self-doubt and anxiety, a bleak outlook
    c. great financial difficulty, possibly divorce
    d. shock, relief, relaxation

Chapter 16   Middle Adulthood: Emotional and Social Development

37. According to Levinson, the phase in adult development in which people come to terms with their youth and work on individuation is called
    a. settling down
    b. age 30 transition
    c. entry into life structure
    d. mid-life transition

Conceptual Questions

1. A 45-year-old woman decides to get a silicone breast implant to please her young boyfriend, just as she pleased him by changing her wardrobe. Robert Peck would view this behavior as a form of
    a. generativity
    b. stagnation
    c. mental rigidity
    d. valuing physical powers

2. John acts extroverted when he is with his friends but very sedate and conservative at work. This observation is the most consistent with which of the following models of personality?
    a. Mischel's situational model
    b. the dynamic model
    c. the trait model
    d. the interactionist model

3. Extroverted adults tend to be drawn toward social situations in which they can meet new people, socialize, and enjoy themselves; whereas they avoid situations where people act aloof, clannish, and antisocial. This observation would be consistent with the _____ model of adult personality.
    a. dynamic
    b. interactionist
    c. situational
    d. trait

4. Based on your text's description, an analogy for maturity is: maturity is like _____
    a. searching for the horizon – it is evident it is there, but it always stays in front of you and you can never reach it
    b. finding a rainbow; it is a phenomenon that is spectacular, then it disappears
    c. working as an architect, where one is striving to complete big projects on time to everyone's satisfaction
    d. completing semesters at college successfully; the satisfaction is in the growth and skills learned along the way, and then you go on to new life challenges

5. Which of the following scenarios is the most likely to occur?
    a. Shirley and Terrence are a married couple in which Terrence is happiest when he does the lion's share of the housework.
    b. Sam and Diane are a working, married couple who measure their financial success in terms of Sam's income.
    c. Anthony and Erica are newlyweds whose primary conflict involves Anthony's contention that Erica spends too much time with her friends.
    d. Naomi and Rupert have been married for twenty years, and they argue frequently about Rupert's demands to spend more time with his buddies.

Chapter 16 Middle Adulthood: Emotional and Social Development

6. Mr. Brown admits to his wife that he's been having an affair with a woman at his office. Mrs. Brown, extremely distraught and hurt by his confession, retorts, "Well, you don't love me, then." According to your text, most men enter into an extramarital affair because they
    a. no longer love their wives
    b. crave a satisfying sexual relationship
    c. crave emotional excitement and proof they are not getting old, but they usually love their wives
    d. want the affair to blossom into a full-fledged love affair so they will no longer love their wives

7. Jacque and Jill were married for 25 years, but at that time found that their lives were unfulfilling and no longer satisfying. Although they were still fond of each other, they were no longer "in love." They sought an amicable divorce, but months later both found that they were almost always sad and depressed. The best explanation that can be offered concerning the situation of Jacque and Jill is
    a. they had grown "used to" and dependent upon one another
    b. divorce exacts a greater emotional and physical toll than almost any other life stress
    c. they were unable to find suitable new partners
    d. their financial resources deteriorated so they could no longer enjoy the lifestyle to which they had become accustomed

8. A 45-year-old adult is being treated by a psychiatrist because of clinical signs of depression (e.g., insomnia, agitation, feelings of worthlessness). This adult is most likely to be a
    a. recently divorced displaced homemaker
    b. divorced mother who initiated the divorce
    c. recently divorced working mother with two children in elementary school
    d. soon-to-be-divorced woman who misses her abusive husband

9. Jim is a 45-year-old divorced man. Without knowing anything else about Jim, we are likely to predict that he
    a. is not likely to remarry
    b. will remarry an older woman
    c. will remarry a younger woman
    d. is less likely to remarry than a divorced woman of the same age group

10. Which of the following scenarios is most likely to take place in a stepfamily?
    a. The stepfather is uncomfortable sitting in the father's favorite chair.
    b. The wife's son starts behaving in an infantile, regressive manner after the remarriage.
    c. On announcing her plans to remarry, the wife is confronted by her daughter who asks, "Why didn't you do this sooner?"
    d. The children do the dishes when their new stepfather asks them to because they know this will make their mother happy.

11. You have been told that one of your grandparents is moving from passive to active mastery. Who is it likely to be?
    a. grandmother
    b. grandfather
    c. can't tell
    d. neither

Chapter 16 Middle Adulthood: Emotional and Social Development

12. Sarah's youngest daughter has just gotten married. Now all her children are gone from the house. We can predict that Sarah, a devoted mother, will
    a. be depressed as a result of role confusion
    b. have so much new "free time" that she won't know what to do with it
    c. become immobilized because of feelings of loneliness
    d. feel closer to her husband than when they were first married

13. Natasha is 68 years old. While she is still ambulatory, she suffers from severe bouts of rheumatoid arthritis. Which of the following predictions can we make about Natasha?
    a. Natasha's daughter sees her mother regularly and helps her with her chores.
    b. Natasha is likely to reside in a nursing home.
    c. Natasha is likely to be living with her married son.
    d. Natasha's son drives fifty miles a day to see his mother, although his own health is failing.

14. You and your spouse both work and are middle-aged. Which scenario is most likely?
    a. you both want private time
    b. you pool your money
    c. you don't pool your money
    d. neither of you want private time

15. Which of the following employees is least likely to change careers?
    a. a nurse who feels that the hospital patients do not appreciate the care she provides for them
    b. an elementary school teacher who feels instead of teaching children he is expected to be their surrogate parent
    c. a psychology professor who feels that her students need remedial help and are unprepared to master the material in her courses
    d. a college administrator who has just helped the college eliminate its deficit and is now being asked to computerize its accounting system

16. Jack is a 43-year-old computer engineer who has become disenchanted with his current profession. The enthusiasm has faded, and he lacks a sense of fulfillment. A psychologist would most likely recommend that Jack
    a. continue with his current job because these types of feelings are normal
    b. consider switching careers because it is common for middle-aged adults to reassess what they are doing with their lives
    c. consider getting psychological help because he is on the verge of a nervous breakdown
    d. retire and channel his energies into caring for his family

17. Jessica is a recent college graduate who aspires to a career in the corporate world and is willing to accept an entry-level position to "work her way up." Her female relatives attempt to prepare her for several employment rejections, but Jessica is optimistic because she is aware that
    a. attitudes toward women in the corporate world have changed dramatically
    b. since 1980, women have taken 80 percent of the new jobs created in the economy
    c. she has no immediate plans to marry and/or start a family
    d. she has the educational preparation

18. Craig's wife just told him it's time for him to go out and get a haircut – all he does is sit around the house. She also said, "While you're at it, why don't you apply for some jobs, too." The most reasonable conclusion one might reach is that Craig
    a. has just received a layoff notice from his employer
    b. has been unemployed for about a month
    c. feels emasculated because he has been unemployed for a long time
    d. will tell his wife, "It's time for you to wear the pants in this family. My turn is up!"

Essay Questions

1. You have been told that stepfamilies are the easiest to grow up in. Do you agree?

2. Do you believe that adults go through stages of development? Some argue that emotional development can only occur when physical development occurs. Argue for or against this.

3. Some argue that fulfilling work is better than a fulfilling sexual relationship. Do you agree?

Chapter 16 Middle Adulthood: Emotional and Social Development

ANSWERS FOR SELF-TESTS

Matching

1. b
2. g
3. l
4. j
5. a
6. m
7. h
8. c
9. i
10. f
11. e
12. k
13. d

Multiple Choice

Factual

1. d
2. c
3. c
4. c
5. c
6. c
7. d
8. b
9. b
10. d
11. c
12. a
13. a
14. b
15. d
16. b
17. c
18. b
19. c
20. b
21. c
22. b
23. c
24. c
25. d
26. d
27. c
28. c
29. d
30. b
31. b
32. a
33. c
34. c
35. d
36. a
37. d

Conceptual

1. d
2. a
3. b
4. d
5. b
6. c
7. b
8. a
9. c
10. a
11. a
12. c
13. a
14. b
15. d
16. b
17. b
18. c

Chapter 17

Late Adulthood:
Physical and Cognitive Development

INTRODUCTION

Chapter 17 focuses on physical and cognitive development during later adulthood. Several topics are looked at in detail, including:

- Aging: Myth and Reality. The age at which an individual is considered elderly differs from one society to another. The demographics of the elderly are presented for various cultures. Why women live longer than men is discussed. A number of myths which cloud the real facts of aging are also outlined, and the overall health of elderly people is covered. In addition, the question of how the nation should allocate its resources among generations is addressed, as are programs for the elderly, such as Social Security.

- Health. Nutrition and health risks are discussed.

- Biological Aging. The physical changes associated with aging are presented, as are ways of combating the effects of aging through physical fitness. Various biological theories of aging are also examined.

- Cognitive Functioning. The first issue covered in this section is the varied course of different abilities. Results of studies on late-adult cognitive development and an overestimation of the effects of aging are presented. Research dealing with the memory processes, information processing, and learning in the elderly is also documented. The topics of senility and Alzheimer's disease are addressed.

- Moral Development. The importance of religion and faith are covered.

LEARNING OBJECTIVES

After completing Chapter 17, you should be able to:

1. Describe some of the common myths for elderly American men and women.

Chapter 17   Late Adulthood: Physical and Cognitive Development

2. Define the terms *ageism*, *gerontology* and *geropsychology*.

3. Compare and contrast the issue of longevity in various cultures, cite some countries where people seem to live the longest, and cite the results of research about people living to be 120 or older.

4. Describe the demographic statistics on elderly Americans and on the elderly in other cultures.

life expectancy

numbers and rate of growth of elderly population

5. List the predicted likely effects of these population changes on the American culture and budget.

6. Briefly summarize from research data several reasons why women are living longer than men.

7. Cite and briefly describe the purpose of several government-sponsored programs to benefit the elderly.

8. Give a brief historical perspective on U.S. government spending on the elderly, cite the current levels of spending in the federal budget, and state projected spending levels.

9. Appraise the concept of *ageism* by stating some common myths concerning elderly Americans and then citing the facts.

10. Describe the health status of older Americans.

11. Describe several physical changes associated with aging.

hair

skin appearance

muscle/fat ratio

visual efficiency

hearing loss

taste bud impairment

olfactory impairment

touch sensitivity

temperature sensitivity

hypothermia symptoms

sleep patterns

sexuality

12. Compare and contrast the following major biological theories of aging.

"notion of inborn limits," supported by James Fries

Chapter 17   Late Adulthood: Physical and Cognitive Development

"small gains in life span," supported by S. Jay Olshansky

13. List and briefly describe other biological theories of aging.

14. Succinctly explain the suggested three primary ways of staving off the aging process.

   •

   •

   •

15. Cite the results of studies which criticize traditional intelligence/ability testing with aging subjects.

Labouvie-Vief

Schaie and Willis

16. Analyze the differing results produced by cross-sectional and longitudinal studies of late-adult cognitive development, and describe the significant effect of the *death drop*.

Chapter 17 Late Adulthood: Physical and Cognitive Development

17. Summarize the research dealing with memory loss.

prevalence of memory loss

recalling people's names

vocabulary memory

recall tasks

recognition tasks

18. Briefly explain the phases in information processing and *retrieval*.

encoding

storage

retrieval

19. Discuss factors that influence memory failure.

decay theory

interference theory

practical implications

20. Describe the research on learning and aging.

Chapter 17   Late Adulthood: Physical and Cognitive Development

21. Discuss the following aspects of *Alzheimer's disease*.

physiological changes/symptoms

psychological changes/symptoms

demographics

effect on family

phases of progression

possible causes

22. List and briefly describe Fowler's 7 stages of Faith Development

-
-
-
-
-
-

Chapter 17   Late Adulthood: Physical and Cognitive Development

WEB SITES

The following web sites deal with some of the concepts and issues addressed in Chapter 17. Additional resources can be found on the text's web site, at http://www.mhhe.com/crandell7.

The Women's Health and Aging Study
http://www.nih.gov/nia/edb/whasbook/title.htm

NIH Resource Directory for Older People
http://www.nih.gov/nia/related/aoaresrc/toc.htm

Web Resources on Gerontology
http://www.usc.edu/isd/locations/science/gerontology/web_resources.htm

Spreading Eternal Youth – Extensive links
http://homepage.esoterica.pt/~jpnitya/science/youth.htm

Chapter 17 Late Adulthood: Physical and Cognitive Development

SELF-TESTS

Matching

Match the key terms with their definitions:

a. ageism
b. Alzheimer's disease
c. collagen
d. death drop
e. decay theory
f. encoding
g. gerontology
h. geropsychology
i. hypothermia
j. interference theory
k. multiinfarct
l. osteoporosis
m. retrieval
n. senescence
o. senility
p. sleep apnea
q. storage

1. ____ "little strokes" that destroy a small area of brain tissue

2. ____ a condition associated with a slow, insidious loss of calcium, producing porous bones

3. ____ a condition in which body temperature falls more than 4 degrees Fahrenheit and persists for a number of hours

4. ____ a lack of consistency and deterioration in cognitive functioning

5. ____ a marked intellectual decline that occurs just a short time before a person dies

6. ____ a progressive, degenerative disorder that involves deterioration of brain cells

7. ____ a sleep disorder in which the person occasionally experiences breathing that stops during sleep

8. ____ a substance that constitutes a very high percentage of the total protein in the body

9. ____ forgetting due to deterioration in the memory traces in the brain

10. ____ perceiving information, abstracting from it one or more characteristics needed for classification, and creating corresponding memory traces for it

11. ____ refers to retrieval of a cue becoming less effective as more and newer items come to be classed or categorized in terms of it

12. ____ the process by which information is gathered from memory when it is required

13. ____ the process by which information is retained in memory until it is needed

14. ____ the process of aging

15. ____ the stereotyping of a group of people and judging them solely on the basis of their age

16. ____ the study of aging and the special problems associated with it

17. ____ the study of the behavior and needs of the elderly

Chapter 17 Late Adulthood: Physical and Cognitive Development

Multiple Choice

Circle the letter of the response that best completes or answers each of the following statements and questions.

Factual Questions

1. Which of the following statements is most accurate concerning aging in American culture?
    a. Aging is viewed positively by both younger and older generations.
    b. Aging is viewed negatively by only those in the older generations who are experiencing it.
    c. Aging does not, for the majority of Americans, destroy the continuity of who they are.
    d. American senior citizens are more likely to be labeled with masculine characteristics than feminine ones.

2. The study of aging and the special problems of the elderly is _____; whereas, the branch of medicine that is concerned with the mental health of elderly persons is _____.
    a. geriatrics; senescence
    b. geriatrics; gerontology
    c. gerontology; geropsychology
    d. senescence; gerontology

3. An area of the world where people typically live until very old is
    a. China
    b. Kenya
    c. Soviet Caucasus
    d. Switzerland

4. A substantial rise in elderly population will most likely occur around what time, when the baby boom generation passes 65?
    a. 2000-2010
    b. 2010-2030
    c. 2020-2040
    d. 2030-2050

5. The fastest growing part of the American population currently is
    a. those under age 25
    b. those reaching age 45
    c. those reaching age 65
    d. those reaching age 85

6. American population changes will have far-reaching socioeconomic impact, including all of the following except
    a. increased movement of Americans to the south and southwest
    b. increased demand for various resources, such as Social Security, and other government-sponsored programs
    c. increased attention to the dependency needs of the elderly, such as housing and health care
    d. increased political action and involvement

Chapter 17 Late Adulthood: Physical and Cognitive Development

7. Women seem to be more durable organisms than men because
    a. of an inherited sex-linked resistance to some types of life-threatening disease
    b. lower levels of late-life estrogen protect them against cardiovascular disease
    c. they eat more balanced diets that are lower in cholesterol
    d. they lead more active and energetic lives

8. A major economic trend in the United States over the past five decades has been
    a. more saving promoted by banks offering higher interest rates
    b. growth in the number of Americans dependent upon government aid
    c. a decrease in the standard of living for most Americans
    d. a decrease in programs and support services for older Americans, allowing fewer people to retire

9. Regarding the future of the Social Security system, one can probably anticipate that
    a. the number of workers who will contribute to this system will be increasing
    b. the support ratio will be decreasing
    c. by the year 2020, on the basis of current trends, the system will be paying out more than it is taking in
    d. those working Americans who have been contributing will be getting all their money back for their retirement years

10. Which of the following statements regarding the Social Security system is the least accurate?
    a. One answer to the problems of the Social Security system has been raising the retirement age.
    b. Today's younger workers must pay Social Security taxes of several thousand dollars a year for their entire working careers.
    c. Critics of the system contend that most people could do much better if they were able to put their Social Security contributions into a private pension plan.
    d. Economists say that we should make Social Security voluntary.

11. Which of the following statements is a fact?
    a. Most old people are in poor health.
    b. Less than one-tenth of the elderly who live at home are bedridden and homebound.
    c. Most Americans over 65 find themselves in serious financial straits.
    d. Most of the elderly view crime as a major concern.

12. Which of the following statements is least accurate?
    a. Most elderly people are in serious financial straits.
    b. Elderly Americans are in better financial shape than they were three decades ago.
    c. Social Security and retirement benefits are the primary sources of income for most elderly persons.
    d. The economic gap between men and women widens in retirement.

13. If a woman is a widow and was not employed during her lifetime, she is likely to receive a monthly Social Security benefit of how much based on her husband's previous benefit of $850?
    a. $850
    b. about $538
    c. about $425
    d. none

Chapter 17   Late Adulthood: Physical and Cognitive Development

14. Elderly Americans are more likely to experience
    a. higher incidence of multiple disorders
    b. lower incidence of chronic disease
    c. higher incidence of acute illnesses
    d. multiple serious disorders

15. Researchers examining the health of elderly Americans find that
    a. 75 percent of adults have sufficiently active lifestyles
    b. increases in so-called desirable weights for men made over the last three decades are unjustified and are likely to result in higher death rates
    c. energy requirements increase with age
    d. elderly people need fewer nutrients than younger adults

16. Elderly women are more likely than men to
    a. experience brief blackouts
    b. absorb drugs rapidly from their intestinal tracts
    c. need calcium supplements to slow or stop osteoporosis
    d. spend a large percentage of their lives without chronic infirmities

17. Regarding prescription drug use,
    a. elderly persons absorb drugs more readily from the intestinal tract than younger persons
    b. the average healthy elderly person takes two different prescription medicines per year
    c. a person over age 60 is more likely to suffer adverse side effects than a younger patient
    d. elderly people need higher doses of all medications than younger people

18. In order to combat the effects of aging through physical fitness, elderly individuals
    a. need to exercise regularly to replace lost muscle mass
    b. need to perform aerobic activities as well as strength training
    c. need not be concerned with strength training because muscle size does not change with age
    d. need to perform only non-vigorous exercises to increase their life span

19. The protein substance that has been implicated in the body's aging process is called
    a. dilantin
    b. primarin
    c. collagen
    d. carotene

20. Regarding tendencies in rates of aging, which of the following statements is most accurate?
    a. Aging occurs in a very predictable pattern for men and women.
    b. Sensory functioning declines precede physical/muscular decline.
    c. The rate of aging varies while the tendencies in aging are predictable.
    d. Genetics plays a major role in the rate of aging.

21. Which of the following is an accurate description of age-related physical change?
    a. a marked loss of hearing, especially in the lower frequencies
    b. gains in maximum oxygen intake
    c. more sleep with less frequent awakenings
    d. a decline in the number of taste buds

Chapter 17   Late Adulthood: Physical and Cognitive Development

22. Most communities, through their own utility companies, accept donations for the elderly poor to heat their living space during the cold months because the elderly are susceptible to a medical condition called
    a. insomnia
    b. hypothermia
    c. hyperthermia
    d. hyposensitivity

23. The perspective that there are biological limits as to how long human beings can live is supported by _____, while the perspective that human beings are not programmed to survive very long past the end of their reproductive period is supported by _____.
    a. Fries; Vaupel
    b. Olshansky; Fries
    c. Vaupel; Olshansky
    d. Fries; Olshansky

24. Which of the following theories of aging implies that the probability of a random happening increases as the number of events increases?
    a. autoimmune mechanism
    b. genetic preprogramming
    c. stochastic processes
    d. error in DNA

25. The biological theory of aging that proposes the body's natural defenses against infection begin to attack normal cells is called _____ theory.
    a. mean time to failure
    b. copying errors
    c. autoimmune mechanism
    d. accumulation of metabolic waste

26. Longevity assurance theory, proposed by Sacher, takes a different perspective on the aging process by supporting that
    a. favorable genes that repair other cells are passed along by evolution
    b. the longer you live, the more likely you will continue to live because you have learned how to avoid disaster and illness
    c. "free radicals" help to repair cell functioning
    d. DNA mutations in molecules promote more rapid cell division

27. Different procedures for studying the effects of aging provide somewhat different results. Which of the following approaches tends to overestimate the effects of aging?
    a. cross-sectional
    b. longitudinal
    c. statistical
    d. case study

28. Research suggests that with respect to aging and memory
    a. a progressive loss of memory necessarily accompanies advancing age
    b. some memory loss is found in an increasing proportion of older people with each advance in chronological age
    c. age-related decreases are more severe for recognition than for recall tasks
    d. there is no clear pattern of problems with memory retrieval

Chapter 17   Late Adulthood: Physical and Cognitive Development

29. Which of the following is not characteristic of senility?
    a. progressive mental deterioration
    b. memory loss
    c. disorientation to time and place
    d. impaired hearing

30. In the first phase of Alzheimer's disease
    a. the patient experiences multiinfarcts that destroy small areas of brain tissue
    b. individuals forget where things were placed and have difficulty recalling events
    c. there are difficulties in cognitive functioning that cannot be overlooked
    d. hyperthyroidism leads to signs of depression

31. Which of the following statements regarding Alzheimer's disease is most accurate?
    a. There is no evidence supporting a genetic source for Alzheimer's disease.
    b. Many adults with Down syndrome eventually develop Alzheimer's lesions.
    c. Alzheimer's-induced senility is an easily treated condition.
    d. Ninety percent of all cases of senility are caused by Alzheimer's disease.

Conceptual Questions

1. Great Aunt Linette is 90 years old, and lives in the same home she's lived in for nearly 70 years. She's been a widow for over 50 years and takes care of herself, her home, and property. She rarely leaves her home but loves to watch her favorite baseball teams on television and read. She is lively, witty, healthy for her age and has a very positive outlook on living until 100.   She writes/receives letters to and from many relatives and friends. Based on this chapter, Linette
    a. fits the positive stereotype for the elderly
    b. fits the negative stereotype for the elderly
    c. fits the stereotype for performing poorly on tasks
    d. would be judged to have more masculine characteristics of aging

2. On the television show *Ripley's Believe It or Not*, a man in the Soviet Republic of Georgia was interviewed and claimed to be 120 years old. We can probably conclude
    a. he eats yogurt
    b. he comes from a rural area and is exposed to less air pollution
    c. his claim to be 120 years old is probably an exaggeration
    d. his dietary habits are healthier than those of most Americans

3. Rosa, who is a healthy 70-year-old, was married to Joseph for 45 years before his death at age 68. We can most reasonably infer that Rosa has outlived Joseph
    a. due to an inherent autosomally-linked resistance to some types of life-threatening diseases
    b. due to her higher levels of testosterone
    c. due to an inherent sex-linked resistance to some types of life-threatening diseases
    d. due to the female hormone estrogen, which dramatically reduces the risk of diabetes in women

Chapter 17 Late Adulthood: Physical and Cognitive Development

4. A major lifestyle factor that affects life expectancy for many males is
    a. estrogen
    b. smoking
    c. their immune system
    d. sex-linked resistance

5. You feel very uncomfortable because you get in the middle of a conflict at a family reunion. Your elderly grandfather is berating your cousin because your cousin has been bad-mouthing the Social Security system and the amount of money he has to pay into it. Your cousin's best defense might be which of the following?
    a. Even though you paid your dues, you're getting ripped off.
    b. Your Social Security isn't providing for all your needs, is it?
    c. Pay me now, or pay me later.
    d. You got more for your money than I will.

6. Your 10-year-old daughter tells you that she understands why old people are so cranky and crotchety all the time. It is because most of them are sick and invalid and cannot take care of themselves. This perception is
    a. very sophisticated for a 10-year-old
    b. somewhat inaccurate but very close to being true
    c. confused because your daughter has paired the wrong causes with the right effect
    d. inaccurate and may inadvertently perpetuate the inferior status of the elderly

7. Your 89-year-old grandmother just fell and broke her hip and is in the hospital. Based on this type of serious injury and her age, what can you predict is likely to happen next?
    a. She will recuperate in the hospital and will go back to her own independent lifestyle.
    b. She is likely to live several more years after recovery.
    c. She has a greater risk of a serious health decline of 3 to 4 months ending with senescence.
    d. She will, most likely, end up living in a nursing home.

8. Adrianne, 67, and her husband Larry, 68, are both retired. We can reasonably infer that
    a. the economic gap between Adrianne and Larry has narrowed during their retirement
    b. Adrianne's Social Security benefits are greater than Larry's
    c. Adrianne's Social Security benefits are equal to Larry's
    d. Adrianne's Social Security benefits are less than Larry's

9. Your grandfather is in the hospital because he fell down and broke his hip. Which of the following problems should you be the most concerned about?
    a. He may receive too much estrogen and therefore develop osteoporosis.
    b. He may develop too much bone mass as a result of calcium therapy and be more likely to break his hip again.
    c. He may develop additional problems as a result of receiving other medications, such as sedatives.
    d. He may leave the hospital suffering from a chronic disease that he contracted while in the hospital.

Chapter 17   Late Adulthood: Physical and Cognitive Development

10. Paul, a 70-year-old retiree, has been exercising regularly for the past forty-five years of his life. It is likely that Paul's physical fitness regimen results in
    a. an increased replacement of lost muscle mass
    b. a decreased risk of developing depression
    c. a doubling in his life span
    d. an increased risk of bone fractures

11. Advertisements for various creams and oils imply that these products can keep women's skin less wrinkled and younger looking. If these products really do make skin younger looking, they accomplish this by
    a. creating more DNA
    b. preventing collagen fibers from changing
    c. attacking defective cells
    d. creating cellular mutations

12. Many state legislatures have passed laws preventing gas and power companies from disconnecting the natural gas supplies of poor and elderly customers. If this legislation were declared unconstitutional, the elderly would be at risk for
    a. decreased ventilatory volume
    b. decreased organ reserve
    c. life-threatening hypothermia
    d. hypoglycemia

13. A biologist places cells from chick embryos in a cell culture to count and determine the number of times the cells divide and re-divide. He finds that there is a finite limit to the number of cell divisions that will occur, thus lending support to which theory of aging?
    a. genetic preprogramming
    b. mean time to failure
    c. DNA error
    d. stochastic processes

14. You are copying a computer file from one disk to another when a power outage shuts down your computer. As a result of this problem, your file is only partially transferred to the new disk. This problem is analogous to which of the following theories of aging?
    a. genetic programming
    b. longevity assurance
    c. DNA error
    d. stochastic processes

15. On which of the following tasks is an elderly person most likely to experience declines in performance?
    a. crossword puzzles
    b. playing poker
    c. putting a jigsaw puzzle together
    d. playing checkers

16. Mr. Gates, 65 and now retired, has decided to enroll in a college class in philosophy and logic. What can we predict about his cognitive performance? He will most likely find that he
    a. can do the work only if he's given extra time
    b. cannot retain the information long enough in long-term memory to be successful on tests
    c. will need to drop the course because he cannot remember names of important philosophers
    d. will make improvements in his deductive reasoning

17. Dr. Firenze has been a math professor for thirty years. Recently, she has noticed that she doesn't always recall her students' names as easily as she used to when she calls on students. Since 1966, she's taught over nine thousand students. However, she knows her math "like the back of her hand." She shares her concern about memory loss with you, a colleague. As a psychologist, you can tell Dr. Firenze that she
    a. must see a neurologist
    b. should relax, because a large percentage of middle age and older adults have some difficulty with memory, usually forgetting names first
    c. should see her doctor for a prescription for estrogen
    d. is under too much stress and should consider working only part time

18. An elderly man has just received a past-due notice on his phone bill. He may have forgotten to pay the bill because he got four other utility bills when he received this one and placed them all in a manila folder labeled "bills." The man's memory failure is due to
    a. lack of encoding
    b. the decay of memory trace
    c. interference from other stored information
    d. retrieval of inaccessible information

19. A psychology professor finds that elderly adults perform more poorly on anagrams than younger adults. However, when elderly adults are given practical problems to solve (e.g., What would you do if your refrigerator were warm inside?), they perform as well as younger adults. We can therefore conclude that
    a. the elderly demonstrate learning competence but not performance
    b. memory is not necessary to solve practical learning problems
    c. the elderly perform well only on familiar, habitual tasks
    d. the second task was more relevant for the elderly, and therefore they were motivated to do better

20. Your elderly mother keeps forgetting where she has put her glasses, checkbook, and keys. You should therefore conclude that
    a. she has suffered a stroke
    b. no definite conclusions are warranted without further information
    c. she has Alzheimer's disease
    d. she is suffering from an irreversible organic brain syndrome

21. You go to visit your elderly grandfather and notice he is disoriented (what day is it?) and very agitated (pacing incessantly in his apartment). You are concerned about his atypical behavior because he is usually calm and aware. What might you reasonably do next?
    a. Call 911 immediately.
    b. Suggest he take a nap to sleep it off.
    c. Prepare a meal for him so he has something in his stomach.
    d. Check his prescriptions and call the pharmacist about side effects.

Chapter 17 Late Adulthood: Physical and Cognitive Development

Essay Questions

1. Some people say that getting old is all in the mind. Discuss both sides to this statement.
2. When and why would you choose to give up work? What would need to be guaranteed for you to feel secure?
3. How would you respond if you and your significant other were both diagnosed with Alzheimer's?

ANSWERS FOR SELF-TESTS

Matching

1. k
2. l
3. i
4. o
5. d
6. b
7. p
8. c
9. e
10. f
11. j
12. m
13. q
14. n
15. a
16. g
17. h

Multiple Choice

Factual

1. c
2. c
3. c
4. b
5. d
6. a
7. a
8. b
9. b
10. d
11. b
12. a
13. c
14. a
15. b
16. c
17. c
18. b
19. c
20. c
21. d
22. b
23. d
24. c
25. c
26. a
27. a
28. b
29. d
30. b
31. b

Conceptual

1. a
2. c
3. c
4. b
5. d
6. d
7. c
8. d
9. c
10. b
11. b
12. c
13. a
14. c
15. c
16. d
17. b
18. c
19. d
20. b
21. d

Chapter 18

Late Adulthood:
Emotional and Social Development

INTRODUCTION

Chapter 18 takes a close look at the period of late adulthood and the psychosocial domain. Several important topics are covered, including:

- The Psychosocial Domain. The psychosocial tasks of later adulthood are described, as viewed by Erikson and Peck. Major personality patterns of late adulthood are introduced. Research data are also presented from an examination of the relationship between self-concept and life satisfaction in later adulthood.

- Theories of Adjustment to Aging. Several theories describing changes in the elderly in terms of the changes in their social environment are examined. These include (1) disengagement theory, (2) activity theory, (3) role exit theory, (4) social exchange theory, and (5) trait theory.

- Family. Topics include being single, and the effects of siblings and grandchildren on the elderly.

- The Psychosocial Aspects of Aging. Several topics are covered in this section, beginning with retirement, changing marital relations, and kin and friendship ties. Data dealing with the roles and functions performed by grandparents are then presented. A close examination is made of different types of institutional, home, and day care for the elderly. Finally, the significance of personal control and choice in influencing the well-being of elderly nursing home residents is discussed.

Chapter 18 Late Adulthood: Emotional and Social Development

LEARNING OBJECTIVES

After completing this chapter, you should be able to:

1. Present the four areas of research called for by the Vitality for Life proposal.

    •

    •

    •

    •

2. Discuss the American stereotype of elderly people.

3. List positive and negative attitudes of the elderly.

4. Describe the views of Erikson and the task and crisis in development in late adulthood.

5. Explain Peck's view on psychosocial development in late adulthood.

6. Describe each of the major late-adulthood personality patterns identified by Neugarten, Havighurst, Tobin, and others.

integrated

armor-defended

passive-dependent

disintegrated

7. Explain *selective optimization with compensation*, as well as third age and fourth age, in later adulthood.

Chapter 18 Late Adulthood: Emotional and Social Development

8. Compare and contrast the following theories of adjustment to aging.

disengagement theory

activity theory

role exit theory

social exchange theory

modernization theory

9. Discuss how the psychosocial aspects of life in later adulthood are affected by personal control and choice.

10. Describe how the psychosocial aspects of life in later adulthood affect marital relations.

nature of relationship

level of satisfaction

improvements

strains/stressors

conflict of time

retirement

11. Discuss how the psychosocial aspects of life in later adulthood are affected by:

becoming widowed

remarriage

lesbian and gay relationships

relationship with children

grandchildren

role of sibling(s)

12. Briefly summarize the research data dealing with voluntary and involuntary retirement.

13. Discuss different living arrangements for the elderly

alone

assisted living

with children

institutions

retirement communities

adult group homes

14. Cite the data dealing with the following aspects of grandparenting.

demographic statistics

roles performed

themes

custodial role

three-generation household

15. Assess the significance of the following factors in the selection of institutional care.

demographics

living conditions

quality of life

16. Discuss *elder abuse* and its effects on society.

WEB SITES

The following web site sites deal with some of the concepts and issues presented in Chapter 18. Additional resources can be found on the text's web site, at http://www.mhhe.com/crandell7.

Vitality for Life Reports
http://www.iog.wayne.edu/apadiv20/vitality.htm

National Institute on Aging (NIA)
http://www.nih.gov/nia

American Association of Retired Persons
http://www.aarp.org

Professional Opportunities in the Field of Aging
http://www.usc.edu/dept/gero/careers/Why_Gerontology.html

Chapter 18 Late Adulthood: Emotional and Social Development

SELF-TESTS

Matching

Match the key terms with their definitions:

a. activity theory of aging
b. adult day care
c. disengagement theory of aging
d. elder abuse
e. integrity vs. despair
f. life review
g. modernization theory
h. role exit theory of aging
i. social exchange theory of aging
j. selective optimization with compensation
k. wisdom

1. ____ a reminiscence and sharing of family history from one generation to another

2. ____ acts of commission and omission that cause unnecessary suffering to older persons

3. ____ expert knowledge about life in general and good judgment and advice about how to conduct oneself in the fact of complex, uncertain circumstances

4. ____ long-term care support to adults who live in the community, providing health, social, and support services in a protective setting during any part of the day

5. ____ refers to the life span model where we are adjusting to our standards of expectation

6. ____ states that an elderly person maintains a fairly stable level of activity for as long as possible and then finds substitutes for those activities they are forced to relinquish

7. ____ states that as an elderly person's level of activity declines, so do feelings of satisfaction, contentment, and happiness

8. ____ the notion that the status of the aged tends to be high in traditional societies and lower in urbanized, industrialized societies

9. ____ the stage in which individuals recognize that they are reaching the end of life

10. ____ the view that people enter into social relationships because they derive rewards from doing so – economic, sustenance, recognition, a sense of security, love, social approval, gratitude, and so on

11. ____ views retirement and widowhood as the termination of the participation of the elderly in the principal institutional structures of society – the job and the family

Chapter 18 Late Adulthood: Emotional and Social Development

Multiple Choice

Circle the letter of the response that best completes or answers each of the following statements and questions.

Factual Questions

1. According to Erik Erikson, those in late adulthood are confronted with which task that might lead to wisdom?
    a. isolation vs. socialization
    b. outwardness vs. inferiority
    c. integrity vs. despair
    d. trust vs. mistrust

2. According to Peck, an elderly person who sees himself as having multiple dimensions and as pursuing new ways of finding a sense of satisfaction is demonstrating
    a. disengagement
    b. ego differentiation
    c. body transcendence
    d. ego transcendence

3. What does Peck say happens to men and women who equate pleasure with physical comfort and well-being?
    a. They do not succumb to their physical aches, pains, and disabilities.
    b. They refuse to become preoccupied with bodily health.
    c. They are affected significantly by the decline in their health and strength.
    d. They find human relationships and creative mental activities to be more fulfilling.

4. By "ego transcendence," Peck means that the elderly
    a. come to see themselves as living on after death through their contributions – children, work, etc.
    b. do not succumb to becoming preoccupied with their declining health
    c. adapt easily to their new stage in life
    d. come to realize that they are multi-dimensional and not just workers

5. According to Neugarten's research on personality and patterns of aging, what term does she use to describe those people who place a premium on staying young, remaining active, and refusing to grow old?
    a. focused
    b. reorganizers
    c. integrated
    d. holders-on

6. In Neugarten's study of personality patterns in the aged, she describes the disintegrated elderly as
    a. revealing defects in psychological and thought processes
    b. well-functioning individuals with a complex inner life and intact cognitive abilities
    c. striving, ambitious, achievement-oriented individuals
    d. having strong dependency needs and eliciting responsiveness from others

Chapter 18 Late Adulthood: Emotional and Social Development

7. Older people have more favorable self-concepts if they
    a. live in their private homes
    b. are healthy and relatively affluent
    c. were happy and emotionally stable in their younger years
    d. all of the above

8. The Harvard graduates' longitudinal study found which personality traits are associated with those making the best emotional adjustments in their later years?
    a. spontaneity and creativity
    b. ability to make friends easily
    c. scholarly and theoretical traits
    d. organization, dependability, and sincerity

9. Research suggests that being close to one's siblings while in college
    a. has little effect on well-being in later adulthood
    b. is a variable that more strongly predicts emotional well-being in later adulthood than having had a successful career
    c. is a weaker predictor of emotional well-being in later adulthood than having had a good marriage
    d. is associated with psychological depression and high divorce rates in later adulthood

10. According to which of the following theories does a gradual and mutually satisfying process occur in the course of aging in which society and the individual prepare in advance for incapacitating disease and death?
    a. role exit
    b. disengagement
    c. social exchange
    d. activity

11. According to activity theory, as people age they
    a. lose their master status as younger people take over their roles
    b. volunteer more to stay active
    c. decrease social interaction (a result of society withdrawing from the aging person)
    d. attempt to extract from society a more favorable distribution of benefits and privileges for themselves

12. The role exit theory, formulated by Blau and supported by Rosow, states as Americans age, they
    a. have decreasing interaction with society
    b. increasingly volunteer to fill in the "gaps" in their time
    c. lose their basic identity by losing opportunities to be socially useful
    d. seek integration through more solitary activities

13. The social exchange theory of aging suggests that the elderly find themselves in a state of increasing vulnerability because
    a. they have less to offer society
    b. role loss is a stressful experience
    c. increasing numbers of elderly individuals are retiring early
    d. as an elderly person's activity level declines, so do feelings of satisfaction, contentment, and happiness

14. The _____ theory assumes that the position of the aged in pre-industrial, traditional societies is high because the aged tend to accumulate knowledge and control through their years of experience.
    a. activity
    b. disengagement
    c. modernization
    d. social exchange

15. According to the Bureau of Labor Statistics, by the year 2000 only one in _____ men 60 years and over will be working.
    a. two
    b. four
    c. six
    d. ten

16. Many Americans view the practice of compelling workers to retire as a
    a. way of ensuring more jobs for young adults
    b. long-term solution to inflation
    c. curtailment of basic rights
    d. way of improving future life prospects for the elderly

17. Surveys conducted by the American Association of Retired Persons (AARP) found that how many older workers and retirees would delay retirement if they could work fewer hours instead of retiring?
    a. 5-20 percent
    b. 25-50 percent
    c. 50-75 percent
    d. 76-100 percent

18. Which of the following is an accurate finding about American retirees?
    a. More are going back to college.
    b. More are doing preplanning.
    c. Involuntary retirees have more satisfaction after retirement.
    d. Most retirees regard retirement with optimism and plan for it.

19. Based on most research of satisfaction in a lifetime of marriage, researchers suggest that, graphically, it resembles
    a. a broken line, – – , with breaks in satisfaction with companionship throughout the marriage
    b. like a W, with lots of ups and downs during marriage and with satisfaction varying at times
    c. like a U, with greater satisfaction at the beginning and later years of marriage
    d. like an S, "go with the flow," where satisfaction varies from time to time

20. Which of the following factors appears to contribute to improved marital relationships in later years?
    a. Problems with issues such as in-laws and sex have often been resolved.
    b. Grown children are more likely to show appreciation and affection toward their elderly parents and ask less of their parents.
    c. Each partner enjoys spending much more time with his or her spouse.
    d. Grandchildren are more likely to help out with chores that the couple cannot perform.

21. About what percent of couples both retire at the same time (based on the National Longitudinal Survey of Mature Women)?
    a. 5 percent
    b. 10 percent
    c. 15 percent
    d. 25 percent

22. It's _____ rather than _____ who researchers find receive marriage's greatest mental and physical benefits; and older _____ individuals are healthier than _____ individuals.
    a. men, women; single, married
    b. men, women, married, single
    c. women, men; married, single
    d. women, men; single, married

23. Which of the following statements concerning the current generation of grandparents is accurate?
    a. More youngsters have living grandparents, particularly grandmothers.
    b. Grandparents have less money.
    c. Grandfathers report greater satisfaction with grandparenting than grandmothers.
    d. The main role for grandparents is that of surrogate parents.

24. According to your text, most nursing homes
    a. have an adequate, qualified staff
    b. are owned by private proprietors and are operated for profit
    c. are rarely used by the terminally ill who require intensive nursing care
    d. are more economical than services such as adult day care and "meals on wheels"

25. Nursing home residents who were told by an administrator that they were responsible for caring for themselves and for shaping the home's policies
    a. became more depressed than comparable residents
    b. were rated as healthier than comparable residents
    c. were overwhelmed by their responsibilities and refused to assume them
    d. expressed a preference to be physically and emotionally dependent

26. Langer and Rodin's study in a nursing home found that patients who were given a choice and asked to make decisions
    a. fell into psychological depression by virtue of the stress
    b. exhibited helplessness in the face of making decisions for themselves
    c. began to take over and order the staff about
    d. were actually healthier than the control group

Conceptual Questions

1. Someone scoring high on positive affect would likely have experienced which of the following?
    a. read the news that day
    b. be living with others
    c. be in several clubs
    d. all of the above

2. An elderly man tells you, "I live every day as if it were the first day of my life, because it might be the last." People say that he did the best he could with the tools he had. This statement indicates a satisfactory resolution of
    a. body transcendence vs. body preoccupation
    b. ego differentiation vs. work-role preoccupation
    c. ego transcendence vs. ego preoccupation
    d. generativity vs. stagnation

3. Your grandfather is a retired corporate executive and has become involved in the retired senior volunteer program helping people start new businesses. He claims he doesn't want to become an old "fuddy-duddy" in a rocking chair – he's going to remain in control of his life! Your grandfather is a(n)
    a. reorganizer
    b. disintegrated type
    c. passive-dependent type
    d. armored-defended type

4. Which of the following situations is most likely to occur to someone in later adulthood?
    a. When given a questionnaire measuring life satisfaction, a group of 60-year-old men score lower than a group of 30-year-old men.
    b. When given a questionnaire measuring life satisfaction, a group of 30-year-old men get nearly the same average score as a group of 60-year-old men.
    c. Your grandfather tells you that his retirement years are far worse than he expected them to be and that he is bored.
    d. A group of 30-year-old men express less satisfaction with their life accomplishments than a group of 60-year-old men.

5. Charles, a 57-year-old member of your local Rotary Club, has quit the organization after being a member for thirty years. Now he hardly even associates socially with the men he used to see each day. We can most reasonably conclude that
    a. his behavior would be more likely to occur in someone much older than he is
    b. his behavior is a normal way of acknowledging that organizations need "new blood"
    c. as people get older, they disengage from activities in which they no longer feel useful
    d. he resigned because he felt that the club didn't want old members, and he didn't want to be a burden

6. William grew up as an only child and never married. He is very scholarly and was a literature major in college. He spent his career analyzing the language of Shakespearean works, traveled the world and was renowned in his field. One can predict, now that he has retired, that
    a. he will die within a year
    b. his emotional health and life satisfaction will improve
    c. he will become more social
    d. his emotional health and life satisfaction will probably decrease

7. All through her life, Deborah and her siblings have remained close (throughout adolescence, college years, raising their families, etc.). What do research studies predict about Deborah's adjustment to her later adult years? She will
    a. experience more difficulty adjusting because she will most likely have health problems
    b. probably have fewer friends because she's remained close to her siblings
    c. most likely retain the capacity to recover from adversity and go on with he life
    d. probably experience poor emotional health and lower life satisfaction

Chapter 18 Late Adulthood: Emotional and Social Development

8. Mr. Bennett, a retired corporate executive and former active community leader, was recognized for his contributions to his community with a banquet in his honor a year ago. Since that time, however, he has chosen to spend more time fishing, visiting his grandchildren, and "catching up" on the reading he put off for years. Mr. Bennett's change in activities supports which theory of adjustment?
    a. disengagement
    b. activity
    c. role exit
    d. modernization

9. According to the predictions of activity theory, an elderly woman who sits in her apartment and watches television all day
    a. will not be as happy as an elderly woman who keeps herself occupied with a variety of tasks and social activities
    b. does so because she feels that slowing down is an inevitable and desirable result of aging
    c. is preparing herself for the "ultimate disengagement" of incurable, incapacitating disease
    d. can be happy with reduced activity levels as long as her health is OK

10. Which of the following individuals should have the highest reported life satisfaction?
    a. a 60-year-old man who retired because of chronic emphysema
    b. a college professor who retired because he reached the mandatory retirement age of 70
    c. an automobile worker who retired because he was about to be laid off
    d. a legal secretary who retired when her law firm implemented a better pension plan

11. Dr. Parsley retired at age 70 after working 45 years as a professor and researcher for a prestigious private university. Upon retirement, he was given professor emeritus status and told he could still be affiliated with the university; however, he had to move everything out of his office immediately to make room for a young colleague. He will have to do his own secretarial and "go-fer" work, to pay for his own copies at the copy machine, and to pay for any phone calls he makes from the college. He's stunned by the loss of privileges, and his self-esteem plummets. Which theory of adjustment to aging seems to be in effect?
    a. role exit
    b. social exchange
    c. activity
    d. disengagement

12. Many middle management workers today in the United States who are near retirement age are being "let go" through corporate downsizing. These skilled workers always felt they would have a secure, comfortable position with their "blue chip" firms in exchange for loyalty, dependability, and hard work. Now that the companies look at the "bottom line" only and can easily discard them, this comes as a devastating blow. Which theory of adjustment seems to apply in this case?
    a. role exit
    b. social exchange
    c. activity
    d. modernization

Chapter 18 Late Adulthood: Emotional and Social Development

13. Which of the following statements about retirement is accurate?
    a. Many of today's workers can expect to live another 5 to 10 years.
    b. Some workers actually work well into their 70s and 80s.
    c. The majority of workers wait until they are 65 before they retire.
    d. Only a small percent of post-retirement work is full time.

14. The American stereotype about retirement is
    a. it's a very satisfying feeling to retire and finally be able to do what you want to do
    b. it's a negative feeling to retire because one's self-esteem has, for many years, been tied to one's role at work
    c. retirement is demoralizing, and workers should continue to work as long as they are physically able
    d. it's a great milestone to retire because one finally gets the respect he/she deserves

15. The best geographical way to describe the relationship between length of marriage and marital satisfaction would be to draw a
    a. hill
    b. plateau
    c. series of hills and valleys
    d. valley

16. Mrs. Marvin, a retired widow, relies on a certain person to be her confidant, chauffeur, etc., and to be available to her whenever she needs help. Most likely, what relationship does the helper have to Mrs. Marvin?
    a. son
    b. daughter
    c. grandchild
    d. sibling

17. An elderly person may feel lonely, isolated, and depressed. Which of the following individuals is most likely to be experiencing these symptoms?
    a. an elderly widow who went to live with her son's family in a distant city
    b. an elderly widower who can be seen playing cards every day with a group of men at the senior citizens center
    c. a widower who takes daily walks with a longtime acquaintance
    d. an elderly lifelong bachelor who lives by himself

18. Your elderly mother fell down on the icy pavement in front of her car and broke her arm. The best course of action would be to
    a. put her in a hospital so that her recuperation will progress more rapidly
    b. hire a full-time housekeeper for her because she will not be capable of caring for herself alone
    c. place her in a residential care facility where her physical and psychological needs can be taken care of
    d. let her recuperate at home and provide her with support when and where needed

Chapter 18   Late Adulthood: Emotional and Social Development

19. The song title that would best describe the relationship between today's grandparents and their grandchildren would be
    a. "The Pretender"
    b. "Five Short Minutes"
    c. "You've Got a Friend"
    d. "When Time is Stolen"

20. Which of the following elderly persons would be the <u>least</u> likely candidate to be placed in a residential nursing home?
    a. a homeless person with no family and nowhere else to go
    b. an elderly victim of Alzheimer's disease who is incontinent
    c. an elderly man who has been paroled after a long imprisonment
    d. an elderly person recovering from major cancer surgery

21. Your mother was alert and talkative when she entered a nursing home. One month later she appears lethargic, and her medical problems have gotten worse. Which of the following descriptions would apply to this home?
    a. Your mother was told upon entering "Don't worry, sweetie, we'll take good care of you; we'll even tell you when it's time to go to bed."
    b. Your mother was told that the staff would take care of her physical needs, but she would be responsible for keeping her room arranged.
    c. Your mother was told that the nursing home would provide recreational activities; but if she wasn't satisfied, she would have to voice her concerns.
    d. Your mother was told upon entering the home that she could decorate her room in any way she saw fit.

Essay Questions

1. Your 85-year-old father and mother just want to be left alone. They say, "We want to enjoy our final years together. We've given enough time to raising children and working. We don't see this as selfish." How would you feel?

2. "Everyone approaches aging the same way. They go out with a whimper." Discuss the different aspects of aging as viewed against this picture of aging.

3. When and why would a person choose to live in a nursing home instead of with family? You might want to investigate the beginnings and acceptance of nursing homes.

Chapter 18 Late Adulthood: Emotional and Social Development

ANSWERS FOR SELF-TESTS

Matching

1. f
2. d
3. k
4. b
5. j
6. c
7. a
8. g
9. e
10. i
11. h

Multiple Choice

Factual

1. c
2. b
3. c
4. a
5. b
6. a
7. d
8. d
9. b
10. b
11. c
12. c
13. a
14. c
15. b
16. c
17. b
18. a
19. c
20. a
21. d
22. b
23. a
24. b
25. b
26. d

Conceptual

1. d
2. c
3. d
4. b
5. a
6. d
7. c
8. a
9. a
10. d
11. b
12. b
13. b
14. b
15. d
16. b
17. a
18. d
19. c
20. a
21. a

Chapter 19

Dying and Death

INTRODUCTION

The concluding chapter of the text considers the antithesis of the life process – the stage of dying and death. Several significant topics are discussed, including:

- The Dying Process. Modern definitions of death and how various societies perceive and recognize death are presented. How the elderly conceive of death, as well as the systematic psychological changes which precede death, is also examined. Kübler-Ross' stages of the death experience are outlined, and a critique of her stage approach is offered. Stress, as a cause of illness and death, is also highlighted.

- The Quest for "Healthy Dying." Research findings are presented regarding an individual's need to die with dignity. Salient features of the right-to-die movement are reviewed (such as preparing a living will and a health care proxy), and the controversial issue of euthanasia is discussed. The extraordinary phenomenon of near-death experiences for some who have been declared clinically dead is explored. A special overview of AIDS is also presented, and within the context of "healthy dying," the role of the hospice in comforting those near the end of life's journey is examined.

- Bereavement. Findings are revealed regarding typical adjustment to the death of a loved one. Finally, the coping experiences of widows and widowers are examined.

LEARNING OBJECTIVES

After completing Chapter 19, you should be able to:

1. Describe the changing American view of death.

Chapter 19   Dying and Death

2. Define *thanatology* and summarize past and present definitions of death.

3. Outline the ways in which elderly people confront death.

4. Define the concept of healthy dying ("death with dignity").

5. Discuss physician-assisted suicide (PAS).

6. Cite the contrasting views on the right-to-die movement.

Chapter 19   Dying and Death

7. Summarize the issues related to the controversial issue of *euthanasia*.

8. Discuss different aspects of suicide:

ideas

attempts

completions

who

why

9. Identify eight steps for approaching patients who request suicide.

-
-
-
-
-
-
-
-

Chapter 19   Dying and Death

15. Define the following terms and discuss the functions and stages of development for each concept related to *bereavement*.

bereavement

grief

mourning

16. Explain some findings about each of the following topics related to bereavement.

ventilating feelings

culture and the expression of grief

consequences of grief

violent and premature death

death of a child

death of a parent

17. Identify and describe the four distinct stages of adult bereavement.

-
-

Chapter 19 Dying and Death

-
-

18. Summarize the data regarding each of the following topics related to widows and widowers.

demographics

coping difficulties

WEB SITES

The following web sites deal with some of the concepts and issues presented in Chapter 19. Additional resources can be found on the text's web site, at http://www.mhhe.com/crandell7.

Thanatology Forum
http://www.rights.org/~deathnet/thana.html

Euthanasia
http://www.euthanasia.com

DeathNet
http://rights.org/~deathnet/open.html

Sociology of Death
http://www.trinity.edu/~mkearl/death.html

Chapter 19 Dying and Death

SELF-TESTS

Matching

Match the key terms with their definitions:

a. anticipatory grief
b. bereavement
c. brain death
d. euthanasia
e. grief
f. hospice
g. life review
h. living will
i. mourning
j. near-death experience
k. thanatology

1. ____ a feeling of having had otherworldly experiences commonly reported by persons who have been gravely ill or injured

2. ____ a legal document that states an individual's wishes regarding medical care in case the individual becomes incapacitated and unable to participate in medical care decisions

3. ____ a program for providing comfort, care, and pain relief to persons dying of long-term illnesses

4. ____ a sharing of family history from one generation to another

5. ____ a state of emotional limbo where the death of a loved one is anticipated

6. ____ an experience involving keen mental anguish and sorrow

7. ____ being deprived of a relative or friend by death

8. ____ cessation of neural activity

9. ____ the act of terminating an ill or injured person's life for reasons of mercy

10. ____ the culturally or socially established manner of expressing sorrow over a person's death

11. ____ the study of death and dying

Multiple Choice

Circle the letter of the response that best completes or answers each of the following statements and questions.

Factual Questions

1. Thanatology involves
   a. the right to die
   b. clinical death
   c. life after death
   d. the study of death

Chapter 19 Dying and Death

2. Life-extending technologies have compelled courts and legislatures to accept a standard for death--one that is agreed upon by the American Bar Association, American Medical Association, and Presidential Commission, death is when
   a. a person is unable to breathe independently
   b. a person's entire brain doesn't register activity, including the brain stem
   c. a person's primitive reflexes cease
   d. a person's heart stops functioning

3. Which of the following attitudes is the most rare attitude towards death?
   a. Death is a form of punishment.
   b. Death is simply the "end" of being.
   c. Death is the end of bodily life and a transition into a new life.
   d. In death, one will be reunited with loved ones who have passed on.

4. The death-drop phenomenon refers to
   a. the systematic psychological changes that occur before death
   b. intense guilt, despair, and depression that occur when one is told that death is near
   c. the otherworldly experiences reported by those who are resuscitated after clinical death
   d. the higher rates of death that follow significant life changes

5. According to your text, which of the following statements is the least accurate conclusion about how modern American society regards death?
   a. Nursing homes and hospitals take care of the terminally ill and manage the "crisis" of dying.
   b. A mortuary establishment, in contrast to the deceased's family, prepares the body and handles funeral arrangements.
   c. The average person has increased exposure to death through the media and has become "numb" to death.
   d. The dying are to be segregated from others and are managed in an impersonal way.

6. According to Elisabeth Kübler-Ross, a thanatologist and leading advocate for restoring dignity to dying, typically a terminally ill person's first response to impending death is
   a. anger
   b. depression
   c. bargaining
   d. denial

7. Kübler-Ross distinguishes five stages of a process through which dying people typically pass. In the middle phase, dying individuals try to arrange a truce with the illness in order to prolong their lives ("If only I can live through our family gathering at Christmas, I'll be ready to go."), and Kübler-Ross calls this the stage of
   a. anger
   b. acceptance
   c. depression
   d. bargaining

8. Dying people often mourn their own deaths, the loss of all the people and things they have found meaningful, and the plans and dreams that will never be fulfilled. Kübler-Ross calls this
   a. death drop
   b. denial
   c. preparatory grief
   d. life review

9. Most people who are aware of their impending death desire to die where?
   a. in the hospital, where all their needs can be met
   b. at a nursing home setting, where people understand the needs of a dying person
   c. at home, among loved ones, and in familiar surroundings
   d. away from most people so they can die quietly

10. Kastenbaum's criticism of Kübler-Ross's stage theory of death includes all of the following except
    a. the specific nature of each disease (pain, mobility, duration, etc.)
    b. differences in dying experienced by women and men
    c. ethnic group membership (perspective on death)
    d. the lack of recognition that people go through a "preparatory grief" time

11. The death awareness movement asserts that
    a. life must be prolonged at all costs
    b. a basic human right is the power to control one's own dying process
    c. "aggressive" medical care should be used to prolong a dying person's life
    d. dying individuals never come to accept death

12. "Any clinical circumstance in which the doctor and consultants conclude that further treatment cannot, within a reasonable possibility, cure, palliate, ameliorate, or restore a quality of life that would be satisfactory to the patient" describes
    a. futile care
    b. mercy killing
    c. the right to die
    d. a living will decree

13. Because of a Supreme Court ruling that states when a permanently unconscious person has left no clear instructions, a state is free to carry out its interest in the protection and preservation of human life, more people are preparing a legal document recognized in most states that describes one's wishes regarding life-sustaining technology and treatment when one is dying. What is this document?
    a. writ of life
    b. living will
    c. living care proxy
    d. health care proxy

14. Concerning terminally ill or critically ill patients (including newborns), the AMA states
    a. physicians may help patients end their own lives through assisted suicide
    b. physicians and nurses may help the critically ill with "mercy killing"
    c. physicians can withhold all means of life-prolonging medical treatment, including food and water, from patients in irreversible comas even if death is not imminent
    d. physicians are to ignore DNR (do not resuscitate) orders from the patient and family and are to use their own best judgment in each case

Chapter 19 Dying and Death

15. Another term for "mercy killing" is
    a. thanatology
    b. euthanasia
    c. senility
    d. convalescence

16. Which of the following findings about AIDS is not correct?
    a. Efforts to devise a vaccine or treatment have been complicated by the fact that AIDS is caused by dozens of strains of the virus.
    b. Behavioral remedies are the only methods available right now for prevention.
    c. When considering random sex, each person is connected to the other person's sexual partners from the past ten years.
    d. Abstinence is the only way to prevent AIDS.

17. Which of the following is a concern about "healthy dying" from the physician's perspective?
    a. Depressed patients or those in severe pain have severely distorted thinking.
    b. Sometimes patients at the brink of death actually recover.
    c. There is a potential for abuse if physician-assisted suicide is legal.
    d. All of the above.

18. Most hospice programs center upon
    a. attempts to prolong the life of the dying person
    b. developing cures for terminal illness
    c. "comfort care" at home rather than attempts to prolong life
    d. new experimental procedures designed to combat genetic disorders

19. Which of the following is not likely to be reported by individuals with near-death experience (NDE)?
    a. passing through a tunnel in a "spiritual" way and entering into an unearthly realm
    b. seeing deceased loved ones and a being of light, believed to be God
    c. intense feelings of joy and peace that change the person's life upon returning
    d. a desire to return to this earthly life to tell others about their other-worldly experience

20. Bereavement is best defined as a(n)
    a. socially established manner of displaying signs of sorrow over a person's death
    b. state in which a person has been deprived of a relative or friend by death
    c. study of death
    d. individual's right to choose a death with dignity

21. Grief work involves
    a. mourning, talking about, and acknowledging the loss of a loved one
    b. heroic measures designed to prolong the life of a terminally ill patient
    c. placing a dying individual in a facility outside the home
    d. the reconstruction of a new life pattern after the death of a loved one

22. Typically, for many people, the culmination phase of adult bereavement is
    a. anger, sleeplessness, loss of appetite, weight loss, preoccupation with image of the deceased
    b. shock, denial, disbelief
    c. assumption of new roles, a sense of self-reliance, strength, new friends
    d. adjustment to the new circumstances; reconnection to friends and family

Chapter 19 Dying and Death

23. Which of the following is the most accurate conclusion concerning people's bereavement behavior?
    a. People's reactions can be easily identified in well-defined stages.
    b. It is normal for the intensity and duration of symptoms of loss to vary from individual to individual.
    c. Nearly all survivors experience deep shock, loss, and denial.
    d. Two percent of survivors do not experience great distress.

24. Which of the following is the least accurate finding about widows and widowers?
    a. Among those over 75, two-thirds of men are living with a spouse, while less than one-fifth of women are living with a spouse.
    b. The life expectancy of women tends to be seven years longer than that of men.
    c. The death rate of widowers is seven times that of married men of comparable age.
    d. Health status remains about the same after the death of a spouse.

25. Concerning remarriage of widows and widowers, which is most accurate?
    a. After age 65, women remarry at a rate of nine brides to every bridegroom.
    b. Healthy widowers remarry relatively rapidly.
    c. Many widowers, compared to widows, have the financial resources to care for themselves (cooking, cleaning, laundry, health care, etc.).
    d. Women in the United States seem to have a more difficult time living alone than men.

Conceptual Questions

1. Absence of spontaneous breath is to _____ as spontaneous brain function is to life.
    a. thanatology
    b. death
    c. life
    d. artificial ventilation

2. Over the past several years, your Uncle Al has developed kidney failure. He now needs to go to the hospital regularly to sustain his life. What medical procedure/machine is prolonging his life?
    a. CPR
    b. mechanical respirator
    c. pacemaker
    d. dialysis

3. A friend of yours sustained a severe head injury two years ago in a motorcycle accident, but his critical life functions, like respiration, were not affected. His parents can no longer deal with this suffering and are requesting to end all life support for their "vegetable" child. Based on the AMA, American Bar Association, and Presidential Commission, can medical staff comply?
    a. No, not if the child can still breathe on his own.
    b. No, not while his brain stem is still functioning.
    c. Yes, and his organs can be donated.
    d. Yes, food and water can be withheld, but organs cannot be donated.

Chapter 19 Dying and Death

4. A family that recently immigrated to the United States from Vietnam has a grandfather die at home. Most likely their reaction to this sorrowful event would be
    a. to call the coroner immediately
    b. to build a coffin while the rest of the family prepares the body
    c. to call a mortuary establishment to handle all funeral arrangements
    d. to call the police to confirm foul play

5. An elderly man is informed that he is suffering from a terminal illness. The man tells his doctor, "You must have mixed up my lab results with someone else's." This response would be characterized by Kübler-Ross as
    a. bargaining
    b. denial
    c. acceptance
    d. rejection

6. A manager who works in your office just had a major heart attack. Everyone who knows the man is amazed because he was in perfect health and had no history of heart problems. A reasonable conclusion might be that the man
    a. was depressed because of a recent negative life review
    b. underwent a major personality change in the last year
    c. was trying too hard to get a promotion
    d. experienced an unusual number of life changes recently

7. A Haitian refugee, who is living in Miami, Florida, is critically ill and desires medical treatment. The patient is brought to a facility and put into a trance while special spirits are called upon to help this patient. This form of medicine is called
    a. hospice
    b. sympathy healing
    c. religious healing
    d. holistic healing

8. A critically-ill woman goes to a special mass where a priest will lay his hands upon her head while saying special prayers. She gently collapses into the waiting arms of others and is laid on the floor while in an altered state of consciousness. A few minutes later she gets up and claims that she's much better. This is an example of
    a. sympathy healing
    b. holistic healing
    c. religious healing
    d. shaman healing

9. Knowing that a little girl has a form of inoperable cancer, Dr. Smith, a traditional physician in the United States, would most likely deal with the information in what way?
    a. prevent the patient from finding out to keep her spirits up, and not inform the family
    b. not tell the patient and medicate the patient so she won't have to be aware of any aspects of dying
    c. share with the patient and family information about the illness, continue with "aggressive medical care," but not inform them about the hospice as a possibility
    d. turn over all care to the hospice staff, and let them tell the family and patient

Chapter 19 Dying and Death

10. Your elderly aunt tells you, "If I ever have a stroke, I don't want you to keep me alive with tubes and needles and machines." This statement
    a. would by unconditionally accepted by doctors
    b. would be approved of by most religious groups
    c. is a death wish that the elderly make when they resign themselves to dying
    d. might not be accepted at face value by a doctor

11. Intolerance of pain is to _____ as a living will is to euthanasia.
    a. the right to die
    b. healthy dying
    c. depression
    d. living wills

12. You talked to your elderly mother's physician about her failing health. He is concerned about her comfort and well-being but seems more concerned about being a medical failure and losing the battle to cure her illness. This doctor's attitude is inconsistent with which of the following concepts?
    a. medical model
    b. hospice
    c. bereavement
    d. right to life

13. Your car plunges off an icy bridge, and you are trapped under the water. Although pronounced dead at the scene, you are miraculously resuscitated. Later, all you can recall of this incident is plunging into the water. Your reaction
    a. was an out-of-body experience
    b. offers evidence for a spiritual existence beyond death
    c. does not support the notion of a life-after-death phenomenon
    d. was probably produced by a hyperventilated brain

14. Your son's friend was hit and killed by a car. You are unsure about whether your son should attend the funeral. A thanatologist might tell you that
    a. attending the funeral will give your son death-related anxieties
    b. not attending the funeral will help your son feel his friend has departed
    c. attending the funeral will help your son see death as a natural end to life
    d. attending the funeral will just raise more questions in your son's mind

15. Your neighbor's husband died recently. Despite her loss, she has shown a positive adjustment to her new circumstances by leaving her home more often. She is currently in which phase of the adult bereavement process?
    a. first phase
    b. second phase
    c. third phase
    d. fourth phase

Chapter 19 Dying and Death

16. Your father died four years ago. Your mother still has all your father's belongings and has left them untouched. She has turned into a depressed recluse, relying more and more on you for support. Psychologists would say that your mother
    a. has not progressed beyond the earliest stages of the grieving process
    b. would have resolved her grief more effectively if your father had died suddenly
    c. has begun the identity reconstruction phase of the grieving process
    d. has passed through the emancipation stage of the grieving process

17. Which of the following vignettes would we be the most likely to observe?
    a. An 80-year-old woman is still living with her husband of fifty years.
    b. A 65-year old widower remarries two years after the death of his wife.
    c. A widower develops new male acquaintances after the loss of his wife so that he can ease his loneliness with others.
    d. A 65-year-old widow decides to move in with her married daughter's family.

18. Katherine is a 75-year-old, recently widowed woman who was a devoted wife. She has a college degree, and her late husband was an attorney. Which of the following predictions could most reasonably be made about Katherine?
    a. She is more likely to remarry than a same-age widower.
    b. Katherine probably will prefer to maintain her kinship links by moving in with her married daughter.
    c. She will be at high risk for suicide because of unresolved feelings of loneliness.
    d. Katherine will idealize her late husband.

Essay Questions

1. Your mother and your children are both interested in talking about your mother's impending death. How will you discuss this issue with them?

2. Your father is dying at an early age and wished to choose the time of his death and to have the family gathered with him. Your mother does not want this to happen. Explain your mother's reaction and argue both his and her position.

3. Some people insist that they are just as moved when a pet dies as when a relative dies. Explain why this might be so.

Chapter 19 Dying and Death

ANSWERS FOR SELF-TESTS

Matching

1. j
2. h
3. f
4. g
5. a
6. e
7. b
8. c
9. d
10. i
11. k

Multiple Choice

Factual

1. d
2. b
3. a
4. a
5. c
6. d
7. d
8. c
9. c
10. d
11. b
12. a
13. b
14. c
15. b
16. d
17. d
18. c
19. d
20. a
21. a
22. c
23. b
24. d
25. b

Conceptual

1. b
2. d
3. d
4. b
5. b
6. d
7. c
8. c
9. c
10. d
11. a
12. b
13. c
14. c
15. c
16. a
17. b
18. d